THE WEAK ARE A LONG
TIME IN POLITICS

THE WEAK ARE A LONG TIME IN POLITICS

SKETCHES FROM THE BREXIT NEVERENDUM

PATRICK KIDD

Biteback Publishing

First published in Great Britain in 2019 by
Biteback Publishing Ltd
Westminster Tower
3 Albert Embankment
London SE1 7SP
Copyright © Patrick Kidd 2019

Patrick Kidd has asserted his right under the Copyright, Designs and Patents Act 1988 to be identified as the author of this work.

ISBN 978-1-78590-533-9

10 9 8 7 6 5 4 3 2 1

A CIP catalogue record for this book is available from the British Library.

Printed and bound in Great Britain by
CPI Group (UK) Ltd, Croydon CR0 4YY

To Toady, Lickspittle and Creep.
May your loyalty be rewarded one day.

CONTENTS

INTRODUCTION

On the evening of 29 March 2019, when Britain was meant to have left the European Union, the BBC showed *Sliding Doors*, the 1998 rom-com starring Gwyneth Paltrow about how a split-second decision can have vastly different impacts on your life. It seemed an appropriate piece of scheduling by the BBC planners (Channel 5 may have been making its own point about a divided nation by showing *Britain's Favourite Crisps* the same evening). How different might British politics look today if events that seemed insignificant at the time had gone the other way?

What would have happened in the 2015 general election if Ed Miliband had been able to eat a bacon sandwich daintily or looked a bit less weird? If David Cameron had not won a majority in 2015, would he have been spared a referendum by the excuse of coalition? Where would the Labour Party be today if just two of the MPs who shuddered at the thought of Jeremy Corbyn becoming their leader after Mr Miliband had not put him on the ballot with minutes to spare to give the far left a voice? How strong and stable would Theresa May have been in 2019 if she had not called a general election with a slender 21-point lead in the polls two years earlier? Or if she had run a better campaign that was not based solely upon her own personality, since it turned out she didn't have one?

Implausibly, at a time when the nation was in greater need of talented leadership than at any point since the Second World

War, the two main parties were led by politicians who seemed remarkably ill suited to their jobs and who had risen to their posts by accident without much idea of what they wanted to do once they got there.

It was my privilege – some may say punishment – to watch The May and Corbyn Show from close range as political sketch-writer of *The Times*. My perch in the Commons was a seat directly above Mr Speaker; my desk was in a Portakabin on top of the chamber with a roof that leaked more often than the Cabinet. From there, I worked as a sort of theatre critic for the Westminster Palace of Varieties, trying to daub colour on an often monochrome canvas. If the protagonists could seem weak and dull, there were always eccentrics, sycophants and weirdos on the backbenches to grab my attention. Toady, Lickspittle and Creep, as I called them, were always good value.

It was a large menagerie. In this anthology alone, which is about a third of the sketches I wrote, you will find 259 MPs, four dozen peers and bishops, three former Prime Ministers, several world leaders, lots of bureaucrats and one grumpy Downing Street cat called Larry. Sometimes I think it would have all run much more smoothly if Larry had been in charge.

I first wrote a political sketch for *The Times* in October 2014, as holiday cover for Ann Treneman. It was a dispatch from Clacton, where Douglas Carswell had just become UKIP's first elected MP in a by-election. By the time I took over the post full-time after the 2015 general election, the route to a referendum, if not the result, was inevitable. And yet who could have predicted what was about to happen?

In May 2015, having won a second term and ditched his coalition partners, Mr Cameron seemed at the height of his powers. He was clearly going to be Prime Minister for years; George Osborne was his obvious successor rather than the editor of a free London evening newspaper; Mrs May was a slightly underwhelming Home Secretary; and Mr Corbyn an anonymous Labour backbencher who had voted against his own party over 400 times.

Donald Trump was best known as the American Lord Sugar; Boris Johnson was known for being a buffoon (OK, not everything changed); and Jacob Rees-Mogg was barely known at all. And if you asked people in 2015 what they thought a Brexit was, they might have gone for a cereal, a decongestant or, if they were The Mogg, a Latin past tense. *Brego, bregere, brexi, brectum*: the supine form of the verb meaning 'We're all buggered'.

The referendum provided a lot of colour, not least in the case of Peter Bone's awful lime and olive Grassroots Out ties. Many of the best images of that campaign involved Mr Johnson: Boris driving a juggernaut; Boris confronted by a man in a gorilla suit; Boris auctioning a cow; Boris waving pasties, bananas and asparagus; Boris kissing a fish. His wacky optimism proved more attractive to the voters than Mr Osborne's 200-page dossier of charts, tables and equations warning of Armageddon. Project Fear was Project Dull.

The Remain camp could not even get their name right. Stuart Rose, the head of Stronger In, told a broadcaster, 'I'm chairman of Stay in Britain... Better in Britain campaign... right, start again... The Better Stay in Britain campaign.' The former boss of M&S later admitted it could have been worse: 'I could have said I was once in charge of S&M.' Meanwhile, Mr Corbyn just wanted to lie back and think of Venezuela. He went on holiday during the crucial final weeks, and the last event of a lacklustre Labour campaign to stay in was outside the Waitrose by the offices of *The Guardian*. Really reaching out beyond their base.

Mr Cameron was right about one thing. In January 2016, he told MPs, 'By the time we get to the end of the referendum campaign, everyone will have had enough of the subject.' And that was certainly the case over the next three and a bit years as

Mrs May, saddled with a policy she did not campaign for and a determined sense of duty to deliver it that belonged in a Gilbert and Sullivan opera, attempted to turn her simple philosophy of 'Brexit means Brexit' into a deal that MPs would vote for.

The May and Corbyn years were a time of tantric politics: lots of grunts and moans and changes of position, and neither side came close to being satisfied. Mrs May turned out to be like an inverse Rumpelstiltskin – no matter how hard she spun, she just kept producing more straw. Perhaps a better choice of film for the night of 29 March 2019 would have been *Waiting for Godot*.

It broke her in the end. What looked like a never-ending hell for Mrs May when I started compiling this anthology in March 2019 finally broke in the summer when she offered herself as a sacrifice for Brexit. Not that it changed the parliamentary arithmetic. As we went to print, her newly elevated successor faced a headache of his own, for all his optimistic talk about letting 'belief in Britain' solve all ills. Meanwhile, Mr Corbyn bumbled along, still Labour leader three years after 80 per cent of his MPs voted to get rid of him. He may even end up in Downing Street himself, only the second man to do so after his 70th birthday. Everything has changed about how politics is done, yet 'nothing has changed' seemed to be the motto of the age. Harold Wilson's dictum about the speed of political change, coined forty-five years ago, needs revising; these days the weak are a long time in politics.

Patrick Kidd
Eltham, August 2019

2014: ENTER THE KIPPERS

Four years into the coalition government, David Cameron was beginning to think about whether he could secure his own mandate in 2015, but a problem had arisen: Nigel Farage's UKIP, once dismissed by Cameron as 'fruitcakes, loonies and closet racists', were riding high, eager to hold the Prime Minister to the pledge he had made in his 2013 Bloomberg speech of an in/out referendum on Britain's membership of the EU. Three months after UKIP won the 2014 European elections with 27 per cent of the vote, Douglas Carswell, Tory MP for Clacton, announced he was defecting to Farage's party and would defend the seat in a by-election, which he won with almost 60 per cent of the vote. My first political sketch for The Times, standing in as holiday cover for Ann Treneman, was the next day.

11 OCTOBER
THE BLESSED DOUGLAS GREETS HIS DISCIPLES

UKIP were right. Clacton is full of immigrants. They swarmed around the town centre. Immigrants from east London, central London, even from as far as west London. Refugees from the Snapperi and Scribbleri tribes as well as hordes of Broadkasti, all had flocked to the Essex coast in search of a better story.

The new (old) MP for Clacton took a stroll round his new

(old) constituency, accompanied some of the way by a toad-faced fellow called Nigel. No one seemed too interested in Nigel, though, as Douglas Carswell was propelled in a giant, rolling maul of supporters and press. It was like the parading of a Catholic icon through the streets of a Sicilian village on a feast day, only without people pinning money to the cult figure. UKIP should look into that; could be a good way of fundraising.

At the centre, the Blessed Douglas stood tall and tieless, looking just a little pious. His arrival was heralded by an angel wearing a football shirt. We knew he was an angel because it was written on his shorts. 'Earth Angel' it said, in bold red letters. God works in mysterious ways. On the fringes, acolytes were muttering their creed, phrases such as 'We're on a roll' and 'They don't like it up 'em' over and over again. This was Biebermania for pensioners.

The maul drove on, the Blessed Douglas preaching as he went about the establishment stitch-up. He stopped dead in his tracks only once, when asked whether Malala Yousafzai, the latest Nobel peace laureate, should have been denied entry to Britain as a health tourist (as was the UKIP policy). The messiah stood still. One nostril flared, his crooked smile slanted further. 'I'm not familiar with that case,' he said carefully. 'She's pretty famous,' someone shouted. The Blessed Douglas looked for deliverance. Up came the cry: 'Wheelchair coming through!' The procession moved on.

The perambulation ended at the constituency office, which used to be a café and still had a whiff of chip fat about it. Down the road sat his former headquarters, next to a tanning salon and nail bar, in case we had forgotten we were in Essex. 'Lovely weather for a honeymoon,' one Tory said. 'And that's all he's going to get. We'll take the seat back next May.'

Mr Carswell knows he has work to do. 'There are two fences in this race and I'm still in the saddle after one,' he said. 'The next is in six months.' The People's Army have miles more to march.

14 OCTOBER
SWORN IN BUT NOT SWORN AT

Douglas Carswell was sworn in as UKIP's first elected MP yesterday. Sworn in, but not sworn at. The brief ceremony was received in near-silence. No jeers, no heckles, no boos nor hisses. The Tories had decided that dignity, for once, was best; Labour simply didn't know what to think. Is he one of us or still one of them? The House was full. It was thirty-two years since a defecting MP had sought an immediate by-election, so there was a novelty in gazing upon an honourable member who had actual honour.

The chamber had a lazy, start-of-term feeling. Michael Fabricant (Con, Lichfield) lounged through the Home Office Questions that preceded the oath like a well-fed leopard, twirling one suntanned calf. Dennis Skinner (Lab, Bolsover), wearing an oxblood tie, perched on the edge of his customary seat yet could scarcely be bothered to swear at passing Tories.

Gradually the seats began to fill. Margot James, MP for Stourbridge, strode in wearing leather trousers; Jacob Rees-Mogg, MP for the nineteenth century, draped himself across the end of a bench as if it were a chaise longue; Sir Alan Duncan (Con, Rutland and Melton) and Alec Shelbrooke (Con, Elmet and Rothwell) – one tiny and trim, the other looking like a mastodon with a fobwatch – came in together, a Tory Asterix and Obelix. Near the back, Sir George Young (Con, North West Hampshire) and Sir John Randall (Con, Uxbridge and South Ruislip), the former Chief Whip and his deputy, chatted with the relaxed air of men who know that controlling the rabble is no longer their responsibility.

Liz McInnes, the new MP for Heywood and Middleton, was sworn in first; then a hush descended as the doors were pulled back and in walked Mr Carswell, flanked by Zac Goldsmith (Con, Richmond Park) and the stately antique that is

Sir Peter Tapsell (Con, Louth and Horncastle), who had been given a fresh coat of varnish for the occasion.

Sir Peter has a passing resemblance to Mr Goldsmith's late father, whose Referendum Party once caused the Tories similar problems to UKIP, but he was supporting Mr Carswell as Father of the House rather than as a chum. Indeed, he barely knew who he was. When the Clacton MP defected in August, Sir Peter was quoted as saying, 'Who is he? Where is his constituency?' Sir Peter, who entered Parliament in 1959, has not bothered to learn a new MP's name since decimalisation came in.

Mr Carswell bowed his head to Michael Gove (Con, Surrey Heath), who gave amiable benediction, one Chief Whip to another, for Mr Carswell will have to discipline himself until another UKIP MP is elected. He bowed, too, to William Hague, who gave a curt nod, swore his oath, signed the book and was off. No time for sitting around.

As he left, he seemed to stare pointedly at Peter Bone, the Wellingborough MP and one of those rumoured to be considering joining the UKIP bandwagon. Did one detect a knowing look, like a Roman senator inviting another to join him in a bring-a-dagger party at the emperor's palace? Time will tell.

All this was watched with pride from the gallery by Nigel Farage, on his first visit to the chamber since he was seventeen. Later, the UKIP leader tweeted that he and Mr Carswell met for tea and a fruitcake. He didn't say which fruitcake had joined them.

A month after the Carswell defection, Mark Reckless, Tory MP for Rochester and Strood, also crossed the floor, on the eve of his party conference, and sought re-election at a by-election on 20 November. I went to watch the meeting when the local Tory members chose their candidate.

17 OCTOBER
CAMERON SHINES AT THE HUSTINGS

The Prime Minister bounded in, late but more shiny than ever. He looked as if he had been having his forehead polished for the cameras. This is what Dave means when he says, 'I give you my Pledge.'

We were gathered in a community hall in the village of Wainscott, part of the Rochester and Strood constituency where UKIP hopes to return its second MP on 20 November. The Conservatives are holding an open primary to select their candidate, in which anyone can vote.

The two contenders could not be more different. Two images came to mind when looking at them and saying 'Wainscott'. For Anna Firth it suggested wood panelling; for Kelly Tolhurst, perhaps the name of her first boyfriend.

Ms Firth was stereotypical Tory Woman. A former banker and barrister who gave up work to raise a family, she was dressed in Thatcherite blue, had sensible hair and an outdoorsy look. If she owns a hockey stick, it is undoubtedly a very jolly one.

Ms Tolhurst was more down to earth, like one of the contestants on *The Apprentice*. The daughter of a Medway boat-builder, who has her own business, she grew up in the heart of this community, unlike Ms Firth. 'I am one of you,' she said in a flat Kent accent. Indeed, she used to attend Guides and Brownies in this very hall.

The Prime Minister ran through a quick stump speech, mentioning 'long-term economic plan' four times and talking up his European referendum promise. A lot done, a lot left to do, please vote for us. That was basically it. 'Some of you', he added, 'may never have voted before.' That seemed unduly pessimistic given the age of the audience, although there was one man, well past seventy, who had arrived in short trousers. Very short, in fact, ending four inches above the knee. Given the weather we've been having, you had to admire his balls. And when he sat down, you were almost forced to.

Questions now came from the floor. 'If you become our MP, will you lie to us?' was the first one. Trust is a big issue here. Mark Reckless, who skipped off to UKIP after Nigel Farage flashed a thigh and some awkward polling at him, is a hated figure locally. Naturally, both candidates swore never to tell a fib.

Further questions followed on immigration, policing and religion, which gave Ms Firth – who grew up in Essex – a chance to hammer home (a shade desperately) that she was confirmed by the Bishop of Rochester. The audience seemed impressed with both. The two women appeared honest, unspun and wanting to enter politics for the right reasons. One suspects they haven't got a chance against UKIP's establishment insider.

The party members chose Ms Tolhurst as their candidate, but she lost the by-election to Mr Reckless by 3,000 votes. Six months later, however, at the general election, she won the seat back for the Conservatives with a majority of more than 7,000.

2015: JEZ WE CAN: LABOUR OPT FOR CORBYN

Parliament was dissolved on 30 March with the Conservatives and Labour neck and neck in the polls and UKIP in a strong third place, forcing Mr Cameron to confirm his pledge for an EU referendum. Against expectation, the Conservatives won 330 seats in the election on 7 May, a majority of twelve, with their Liberal Democrat coalition partners slipping from 57 seats to just eight. UKIP won 12.6 per cent of the vote but only one MP – Mr Carswell holding on in Clacton. After Labour won only 232 seats, Ed Miliband stood down as leader. Four MPs put themselves forward to succeed him: Andy Burnham, Yvette Cooper, Liz Kendall and Jeremy Corbyn, a veteran tribune of the far left who reached the required thirty-five nominations from MPs to be on the ballot paper with only minutes to spare after several political opponents agreed to lend him their votes to ensure his wing of the party had a voice. It was at this point that I took over full-time as the Times sketch-writer.

5 AUGUST
THE COMRADES FIND THEIR MESSIAH

Jeremy Corbyn was running late. Six hundred fellow travellers had gathered in Croydon to hear the prophet speak but the man himself had been let down by a train. When Mr

Corbyn spoke of wanting to stand on a platform, he didn't mean a crowded one at London Bridge.

The Jezmaniacs didn't mind. It was a sunny evening, the bar stocked real ale and the second-hand book stand was doing a roaring trade in such titles as *A History of London Busworkers*. Woody Guthrie and the Byrds played over the speakers and cigarettes were being rolled. Corbstock was extremely pleasant.

There was something almost religious in the air. People were wearing badges saying, 'I believe in JC.' Others spoke of keeping the faith. They see Mr Corbyn as the Messiah. They may even have their own Creed that ends: 'And I believe in one wholly drastic and catastrophic lurch; I acknowledge one socialism for the remission of spin; and I look for the resurrection of the Jez, and the strife of the world to come. Our Benn.'

Good news came at last. 'Jeremy is in the building,' the announcer said. 'Someone is making him a cup of tea.' Green tea or something herbal, I assume, since his fans think proper tea is theft.

Eventually, he strode out as Bob Marley sang, 'Get up, stand up.' The audience did not need encouragement. Mr Corbyn plays a crowd well. He spoke of the need to respect your opponents before laying into George Osborne and Lord Mandelson. He conceded that Labour ought to consider winning elections, but wouldn't give an inch on austerity. 'Let this be the summer of hope,' he thundered.

Mr Corbyn was here to answer questions, too. 'Please keep them to two minutes,' the MC warned. 'No fifteen-minute treatises.' A few sighed and put away speeches, but the first was succinct. 'Do you share our vision for a socialist cooperative commonwealth?' he asked. Mr Corbyn beamed and called for the abolition of hedge funds. It was like 1968 all over again.

11 AUGUST
LABOUR CANDIDATES SEEK TO BE TOP TWIT

Political campaigns work best if the message can be boiled down to a three-word innocuous treatise, or 'twit' for short. 'Labour Isn't Working' (Thatcher, 1979), 'Britain Deserves Better' (Blair, 1997), 'Yes We Can' (Obama, 2008). Two more twits arrived yesterday as Andy Burnham (Lab, Greater Manchester) and Liz Kendall (Lab, Leicester West), contestants in the summer's reality show *Labour Lacks Talent*, unveiled the videos and slogans that they hope will enable them to become the next former Leader of the Labour Party.

They differed only in one word. Mr Burnham ended his film with 'I won't change'; Ms Kendall went for 'I won't rest'. The restless Ms Kendall's video has all the passion of a British Gas commercial. There she is, alone in her office late at night, trying to write a letter. 'Dear supporter,' the voice in her head begins, alienating the 92 per cent of the party who say they support others.

Oh, how she wants to get this letter right. She scribbles on a notepad, then types up her thoughts. She gets up and paces round the room, looks out of the window, sits back at her desk. Types some more. Nods a bit. This is a vision of Prime Minister Kendall, taking all night to write a one-page letter.

Prime Minister Burnham, on the other hand, would be the Same Old Andy. A family man, stalwart of his northern community. Andy was shown making cakes with his children, riding on a train, wearing an Everton strip, marching with trade unionists, talking about rugby league. Normal. Northern.

If Ms Kendall is British Gas, Mr Burnham is Hovis. 'He's got the right balance. Genuine and rooted,' said a working-class yeoman captioned as 'Charlie Falconer, Andy's friend', though he looked an awful lot like Lord Falconer of Thoroton, PC,

QC, the former Justice Secretary and grandson of a Lord Provost of Edinburgh. I suppose even a normal man of the people has to find friends where he can.

21 AUGUST
'JEZ WE CAN', THE FAITHFUL SING, AS THE ISLINGTON OBAMA STEAMS IN

'Has he got a railcard?' The ticket inspector spoke to Jeremy Corbyn's aide as if the subject of her question was a catatonic patient in a geriatric ward, rather than the would be leader of Her Majesty's Opposition. Corbynmania had clearly not reached the 4.15 from St Pancras.

'Wait a second, I've got it here,' Mr Corbyn said, fishing his senior citizen's pass out of a coat pocket. 'You didn't believe I'm over sixty, did you?' The inspector wordlessly scribbled on his ticket and carried on, seemingly oblivious that she had just spoken to the Man of the People. She'll be first up against the wall come renationalisation.

They knew him when we got to the Albert Hall. Not *the* Albert Hall, obviously, but one in Nottingham, an appropriate destination for this modern Robin Hood who wants to rob the rich and give to the poor.

This was, Mr Corbyn estimated, the eightieth event he had done since the leadership campaign began and the movement is gathering pace. The hall holds 900 and there were 500 more queueing outside. When he entered the foyer and was told how many people would be turned away, he decided to make it two events instead. 'All out, all out!' went the cry from his comrades, just like in 1926.

'Our movement has been invaded by hope,' he told the crowd outside. 'People are coming together because this is an optimistic and interesting campaign. This is not a campaign against things.' Then he slagged off the bankers, since 'against' has a very narrow definition in the Corbyn dictionary.

Indeed, he is a mass of contradictions. Taking questions, he was asked how the party could unite under someone who had been so frequently disloyal to previous leaders. Mr Corbyn looked pained.

'But those were issues where I disagreed with the leadership,' he said. He has been as loyal as a sheepdog on the handful of subjects he has no problem with.

'But what about all those high-ranking members who disagree with you?' he was asked. He looked confused. 'What's this about ranking party members? We don't rank our members,' he said. Ranking people sounds like competition, with winners and losers, and Mr Corbyn does not like that.

Then someone asked him about trains and his eyes lit up. He spoke for several minutes about franchises and rolling stock. Inside the hall, 900 people looked at their watches and wondered if he was ever going to speak to them. 'Jez we can, Jez we can,' they chanted, politely. Everyone wants a piece of the Islington Obama. Apart, that is, from the inspector on the 4.15 from St Pancras.

11 SEPTEMBER
MY BLAIR LADY SHUTS EARLY

The curtain finally came down on *My Blair Lady* yesterday after a difficult few months. Tipped by many in May to be this summer's hit, the musical flopped badly, hamstrung by a lack of catchy tunes, a mediocre book and a leading lady, Liz Kendall, who was short on stardust.

Revivals have often done well on the Westminster stage. *Jezza Corbs Superstar* is receiving rave reviews, despite not having been updated since it first appeared in the 1970s, while *Fiddler on the Roof* was a favourite until the expenses scandal.

My Blair Lady was a new take on an old classic. The story of a Watford flower girl who is taught to pass herself off as a party leader, while appealing on paper, failed to stir the emotions on stage. This was a Liz Doolittle who lived down to her name.

Yesterday, Ms Kendall performed a farewell selection from the show in front of a gathering of supporters and friends, including the fourth most interesting member of the pop group Blur. In a small upstairs room of the Methodist Central Hall, the sort of space that Jeremy Corbyn now uses for his pre-rally cups of tea, Ms Kendall came out smiling and blowing kisses and launched into such songs as 'The Painful Gains (Fall Mainly to the Tories)', 'A Hymn to Her' ('Why can't a leader be more like a woman?') and 'Wouldn't It Be Loverly (To Be Electable)'.

There was polite clapping, but, as has been the case all summer, Ms Kendall lacked oomph. She called teachers 'amazing and brilliant' without giving one idea for improving education, and spoke repeatedly of her 'passion' without showing much policy. It was like this for most of the run.

Near the end, Ms Kendall's voice choked a little as she said, 'We are the greatest champion of equality and opportunity this country has ever seen,' and there was still time for one more 'amazing' before she went. It got a standing ovation, but this was still the end. The next time *My Blair Lady* is revived, it needs a bigger leading star and better songs.

Ms Kendall could read the writing on the wall. The result of the Labour leadership contest was announced at the Queen Elizabeth II Conference Centre in Westminster and she came last, with 4.5 per cent of the vote. On a turnout of more than 420,000 members, Mr Corbyn received almost 60 per cent.

14 SEPTEMBER
A NEW DAWN BREAKS

It was the morning after the revolution and the Heralds of the Red Dawn were anxious to hail the conquering comrade, but Jeremy Corbyn was in no hurry to leave the house.

Having turned down the chance to share Andrew Marr's sofa with Michael Gove, Mr Corbyn lingered over his muesli and reflected on the extraordinary events of the previous day. Who could ever have believed that the Labour Party would elect a privately educated white man from north London as its leader?

Over and over, Mr Corbyn rewound his Betamax player and watched the moment he became leader. His precise tally of votes was inaudible. 'Andy Burnham 80,462, Yvette Cooper 71,928, Jeremy Corbyn two-hundred-and-ROAR...'

In the QEII Centre, the Heralds of the Red Dawn burst into a chant of 'Jez we did! Jez we did!' Above the lectern, where Mr Corbyn would soon give his first speech as leader, was the slogan 'Your Choice'. One suspects there had been a conversation in party HQ about whether to add, '... so don't blame us.'

As Mr Corbyn took to the stage, Mr Burnham sat impassively. It may have had something to do with the Gorgon glares that Ms Cooper kept shooting him. While Liz Kendall, a distant fourth, was wearing a fixed maniacal smile.

Sitting behind them, soon-to-be-former members of the shadow Cabinet competed to see how slowly they could applaud, Tristram Hunt winning by some way. It had been felt that the party would never elect someone with a posh name like Tristram. Instead they went for a Jeremy, who has a brother called Piers.

15 SEPTEMBER
A QUIET DEBUT FOR MR PUNCH

It has been a long march from Islington to the Labour front bench. At 3.25 p.m. yesterday, Jeremy Corbyn shuffled into the Commons chamber through the door behind the Speaker's chair and had a whispered conversation with John Bercow. 'Where do I sit?' he probably asked.

When Mr Corbyn made his maiden speech back in 1983, he said that the building seemed 'a million miles away from the constituency that I represent'. For the past thirty-two years, he has kept a similar distance between himself and the centre of power.

It felt strange yesterday to look at the seat in the farthest corner where Mr Corbyn used to skulk and see vacant green leather. His comrades had left the place empty out of respect.

Having finally got his bearings, Mr Corbyn slid next to Chris Bryant (Lab, Rhondda) on the end of the front bench nearest the exit, looking like an intern who has been allowed to sit in at a board meeting. He appeared nervous, but also chuffed to bits. He had even put on a tie.

Some leaders on their first appearance in the Commons after their election might have got a cheer, but Mr Corbyn's presence was so low-key as to seem an irrelevance. He had to be beckoned down to the important end of the front bench as the Trade Union Bill debate began. 'Over here, Jeremy. Sit behind this big wooden box.' And there he nestled quietly for the next couple of hours, not causing a fuss.

'We have two things in common,' said Sajid Javid (Con, Bromsgrove), the Business Secretary, as he welcomed the Leader of the Opposition. Mr Corbyn looked up with interest. Does this bald man also own an allotment? 'You'll never catch either of us eating a bacon sandwich,' Mr Javid, a Muslim, told the vegetarian opposite. Mr Corbyn gave a smile. 'Ah yes,' he thought. 'A joke. I've heard about these.'

Some new leaders might have geed up the troops by barracking the minister, but Mr Corbyn just sat there looking bored, fiddling with his phone and occasionally speaking to Diane Abbott (Lab, Hackney North and Stoke Newington).

Instead, it was Mr Javid who united the Labour benches in anger. 'This is not a declaration of war on trade unions,' he said. 'Oh yes, it is,' they shouted back. 'We are the party of working people,' Mr Javid declared. 'Oh no, you're not,' they replied. Punch and Judy politics is back, but this time it seems that Mr Punch is a non-speaking part.

16 SEPTEMBER
CORBYN SWIPES A VETERAN'S LUNCH THEN VISITS THE TUC SHOP

What delightfully archaic things we keep discovering about Jeremy Corbyn. On Sunday, we learnt that one of his hobbies is photographing manhole covers, especially the cast iron opercula through which Victorian tradesmen made deliveries. They open up a window to a man's coal.

Now it turns out that he is the love child of Captain Mainwaring and Warden Hodges. 'My mum served as an air raid warden and my dad was in the Home Guard,' Mr Corbyn said before his first official engagement as leader of Her Majesty's semi-loyal opposition, attending a service to mark the 75th anniversary of the Battle of Britain.

I imagine a *Dad's Army* kind of childhood in which the adolescent Corbyn was told by one parent to 'put that light out' as he tried to read Engels under the blankets, while the other simply muttered 'stupid boy'. There will be a few who say the same thing about him today after seeing the footage of Private Corbyn at St Paul's, his top button undone, refusing to sing the national anthem.

Perhaps he should be commended for a lack of hypocrisy. It may have been a ceremony to honour those who died in the skies over Britain in 1940, but Mr Corbyn is for the many, not The Few. Who really cares if he looked a bit of a scruff? And then Jeremy went and swiped a veteran's lunch.

Two lunches, in fact. Mr Corbyn left the ceremony in a hurry and headed straight for a table where bags of sandwiches had been laid out for veterans and volunteers. Aware that he had a train journey ahead, the Labour leader grabbed two. That's redistribution for you.

From the Battle of Britain to the People's Republic of Brighton, where Mr Corbyn was due to address the TUC conference, the first bearded Labour leader to do so since Keir Hardie in 1907. The hall was packed and the band started to play 'Big Spender'. What an appropriate campaign song for 2020. Mr Corbyn walked in the joint, good looking, so refined, and anxious to tell the comrades what's going on in his mind. If only he had written it down first.

Some can busk a big speech; Mr Corbyn cannot. It is not just that he rambles; he barely draws breath. It's like listening to a waiter reading out a long list of the specials of the day, not allowing you time to take in each dish and decide whether you fancy it.

There was a lot of ground to cover. He had a pop at China for not being communist enough; praised trade unionists in Colombia; and told 30,000 new party members that they will all be invited to shape his agenda. 'Let us make policy together,' he declared. The shadow Cabinet room's going to be awfully cramped. The only issue he didn't mention was manholes. I hope he's got someone looking into them.

17 SEPTEMBER
ENTER JEREMY... MARIE, STEVEN, PAUL, CLAIRE, GAIL AND ANGELA

The chamber was packed and the gallery rammed to the gunwales for the first Prime Minister's Questions of the Corbyn Era.

David Cameron was in his usual place, looking a bit leathery after his summer holiday. Indeed, the whole Tory front bench had caught some rays. Theresa May (Con, Maidenhead) resembled a lightly grilled camembert; Michael Fallon (Con, Sevenoaks) glowed painfully; and Chris Grayling's head (Con, Epsom and Ewell) was so brown and smooth when viewed from above that it would score four at snooker.

Toady, Lickspittle and Creep, the Tory backbenchers, were lined up to ask questions about hard-working powerhouses, and the Labour troops had their angry faces on. All that was missing was the Leader of the Opposition. But she wasn't there. Marie from Putney had sent a bearded gentleman in a beige jacket, looking like Dumbledore in mufti, to ask her question instead.

'Marie says: "What are you going to do about affordable housing?"' Jeremy Corbyn, tribune and mouthpiece of the people, began. When Marie was finished, a man called Steven was made Leader of the Labour Party for thirty seconds. Then Paul led the party, then Claire, then Gail and Angela. Give Mr Corbyn long enough and everyone will have their turn.

It was more like *Gardeners' Question Time*, with Mr Corbyn as Eric Robson and Mr Cameron as Bunny Guinness. As the format develops, viewers may get Mr Corbyn to ask the Prime Minister for his advice on pruning their wisteria or whether he knows a good recipe for quince jelly.

Welcome to the New Politics. People don't want their leaders to think up questions, Mr Corbyn claimed. They want to do it themselves. As their conduit, he had received an awful lot of suggestions. 'There is not time to ask 40,000 questions today,' Mr Corbyn said, with a hint of sadness that made you wonder if he had asked the Speaker if it was possible.

The House seemed bemused by how pleasant it all was. Mr Cameron reined in his customary crowing and tried to give straight answers and Mr Corbyn thanked him for doing so.

Perhaps in future editions, this Jimmy Young-style PMQs can be taken a step further. Mr Corbyn can be given an earpiece and take live questions. 'I've got Sheila from Ipswich on line four, Mr Cameron. She wants to know what you're going to do about potholes on the A12. But first: Chris de Burgh.'

Not long after Mr Corbyn's first PMQs, Parliament broke up for the conference recess, which meant another first for the Labour leader: the first time he had delivered a speech using an autocue, which became apparent when he accidentally read out the speaking instruction 'Strong message here'. The Tories began their conference in Manchester a week later, in a mood of confidence that with an opponent like this, life was going to be easy.

6 OCTOBER
THE MASTER BUILDER REACHES FOR THE SKY

George Osborne strode onto the stage wearing an enormously smug grin, representative of all hard-smirking people, but he was not here as Chancellor of the Exchequer. Mr Osborne has a much higher role to play. This was the entry of the Master Builder. The man with the Caesar haircut intends to be a new Augustus and rebuild the country, turning rubble into marble.

'Some people stand on the sidelines. Some want to knock things down. But we – we are the builders,' Mr Osborne said, a verse he returned to several times. This was to be a constructive dialogue. Where Labour politicians – 'the wreckers' – spoke only to their base at their conference in Brighton last week, Mr Osborne wanted his message to spread beyond the room: to those who had voted Tory and those who might.

'We won't duck decisions,' he said. 'Even if the decisions are unpopular and bitterly opposed, if they turn out to be the right ones, people will go on putting their trust in you.' In doing so, he was echoing another Caesar, Augustus's heir. '*Oderint dum probent*,' Tiberius said. Let them hate me, so long as they approve.

Mr Osborne said that the past five years had been about laying the foundations; the next five years will be about re-forming welfare, lowering taxes, raising wages and building new infrastructure.

'We are the only true party of labour,' he said.

He had a lot of ground to cover. A bit on reforming Europe, quite a large chunk on regenerating the north and several policy ideas on devolving the collection and spending of business rates to local government that had all the besuited Rotarians in the audience purring. It could be described as a 'wide-ranging speech' (code for 'leadership bid').

The Master Builder has great ambitions. So great, in fact, that he was happy to quote John F. Kennedy: 'We do these things not because they are easy, but because they are hard.' It is probably the first time that carriageway improvements on the A14 have been compared to the Apollo moon landings.

'I don't want to do this job just to occupy the office,' Mr Os-borne said. No indeed. There was one person in the room whose office he would prefer. However, the Master Builder should read his Ibsen. You may mount right to the top and hear harps in the air, but the higher you build, the greater the risk of a fall.

13 OCTOBER
LORD ROSE OF HABERDASHERY TRIES TO SELL THE EU

Brave move, holding a press opp in a brewery. I love a good metaphor. Your organising skills had better be tip-top if you're going to launch your campaign in a warehouse with the faint whiff of yeast in the air.

Brave, too, to give your campaign name a set of initials

that conjures up an image that helps your opponents. Britain Stronger in Europe – BSE. It brought to mind a queue of mad cattle shuffling off to the abattoir and a Brussels ban on British beef. Perhaps not the picture that the In crowd were hoping for.

Since their chief argument for staying in the EU is that it may be bad for British businesses to leave, they could have gone for a different slogan. Leaving Europe Probably Risks Our Shareholders' Yield, say – although LEPROSY may not be the image they want either.

BSE was launched in the old Truman Brewery in Brick Lane, east London, where immigrants, from Huguenot weavers to Jewish merchants and Bengali chefs, have often settled. These days it is home to hipsters: young arty-techy people with exuberant facial hair and an addiction to coffee. Lots of keen-looking young people stood around in red, white and blue T-shirts, waiting for a June Sarpong, which sounds as if it should be a post-finals cocktail party at Oxford but turned out to be a TV presenter.

Ms Sarpong told us that the EU was a perfect mixture of 'the efficiency of the Germans, the pragmatism of the Finns, the innovation of the Swedes, the creativity of the Italians and the, er, Frenchness of the French'. She didn't mention what Britain contributes. Queueing, perhaps.

She was the warm-up act for Lord Rose of Haberdashery, the man who went from the shop floor to the boardroom of Marks & Spencer and could thus get away with opening his speech by saying that the chilly weather would be good news for sales of knitwear.

Speaking rapidly and a bit repetitively, Lord Rose said he wasn't much of a fan of Europe but that it would be too dangerous to drop out. 'The benefits outweigh the costs,' he said. 'It's a leap in the dark, not a risk worth taking.' He also said that being in the EU 'saves every person around £480 million a year'. God help our overdrafts if that wasn't a slip of the tongue.

15 OCTOBER
HEAD BOY MULTIPLIES BUMBLEBORE'S DIVISIONS

Professor Bumblebore rose to his feet and looked disapprovingly over his glasses at the smug, sullen forms opposite. Disrespect hung in the air – in front of him and behind, for the staff had hardly given him a resounding welcome – but the headmaster wanted to show that he was in charge of assembly, not David Cameron, the head boy, nor any of the teachers anxious to see him fail.

Cameron perched eagerly on the edge of his seat, a 'Can I help you, sir?' expression on his face, while Toady, Lickspittle and Creep, his goons, slipped stink bombs into their catapults. 'I want to talk to you about Kelly,' the professor began. The less able members of Tory House began to groan. Not the outside world again.

This assembly, though, was going to be more nuanced than the last. Instead of just reading out letters, Bumblebore had a maths test. 'If Kelly, a single mum with a disabled child, works 40.5 hours a week at £7.20 an hour but is losing her tax credits next April, how much worse off will she be?' he said.

'Let me answer him directly,' Cameron replied, a sure sign he was going to avoid the question. Then he started thinking out loud: 'So... £20 a week pay rise for those on the living wage, going up to £9 an hour in four years, plus a rise in tax threshold to £11,000, thirty hours of childcare, cheaper council house rent, rising employment...'

The answer did not please the headmaster. 'It's £1,800, ignoramus,' he tutted. Cameron looked doubtful. Bumblebore threw a few more numbers at him; Cameron gave different ones back. The headmaster wanted to do subtraction and division; the head boy preferred addition and multiplication. Cameron's gang yawned and some of the staff shouted at them.

'He is doing his best,' Bumblebore said, witheringly, and tried another question: 'If Matthew and his three friends, all on an above-median wage, share a privately rented house, how long must they each wait to be able to afford to buy?' There was some sniggering at the back from Toady, Lickspittle and Creep. Perhaps they were reading *The Beano* inside a copy of Hansard. 'You might find this funny, but it's not funny to me or Matthew,' the professor snapped. More sniggering.

Cameron said that his dad's friends were building new starter homes and that people like Matthew would have the right to buy one from a housing association. Teachers jeered.

'Oh yeah?' Cameron said. 'How many council homes did you build?' Bumblebore suggested that he take this problem away as homework and send in his answer later. The head boy, though, had his confidence back. Cameron boasted of a new after-school club called the National Infrastructure Commission.

'That was one of our ideas,' shouted a teacher. 'When you have a good idea, I implement it,' Cameron said. 'A bit like that idea you supported until last week about running a surplus to fix the chapel roof while the sun is shining.'

The bursar, Mr McDonnell, who had upset half the staff room by changing his mind on this policy, was nowhere to be seen and the pupils were baying. Cameron stood, his arms raised in triumph, and Bumblebore looked at his feet. He had done well – much better than at the previous assembly – but it was clear who was still in charge.

6 NOVEMBER
BASHING THE BISHOP

The day after Theresa May announced new powers to look at what websites we are accessing, the House of Lords debated pornography. Better to get it out in the open, I suppose, although doing that sort of thing has landed some politicians in hot water.

It was announced last week that they are reviving the *Carry On* films. The next one should be set in the Lords: *Carry on Scrutinising*. There are plenty of suitably named peers who could have a small part in it. Lord Adonis would be the ladies' favourite, while Lord Griffiths of Fforestfach and Lord Rogers of Riverside would be forever trying to lure Baroness Bottomley outside. Lord Foulkes of Cumnock and Lord Ryder of Wensum sound like the new Sid James and Charles Hawtrey, and Baroness Stern could be the Chief Whip.

Sadly, none of them seemed to be present for the porn debate. Instead, the business began, as it may do on certain special-interest websites, with a bishop. 'My first-hand knowledge of pornography is very limited,' the Bishop of Chester confessed. 'Of the range of vices available to me, I have been tempted by most but not in a significant way by pornography. That makes me a rather unusual, if not exotic, creature.'

He did, though, admit to having an 'unexpected bedfellow' in D. H. Lawrence. One imagined him reading *Lady Chatterley's Lover* under the blanket at theological college, although it was from a more prudish essay of Lawrence that the bishop wished to read. 'Pornograpy is the catastrophe of our civilisation,' he said in his celestial voice, before going on to quote with disapproval of 'degraded nudity and ugly, squalid, dirty sex'.

The Bishop of Bristol clearly preferred the more earthy bits of Lawrence. 'When I was in school there were three pages of his book that captured our attention,' he said wistfully. I suspect that the Bishop of Bristol finds it hard not to snigger whenever he meets the Lord Chief Justice, who shares a name (John Thomas) with Lady Chatterley's favourite garden tool.

Others were quite informed. Lord Giddens, talking about cybersex, said, 'The complete range of human inventiveness is there.' Lord Cormack was eager to differentiate between the filth on the internet and the wonderful Japanese erotic prints that he saw at the British Museum, as well as the 'vigorous cartoons' of the eighteenth-century caricaturist Thomas Rowlandson.

Baroness Murphy was the most candid. 'I come at this from a different angle,' she said, speaking as an academic psychiatrist and as a woman who once submitted a hoax paper on 'cello scrotum' (a musical version of tennis elbow, she claimed) to the *British Medical Journal*.

'The debate has made me feel a little mischievous,' she added, before confessing to a wide experience of top-shelf magazines, hotel channels and dodgy videos, especially, for some reason, ones made in Japan. 'Much of it is pretty silly and highly enjoyable,' she said.

As she went on to talk in specific terms about the importance of fantasies, some faces began to turn the same colour as the benches. Baroness Murphy's browsing history must be fascinating.

11 NOVEMBER
MASTER OF UNIVERSITY CHALLENGE LACKS ANSWERS

It is hard to know what David Cameron could ever do about Europe that would satisfy some of his backbenchers. Blocking up the Channel Tunnel, perhaps, or banning the production of croissants. Certainly, the plans that he outlined yesterday for EU renegotiation were thought by ardent Outers to be wetter than a whale's hanky.

Standing at Chatham House in front of a huge map of the world, as if to show what a global force Great Britain is, Mr Cameron set out four requests (he wouldn't go so far as to call them demands) and made a semi-threat that if they were met with a deaf ear by EU leaders then he would have to think jolly hard about whether Britain should be in their club. He might even withdraw from the wine committee in protest.

Mr Cameron insisted that Britain had a pragmatic approach to Europe. 'We are natural debunkers,' he added. It did not win over the Eurosceptics. Many of them think that debunkers are things you try to avoid on de golf course.

In a debate that followed in the Commons, David Lidington (Con, Aylesbury), the Europe minister, went out to defend the line. Mr Lidington is a charming and intelligent man – twice a winner of *University Challenge* – with a donnish affability. You sense that his colleagues would prefer someone in Brussels who is more of a bastard.

The punching was led off by Sir Bill Cash (Con, Stone), who wanted treaty changes rather than fine words. Douglas Carswell attacked 'Eurosclerosis'; David Nuttall (Con, Bury North) said Mr Cameron was 'tinkering on the fringes'; and Peter Lilley (Con, Hitchin and Harpenden) said Britain should not use up its 'limited bargaining power' on 'purely symbolic changes'.

Peter Bone sarcastically wanted to thank the Prime Minister for his honesty in making clear that little real change was being sought. 'No longer do we have to pretend there's going to be a substantial renegotiation,' he said. 'We can get on with campaigning to come out.'

Jacob Rees-Mogg (Con, North East Somerset) seems to be reading what passes for modern literature in the Moggstead and gave us his best *Oliver Twist*. 'This is pretty thin gruel,' he said, asking Beadle Lidington for more. Bernard Jenkin (Con, Harwich and North Essex) was similarly unimpressed. 'Is that it?' he said, sounding like a disappointed virgin bride on her wedding night. 'Is that the sum total of the government's position in this renegotiation?'

Mr Lidington could only smile and shrug. He is like a Weeble, those once-popular toys that wobbled but never fell down. 'I always strive to be cheerful in this job,' he said, when one Labour MP expressed sympathy for his position. He's going to need bucketloads of cheer to survive the referendum.

On 13 November, a series of co-ordinated terrorist attacks by Is-lamic State in Paris killed 130 people, ninety of them at a rock concert at the Bataclan theatre. Parliament gathered at the earliest opportunity to express its shock and sympathy. It was a chance for Theresa May, then a rather unremarkable Home Secretary, to act as a stateswoman.

17 NOVEMBER
VIVE LA FRANCE AS MPS SHOW *SOLIDARITÉ*

Charles James Fox, rival of Pitt the Younger, had advice for poli-ticians who like to show off in the chamber. 'No Greek; as much Latin as you like,' he said. 'And never French in any circumstances.'

When Parliament debated the atrocities in Paris, though, a few could not resist dusting down *Larousse* in order to demon-strate that they stand *épaule contre épaule avec les grenouilles*.

Tom Brake (Lib Dem, Carshalton and Wallington), the Liberal Democrat foreign affairs spokesman, had at least been schooled near Paris. He wanted to tell our French friends in their own tongue that Britain was on their side and we would *combattre le terrorisme ensemble*. A trickle of *oui-oui* passed around the room.

Soon after, Sir Edward Leigh (Con, Gainsborough) flexed his tongue across the Channel. '*Maintenant et pour toujours, vous avez nos prières et notre solidarité,*' he said, promising our eternal prayers and support. '*Vive la Republique. Vive la France.*'

Theresa May, who had given a statesmanlike and sombre performance entirely in English to that point, sensed that she would have to respond in kind. There is something rather Parisian about the Home Secretary with her stern, birdlike face and sophisticated fashion sense. You could imagine her owning a bistro in the sixth *arrondissement*, one where the food is not all that tasty or filling but the service is efficient.

Madame May was not going to be intimidated by these show-offs. She hoiked up her metaphorical culottes and leapt in. 'I can only say that *nous sommes solidaires avec vous,*' she said. '*Nous sommes tous ensembles.*'

The words were unshowy, but they did the job. Much like Madame May herself. Her statement had been heard in silence. ISIS possess, she said, 'an empty, perverted and murderous ideology. They represent no one. And they will fail.' It was the right tone on a grey day. 'France grieves,' Madame May went on, 'but she does not grieve alone.'

18 NOVEMBER
KING CORBYN UNMOVED BY THE RAGING STORM

It was a *King Lear* sort of a day. Jeremy Corbyn, the elderly ruler of a divided dominion, sat stubborn and intractable, seemingly oblivious to the storm that was lashing around him. Backbenchers on all sides blew winds and cracked their cheeks, and steadily his retinue diminished until Lear was left with just the Fool (Diane Abbott) and loyal Brent (Barry Gardiner). No sign of Poor Tom: the deputy leader had something better to do.

This was not a day for David Cameron to play party politics with his statement on security. He didn't need to. Mr Corbyn's own side were happy enough to attack their leader. Plenty voiced objection to Mr Corbyn's belief that the police should not shoot men in suicide vests, or his regret that ISIS's chief executioner had been bombed rather than invited for a chat about his methods over tea.

Chris Leslie (Lab, Nottingham East), former shadow Chancellor, said that the 'proportionate use of lethal force' should be obvious to everyone, pointedly repeating, 'To everyone.' Mr Corbyn looked at his phone.

Emma Reynolds (Lab, Wolverhampton North East), former shadow Communities Secretary, said it was 'wrong and disgraceful' to blame the West for the terrorist attacks. Mr Corbyn scratched behind his ear.

Ian Austin (Lab, Dudley North), one of Gordon Brown's former henchmen, said he agreed with everything that Mr Cameron said and accused his own leader of inflaming the situation. Mr Corbyn yawned.

His reply was rambling and incoherent. It was met with silence from his own side. Even the Tories couldn't be bothered to jeer, save one idiot who softly said 'hooray' when Mr Corbyn announced his final point.

Then came the backbench attacks and the rapid departure of Mr Corbyn's retinue. Hilary Benn (Lab, Leeds Central), the shadow Foreign Secretary, who had looked away from his leader when the first comments were made about shoot-to-kill, left when Nigel Dodds of the DUP (Belfast North) said it was shameful to blame the victims. Andy Burnham and Chris Bryant soon followed.

One by one, as attack followed attack, the front bench emptied, but poor loyal Brent remained. Mr Gardiner, a junior shadow energy minister, probably felt that it would look rude if he slipped off when it was just down to him, Mr Corbyn and Ms Abbott. 'My master calls me, I must not say no.' One hopes his loyalty will be rewarded with more than an invitation to the Stop the War Christmas dinner.

26 NOVEMBER
CHAIRMAN MCDONNELL THROWS THE BOOK AT OSBORNE

A century ago yesterday Albert Einstein set out a general theory of relativity that identified parts of the universe where space and time have become so distorted that all light has been swallowed up. This is what it must feel like to be a moderate Labour MP.

'Let's quote from Mao,' John McDonnell (Lab, Hayes and Harlington) said in his response to George Osborne's autumn statement. And from his pocket, the shadow Chancellor pulled a Little Red Book. Perhaps he always keeps it close to his heart for when he needs inspiration.

'We must learn to do economic work from all who know how, no matter who they are,' Chairman McDonnell read. 'We must not pretend to know when we do not know.' Well, it could have been worse. 'Revolution is an act of violence by which one class overthrows another', another Maoism, would have gone down very badly in Windsor.

But he didn't seem to have considered the symbolism of quoting from a brutal dictator. Imagine the uproar if a Tory had embellished his speech with a spot of *Mein Kampf.* He then chucked the book across the table at Mr Osborne, who could not believe his luck. Looking inside, he joked, 'It's his own personal signed copy.' Or maybe it wasn't a joke. This was not what Labour supporters meant when they called on Mr McDonnell to throw the book at the Chancellor.

'Bring back Ed Balls,' someone shouted. It was probably a Tory, but these days you can't be sure. Like light in a black hole, moderate Labour MPs are devastated by the gravity of their situation.

The end of 2015 was overshadowed by a debate on whether Britain should join the military action against Islamic State in Syria. It was gripping, especially in what it meant for Labour, with Mr Corbyn arguing against military action at the start and Hilary Benn, his shadow Foreign Secretary, wrapping it up to argue the other way. On the morning after, normal mundane business was resumed.

4 DECEMBER
RELIEF FLOODS IN, ESPECIALLY FOR SPEAKER

Never let it be said that the House of Commons lacks breadth. On Wednesday, MPs debated attacks on targets in Syria for almost eleven hours; yesterday, they talked about Dolly Parton, *Doctor Who* and hedgehogs. Which is more in the national interest? Let us begin, though, with news of Mr Speaker's bladder. John Bercow had stoically sat through the entirety of the Syria debate – all 684 minutes of it – without a single comfort break and was rightly congratulated for his self-control.

Pete Wishart of the SNP called him 'golden bladder', while Chris Bryant, the shadow Leader of the House, wondered whether, like Davros in *Doctor Who*, he secretly had a feeding and filtration system fitted into the chair.

In fact, in days gone by, a commode was built into the chair, and a curtain provided to grant privacy when emergency called. Bernard Weatherill, Speaker in 1983–92, once said that he stopped using it because it gave him back pain.

Mr Bercow, on the other hand, had no such protection. He had simply guarded against nature by not drinking. Mr Bryant speculated that he might have been on drugs, an excuse for a joke. Noting that the owners of Viagra and Botox have recently merged, he suggested that Mr Bercow was being used as a guinea pig for a combined drug that would allow him to keep a stiff upper lip all day.

Perhaps some levity was needed after such a serious Wednesday. Mr Bryant is a puckish character – he began yesterday's weekly grilling of the Leader of the House by telling Chris Grayling to straighten his tie – and he may have been put in a frisky mood by the presence of Hilary Benn, star of the previous evening.

Mr Benn had no obvious reason for showing up, but he seemed very jolly, laughing with Mr Bryant. There is a spring in his step and a glint in his eye after his rollicking performance on Wednesday night.

If Mr Wishart had got his way, Mr Benn would have rounded up the debate yesterday – or perhaps next week. He complained that Syria was of such importance that the debate should have run over at least two days. Oddly, he then moaned that the next Scottish Questions had been postponed a week because of the emergency session. You can't have it both ways.

Martyn Day, his comrade from Linlithgow and East Falkirk, also raised the workload, saying that his staff had to work 'unreasonable, family-unfriendly hours'. Thérèse Coffey (Con, Suffolk Coastal), the deputy Leader of the House, said that there was nothing stopping him from letting his staff go home at a normal hour. She then added, by the by, that '9 to 5' was her favourite Dolly Parton song.

The contribution closest to *The Times*'s heart, though, came from Oliver Colvile (Con, Plymouth Sutton and Devonport), who is a fearless champion of the hedgehog and again raised the plight of the nation's Tiggy-Winkles.

This had the rare effect of making Mr Grayling look rather sweet. Noting that this paper has been encouraging people to make holes in their garden fences to create a hedgehog superhighway, Mr Grayling said that his fence had such a hole.

'Sadly,' he sniffed, 'I do not have any hedgehogs in my garden. I hope they will arrive.' And I swear that a tear began to form in the corner of his eye. Perhaps he should write to Father Christmas.

2016: DAWN OF THE NEVERENDUM

Mr Cameron and Mr Corbyn began the new year hoping to reboot their weary parties. The Labour leader took several days to shuffle his front bench, which said little for his decisiveness, while the Prime Minister, having been on a round of tours of European capitals at the end of 2015, hoped to convince his MPs that he was able to reform the EU from within.

6 JANUARY
LEADERS TRY A NEW POSITION IN TANTRIC RESHUFFLE

After more than a day of tweaks and fiddling, Jeremy Corbyn took a break from his tantric reshuffle to listen to a leader who is the master at teasing his members to the brink of ecstasy without quite giving them what they want.

David Cameron has been toying with the Tory backbenchers for some time over the big in/out. Some will never be satisfied, but Mr Cameron spoke honeyed words to them yesterday about his latest EU referendum negotiations.

There is a 'great deal of goodwill' towards Britain among Europe's leaders, the Prime Minister said. They want to find 'mutually satisfactory solutions' to his demands for change and if they don't, well, he will 'rule nothing out'. Some of the more ardent Europhobes developed a dreamy look, already imagining the bombers taking off from Biggin Hill.

Meanwhile, Mr Corbyn sat opposite the PM, scribbling away in a small notebook. Perhaps he was still tinkering with the detail of a reshuffle that had taken so long, one could only assume that the Leader of the Opposition was working to rule in a dispute over the returns he was getting for his labour. Oh, for the days when a reshuffle just meant rotating the crops in his allotment.

Or maybe he was writing poetry, a hobby in the days before he became leader. It could even have been an ode about the reshuffle. 'When I phoned to dismiss Michael Dugher, he was cross and declared, "What a bugger"...'

Mr Cameron called it 'the longest reshuffle in history' and said that we could have watched all the *Star Wars* films in the time it had taken. This shows how far Tory modernisation has come. In the past, the comparison would have been to Wagner.

The Prime Minister also made a decent joke about the Labour upheaval. Referring to the twin sisters in the shadow Cabinet, he said, 'Never mind how many Eagles we end up with; they have an albatross at the head of their party.' It amused the members who know their Coleridge, but perhaps confused the golfers.

As usual, the opposition were only the people sitting across from Mr Cameron; the enemy were all on the seats behind him and some were still not fulfilled by his seduction. Sir Gerald Howarth (Con, Aldershot) praised him for agreeing that ministers could campaign to leave the EU without being sacked but wanted him to get on with it. 'It will not be done in any unnatural haste,' Mr Cameron said.

He and George Osborne – the Sting and Trudie Styler of tantric politics – have plenty of new positions they want to try. The Prime Minister went a bit further in answer to Cheryl Gillan (Con, Chesham and Amersham). The European Council might reach an agreement next month, but he wants another three months of national debate before the vote. 'Believe me,' he promised, 'by the time we get to the end of the referendum campaign, everyone will have had enough of the subject.'

As he looked across at the scribbling Mr Corbyn, now apparently trying to come up with a rhyme for Rosie Winterton, perhaps the Prime Minister felt a pang of envy. How nice it must be to seem so oblivious to the sharpening of knives on your backbenches.

21 JANUARY
CRISPIN SAYS 'RELAX'

The problem with wanting politics to be more reflective of real life is that it inevitably leads to a bald, middle-aged man explaining to the House of Commons how party drugs help him to enjoy anal sex.

'I out myself as a popper user,' Crispin Blunt (Con, Reigate), the chairman of the Foreign Affairs Select Committee, declared. Fifty years ago, such a statement would have indicated an appreciation of modern philosophy; any politician who confessed to enjoying a hit of Popper was probably referring to one of Sir Karl's critiques of teleological historicism. Those who were into the heavy stuff would take a snifter of Bertrand Russell.

Today, though, poppers are a chemical product popular on the club scene that have, as Keith Vaz (Lab, Leicester East) explained, 'a beneficial … effect in enabling anal sex'. Lyn Brown (West Ham), Labour's drugs spokeswoman, said that until she took on the brief she thought poppers were 'the little things with the string that we had at parties'.

Mr Blunt, 55, is far more worldly and during yesterday's debate on whether to ban psychoactive drugs, or 'legal highs', he said that poppers should be placed, with coffee and incense, on an exempt list, or else gay men would turn to other, more risky, drugs instead.

Amyl nitrite, the principal chemical in poppers, has been around for more than a century. Andrew Gwynne (Lab, Denton and Reddish) said that Ernest Bevin, the Foreign Secretary under Clement Attlee, used to sniff it at the Cabinet table on the advice of his doctor because he had a heart murmur.

Doubtless many MPs have also used it to aid their intimate encounters but politicians are rarely so open about their sexual habits in public. Norman Fowler, the former Health Secretary, is said to have remarked 'Crikey' when a Cabinet colleague explained oral sex to him, while Eric Heffer, the former Labour chairman, was bemused when the subject came up in Annie's Bar. 'They never taught us that in the RAF,' he said. 'I wouldn't ask Doris to do it.'

Then there was the time when Jerry Hayes, the former Harlow MP, found Willie Whitelaw looking ashen-faced and nursing a bucket of Scotch. Asked what was the matter, Thatcher's Deputy Prime Minister groaned, 'I've just had to explain to Margaret what anal sex is.'

Yet here was Mike Freer, who now represents Thatcher's Finchley seat, talking quite cheerfully about relaxing the anal muscles and adding, by way of an interesting aside, that poppers can also be used as an antidote for adder venom. A useful tip for those who go cruising for gay sex in areas where snakes lurk.

23 JANUARY
MOGG'S DRONE ATTACK SHOOTS DOWN BILLS

The House of Commons on a Friday morning is where good ideas go to die. It is here, thirteen times a year, that private members' bills can be debated. Almost all of them fail through being 'talked out'.

It is a parliamentary irony that MPs can be limited to two minute speeches on such trivial matters as whether to bomb another country or how to raise taxes, but when it comes to private legislation they can drone on for as long as they wish, until the Speaker draws stumps.

Fifteen bills were up for debate on such topics as no-fault divorces, putting mothers' names on marriage certificates and abolishing the Department for Energy and Climate Change. At the end of the five-hour session, they had just begun bill No. 2. The rest must hope for better luck another day.

This may seem a waste of time, but there is something admirable in the way that politicians can speak on a subject for well over an hour without nodding off. Sir Ivan Lawrence spent four hours and twenty-three minutes talking about fluoridation in 1985. He only stopped because he had to go and defend a bank robber in his other job as a barrister.

The new Sir Ivan is Jacob Rees-Mogg, MP for Much Wittering, a man who once used parliamentary time to argue that Somerset should have its own time zone. If there were an Olympic event for sesquipedalian circumlocution, as The Mogg would call it, he'd be there in his pinstriped leotard winning gold for GB.

The Mogg debated the precise meaning of 'appropriate', 'cautiously' and 'may' in amendments to the first bill and attacked the idea of consultation. 'It has become immensely fashionable, and we should always be cautious of fashion,' he said.

MPs then spent a few minutes discussing whether The Mogg had ever been called fashionable. 'Only by accident,' Speaker Bercow ventured. 'I would take it as a grave insult,' The Mogg replied, although he later claimed that he was '"with it", in the current phraseology' on knowing that judicial reviews were unfashionable.

There are others keen to be the next Mogg. Kit Malthouse, MP for Prate and Blather, spoke wistfully about going camping with his parents and compared the Bay of Pigs disaster to one of Marks & Spencer's bad reinventions. This gave Seema Kennedy, MP for Upper Rambling, a chance to talk about buying M&S pasties when she was a student. There was some vague link to the subject at hand.

Eventually, after four and a half hours, MPs ran out of things to say and agreed to give the bill a third reading. It may even become law, since the government is quite keen on it. All this filibuster had been about holding up the other fourteen bills.

This lucky one would allow Great Ormond Street Hospital children's charity to keep all the royalties from Peter Pan that J. M. Barrie had willed to the hospital. It seemed an appropriate topic. Thanks to the ticking crocomogg, all the other bills remain stuck in Neverland.

With the European Union Referendum Act getting Royal Assent just before Christmas and Mr Cameron announcing the referendum would be on 23 June, the opening months of the year were spent waiting to see what the Eurosceptic members of the Cabinet would do. Boris Johnson finally decided to support the Leave campaign but only after writing two different columns, advocating alternative courses, and seeing which most persuaded him.

23 FEBRUARY
BULLER BOYS BLUSTER OVER BREXIT

Hell hath no fury, one Labour MP observed, like a Bullingdon boy scorned. Boris Johnson's decision to throw in his lot with the Out crowd was seen in Downing Street as a declaration of war, and yesterday the Prime Minister was happy to take the fight to his old chum.

'I won't dwell on the irony that some people who want to

vote to leave apparently want to use a Leave vote to remain,' David Cameron said, in reference to Boris's suggestion that a Leave vote could lead to a better deal from Brussels.

'I know couples who have begun divorce proceedings,' he went on, 'but I do not know any who began them in order to renew their wedding vows.' There was awkward laughter. Then came the big hit.

'I am not standing for reelection,' Mr Cameron said. 'I have no other agenda than what is best for the country.' Sock! He may as well have added that Boris was only following that old Groucho Marx maxim: 'These are my principles. If you don't like 'em, I have others.'

Boris, his arms folded firmly across his chest and his hands wedged in his armpits, glowered. He had been sitting on the EU fence for so long it almost seemed that he would form a splinter group. Eventually, he had made his mind up. '*Alea iacta est*,' he said. (Or, more likely, knowing from his Plutarch that Caesar declaimed in Greek, 'Ancrriphtho kybos.')

Kibosh it certainly was. The front pages were all about the civil war in the Tory Party. Mr Cameron was keen on a swift revenge. If you're going to cross the Rubicon, be prepared to get your sandals wet.

When the Prime Minister finished his statement, the Speaker called on the Leader of the Opposition. Oddly, this wasn't Boris but a bearded man on the Labour front bench. 'Last week I was in Brussels, meeting with heads of government and leaders of European parties,' Jeremy Corbyn said, 'one of whom said to me—' 'Who are you?' interrupted Chris Pincher (Con, Tamworth). The House fell apart in what Boris would have called paroxysmal hilarity while Labour frontbenchers bit their lower lips to avoid joining in.

Eventually, Boris got his turn. 'Speak for England, Boris,' one Tory backbencher shouted. 'Tuck your shirt in,' another told him. Boris asked what sovereignty the PM had won back from Brussels, which received a dismissive answer. 'Rubbish,' Boris chuntered.

Half the parliamentary party are on his side, though. One of them is Anne-Marie Trevelyan, MP for Berwick-upon-Tweed, who got the second biggest laugh of the day for this opening: 'Having spent recess in the Arctic Circle with the Royal Marines, I'm extremely conscious…'

Mr Cameron laughed along. 'It sounds like you had a more exciting recess than I did,' he said. 'There were times when I wished I'd been in the Arctic Circle.' Or, more accurately, when he wished he could exile Boris to it.

25 FEBRUARY
MUM'S THE WORD FOR PMQS

It was bring your mother to work day in Parliament. David Cameron arrived for his weekly playground scuffle clutching a folder full of statistics and attack lines, a weakish prepared dig at the shadow Defence Secretary and a white-haired retired magistrate from Oxfordshire.

The essence of Mary Cameron sat quietly on the front bench as her son handled a string of questions from Jeremy Corbyn about those bolshie junior doctors, while ten feet away Jeremy Hunt, the Health Secretary, provided sign language for the hard of hearing. 'Rash and misleading,' Mr Corbyn said of Mr Hunt's figures. The Health Secretary shook his head vigorously. 'Scaremongering,' countered the Prime Minister. Mr Hunt nodded so hard you feared his head would fall off.

Then Mr Corbyn raised the massive overspend by the Prime Minister's own local NHS trust. What was he going to do about it? 'Ask your mother!' shouted Carolyn Harris (Lab, Swansea East). Mama Cameron got attention recently for signing a petition against cuts to Oxfordshire services.

This was it. Time to weaponise Mater. 'Ask my mother?' Mr Cameron scoffed, pushing the octogenarian into the front line. 'I know what my mother would say. She would look across the dispatch box and say, "Put on a proper suit, do up your tie and sing the national anthem."'

And then he did that trademark smirk that he gives when he thinks he has been clever. The toadies and sycophants loved it, of course, but when the howls and guffaws had stopped echoing round the hall, Mr Cameron seemed diminished. Was this necessary? It would have been better to keep mum, rather than deploy her.

Mr Corbyn did not seem wounded. Is that the best you've got? Your mum says I'm scruffy? 'Well, if we're talking of motherly advice,' he said, 'mine would have said, "Stand up for the principle of a health service free at the point of use for everybody."' It seems that Ma Corbyn had the same difficulty with snappy soundbites as her son.

26 FEBRUARY
CHURCHILL'S GRANDSON ENJOYS HIS FINEST QUARTER-HOUR

With respect to Mary Cameron, no politician can deploy a more impressive relative than Sir Nicholas Soames (Con, Mid Sussex), who has spent a third of a century as an MP in his grandfather's shadow.

Sir Nicholas learnt his place at an early age. He once recalled visiting Winston Churchill in his bedroom as a five-year-old. 'Is it true, Grandpapa, that you are the greatest man in the world?' Soames asked. 'Yes, I am,' Churchill said. 'Now bugger off.'

Both sides in the EU referendum debate have claimed Churchill's spiritual support, but Sir Nicholas has been a Europhile all his life and told the Commons that he receives 'vile emails' every day from people saying that he was a traitor to his grandfather's memory.

There was no disrespect shown to him in the chamber during a fifteen-minute speech, even from those who disagree with him. He was heard in total silence.

Europe at the end of the Second World War, he said, had been 'a vast mass of bewildered human beings, who gazed forlornly at the wreckage of their homes, their nations, their lives, their families, their possessions and everything that they loved'. The EU gave them and their descendants freedom, security and prosperity.

He admitted it had its flaws and 'now appears weak and uncertain', but said it was Britain's duty to drive the big reforms that Europe must swallow, rather than to leave and let it collapse. Quoting a speech his grandfather gave in 1948, he said a 'high and solemn responsibility rests upon us ... to pool the luck and comradeship and firmly grasp the larger hopes of humanity'.

Hilary Benn knows the burden of a famous forebear and has received similar criticism for betraying the Benn name. He said yesterday that those who want Britain to stay in the EU must praise its benefits. One of these was paternity leave. Jacob Rees-Mogg, who became a father for the fifth time on Tuesday, did not look enthused. The Mogg, as old-fashioned as a sundial, has given his children unusual names. Alfred Wulfric Leyson Pius has joined a pack of siblings who share such names as Wentworth, Anselm, Fitzwilliam, Somerset, Dunstan, Theodore and Alphege. It is unlikely that The Mogg will call a sixth child Juncker Tusk Merkel.

Some people will never be happy, observed David Lidington, the Europe minister. 'Frankly,' he said, 'if the Prime Minister had come back brandishing the severed heads of the members of the Commission and proceeded to conduct an *auto-da-fé* in Downing Street with copies of the Lisbon Treaty, they would still be saying this is feeble.' He had a point.

4 MARCH
CORBYN PROVES TO BE MASTER OF THE BORED ROOM

There is something almost admirable about the way that Jeremy Corbyn refuses to behave like a normal politician. Compare his unpolished display at the British Chambers of Commerce conference with the professional who had preceded him.

Sajid Javid, the terminally bland Business Secretary, took his shiny suit and his shiny tie and his shiny head on to the stage at the Queen Elizabeth II Centre and delivered half an hour of forgettable flannel, much of which was about how much he hates Europe. 'I'm a Brussels basher!' he declared, and he will be showing the depth of that contempt by campaigning for Britain to stay in the EU. Apathy spread.

Then out came Mr Corbyn and proved that you don't need to wear a sharp suit or stick rigidly to prepared lines to deliver a poor speech. He had dressed down for his first talk to a group of businessmen: his favourite brown jacket and unmatching trousers, his top shirt button undone and his tie knot loosened like a schoolboy. Some might think this disrespectful – like David Cameron attending the Durham Miners' Gala in white tie – but Mr Corbyn was only showing how in-tune he is with the great business leaders of today.

Mark Zuckerberg, founder of Facebook, is never seen in anything but a grey T-shirt; Apple's Steve Jobs always wore jeans and black turtlenecks. Less time thinking about your appearance means more time for big ideas. I predict that the granola jacket, navy slacks and skewed red tie will become this year's look for every thrusting digital executive.

Mr Corbyn then ignored all the usual rules about speech-making – structure, clarity etc. – and delivered a twenty-minute ramble rapidly and with minimal eye contact, fluffing every seventh word. He was flying solo before the end of the first page. Keen to show that he understands business, Mr Corbyn moved away from the distributed script. 'I went to my local café this morning and had a coffee,' he said. 'I support businesses like them. I hope they do well.'

The rest of the speech was textbook Corbyn. Never use one word where seventeen will do. The only time he was succinct was on Europe, spending fifty-six words on the EU. Other politicians might talk for hours about the neverendum, but it's a fringe issue for Mr Corbyn.

At the end, the conference chairman asked Mr Corbyn to give 'a quick elevator pitch' to explain what Labour has to offer businesses. This device is supposed to be succinct. Mr Corbyn spoke for four minutes. That was some elevator ride, the host said. Well, said Mr Corbyn, it had thirteen flaws. Or perhaps he meant floors. It's so hard to tell when he's joking.

12 MARCH
BORIS HAS A POP AT THE GLOOMY THEN TRUCKS OFF

'Do not be conned by the Gloomadon Poppers!' Say what you like about Boris Johnson but no one on either side of the Brexit debate explores the full potential of our rich language more than the Mayor of London.

It sounded like a line from Jabberwocky or perhaps a future book by J. K. Rowling. *Harry Potter and the Gloomadon Poppers*, in which our hero, nearing forty, finds life at the Ministry of Magic less than fulfilling and begins to frequent the nightclubs at the dodgier end of Diagon Alley.

Perhaps the Gloomadon Poppers were a 1972 prog rock band, or they could be an American football team. Boris did not provide a crib sheet. Either way, though, his advice was firm. Do not be conned by them.

We had gathered in a warehouse in Dartford to hear Boris's first big speech since he decided to throw in his fortune with the Leave campaign. Glasses perched on the end of his nose and forefinger poised to stab the lectern in front of him, Boris embarked upon a trademark flight of fancy about what a lark leaving the EU would be.

Let's give it a bash, he said. What's the worst that could happen, I ask you? Who needs economic arguments when you've got gargantuan optimism? We have nothing to fear but fear itself and, frankly, you'd have to be a bit of a Walter the Softy like my old mate Dave to be afraid of this.

What is more, he went on, the French want our cake. 'We export cake – a rather dense and glutinous chocolate cake – from Walthamstow to France,' he said. 'They love our cake in France!' How could anyone suggest we would get a bad deal on leaving the EU when they love our gateaux so much? And what is Europe giving us in return? A pretty dashed rotten deal, that's what. All is not sunny on the other side of La Manche. 'This club sounds a bit deranged,' Boris said, almost sending his glasses flying.

'They have all these silly rules,' he went on, 'about how old a child must be to blow up a balloon and the height of trucks. Well, we have a perfectly sensible rule about trucks in Britain. It says, "Don't crash into a bridge."' Later, he would test that rule by getting behind the wheel of a forty-tonne lorry. 'Take Back Control' it said on the side. Boris is never one to ignore an order.

'He's not going to drive the lorry,' his minder insisted. 'It's just for a photo.' The engine started. 'He's definitely not going to drive it. Oh Christ, he's driving it.'

The lorry set off at a lick, photographers flying in all directions. A jobsworth pointed at the 'strictly 5 mph' signs as the Johnson juggernaut thundered down the car park before screeching to a halt in front of the fence. Boris leapt out, thumbs raised, chest thrust forward like a gorilla. Take that, Dave, he may as well have said. You and your gloomy poppers.

23 MARCH
TORY TOADIES GET BEHIND THEIR MAN

Michael Ellis (Con, Northampton North) stood eagerly by the door behind the Speaker's chair. It was a big day for George Osborne, which meant it was a big day for Mr Ellis, the Northampton North MP, who seldom misses an opportunity to crawl.

His shoes and tie pin were gleaming, his hair was neatly combed over and a helpful smile was on his face as he gazed through the door for his patron. Thinking he had spotted the Chancellor, Mr Ellis flung it open like a hotel porter and prostrated himself at the feet of a rather surprised fellow non-entity. Mr Ellis looked saddened as the door swung shut. Mr Osborne then strode through the other one, barely looking at the crawler.

He was not the only sycophant on display. The whips had been working hard. As Mr Osborne rose to open the final day of the debate on his ailing Budget, Toady, Lickspittle and Creep were yodelling away like Genevan goatherds. The first helpful question fell to Gareth Johnson (Con, Dartford), who said how lovely it was that Mr Osborne hadn't put fuel tax up. The Chancellor said it was sweet of him to notice. Chris Philp (Con, Croydon South), maturing nicely as a bottom-kisser, then bellowed a helpful attack on Labour like a Billingsgate fish merchant. Mr Osborne beamed.

The shadow shadow Cabinet (the one sitting on Labour's fourth bench) went to work early. Chris Leslie, Yvette Cooper (Normanton, Pontefract and Castleford) and Rachel Reeves (Leeds West), three shadow Chancellors in exile, all made stinging attacks. Mr Osborne took them all in his stride. He enjoys being the pantomime villain; the more they boo, the more he hams it up.

When Ms Cooper asked for an apology for cuts to disability

benefit, he sneered that he wouldn't say sorry until she apologised for the £80 billion rise in the deficit when she was Chief Secretary to the Treasury. Ms Reeves wanted a clarification about whether there would be more welfare cuts, so he asked why she wasn't saying thank you for the money he'd just given to flood defences in her constituency. Call it arrogance, but a man's got to play to his strengths.

John McDonnell, the actual shadow Chancellor, then rose. Speaking even more like a funeral director than usual, he questioned Mr Osborne's fitness for office and said he should concentrate more on economics than party politics. It drew some odd attacks, two of which accused him of disrespecting those killed by terrorism in talking about the economy during a Budget debate.

As his footsoldiers went to work, Mr Osborne slumped in his seat, his arms folded, a smirk working on his lips. He resembled a schoolboy being told off by a teacher he doesn't respect. I almost expected Mr McDonnell to ask whether he was ignorant or apathetic. And Mr Osborne to reply, 'I don't know. And I don't care.'

24 MARCH
CORBYN CRUCIFIED AT PMQS

It's Holy Week and the House of Commons put on a mystery play instead of Prime Minister's Questions. The Passion of the Corbyn began with the bearded JC trying earnestly to help the poor and disadvantaged in society but ended with him being nailed and mocked as all around, even those on his own side, shouted, 'Crucify him!'

John Bercow, that pompous pilot, tried in vain to calm the noise. 'What evil hath he done?' he asked. 'What's more, people watching this on TV always complain that they hate this sort of thing.' But the crowd kept yelling, 'Let him be crucified,' so Mr Speaker washed his hands of it.

It had all started so well. Relatively well, anyway. The bar is set very low for Mr Corbyn at PMQs. He wanted to talk about the Budget and George Osborne's belief that five loaves and a couple of fishes would be sufficient to feed 5,000. Talk about miracles.

Especially, Mr Corbyn wanted to talk about the cuts to disability benefits. He demanded an apology from David Cameron for driving disabled people into poverty. Mr Cameron said that they could always rise, take up their beds and work. That got Mr Corbyn's disciples baying at him.

Then we came to the grand unravelling. Mr Cameron had read about a list that had been drawn up by the Corbyntariat, dividing the parliamentary party into five groups according to their perceived loyalty. The Prime Minister read from it with glee.

Angela Eagle (Lab, Wallasey), who had been shouting harder than most, was, he said, 'neutral but not hostile'. That silenced the shadow Business Secretary. Rosie Winterton, sitting a few seats away, is regarded as being in the 'hostile' camp, which is a bit awkward for a Chief Whip. She giggled nervously.

'Then there is "core support",' Mr Cameron said. 'You can include me in that very strongly.'

Mr Corbyn was not amused and wondered, now that the disability cuts had been reversed, where the Chancellor would find a spare £4.4 billion to plug his economic black hole. The Prime Minister laughed. 'Art thou the king of the prudent?' he mocked.

Then he started to tease the Labour disciples. 'Hands up, who is "core plus"?' he asked. Lots of hands were thrust into the air from Tory sycophants. Not many from Labour.

Rushanara Ali (Lab, Bethnal Green and Bow) tried to turn the attention back on to disability benefit. 'I see that she is "neutral but not hostile",' Mr Cameron said. 'She would be very welcome with us in "core group plus".'

While the cock was crowing, some Labour MPs wanted to deny JC. John Woodcock (Lab, Barrow and Furness) tweeted, 'F***ing disaster. Worse [*sic*] week for Cameron since he came in and that stupid f***ing list makes us into a laughing stock.'

The sombre, thoughtful atmosphere had gone. The Tories were overjoyed, the opposition dismayed. Up in the gallery, the scribes and elders were just bemused at how, yet again, Mr Corbyn had somehow turned a winning position into a losing one. And this time it wasn't even his fault.

'Why hast thou forsaken me?' JC muttered to no one in particular as he finally gave up the ghost. A watching centurion might be minded to observe: truly this was the law of sod.

15 APRIL
A GLORIOUS VICTORY FOR DOUBLETHINK

It was a bright cold day in April, and the clocks were striking thirteen as the Labour leader walked into the building that had been George Orwell's model for the Ministry of Truth in *Nineteen Eighty-Four*. 'You can never have too many strikes,' Jeremy Corbyn thought.

He had come to Senate House in Bloomsbury to demonstrate the power of doublethink, or how you can hold two contradictory beliefs and accept both. In his case, it was by making a speech in favour of remaining in an institution he has spent most of his career opposing.

Indoctrination had taken a long time. He had easily accepted that two plus two is five: John McDonnell's economic plan relies on it. The rest was harder. All that 'war is peace' nonsense.

Gradually, though, he had become convinced. If you want a picture of the future, imagine Tory boots stamping through the lobbies of Westminster – for ever.

Mr Corbyn realised that if Labour won't win a general

election under his leadership, it is better to support an institution that can deliver his agenda. That's what Yanis Varoufakis had told him, anyway.

There is, Mr Corbyn said, 'a strong socialist case' for staying in, even though, until seven months ago, he thought there was a strong socialist case for staying out.

So he stood there in a lecture hall of the Minitrue and spoke of the EU as being the friend of the working class. 'There will be a bonfire of workers' rights if we vote to leave,' he said. 'Workers need to make common cause across borders.'

He then ran through a list of everything that is goodthink: steel, paternity leave, junior doctors. And then all the things that are doubleplusbad, like air pollution, tax avoidance and 'unscrupulous employers who want greater exploitation'.

It seemed to be more of a speech against Conservatives than in favour of the EU, ironic given that a Tory Prime Minister is relying on Mr Corbyn's support to stay in his job.

His commitment to the cause has seemed rather half-hearted so far. David Cameron has been doing a couple of gigs a week for the past two months. This was Mr Corbyn's first.

As his talk finished Mr Corbyn reflected on his journey from 1975 to now. Forty years it had taken him to learn what kind of smile was hidden beneath the dark-blue star-circled flag. But it was all right, everything was all right, the struggle was finished. He had won the victory over himself. He loved Big Brussels.

20 APRIL
BEAMING GOVE TRIES TO BE THE GOOD NEWS BUNNY

Michael Gove stood under a sweltering spotlight in the Vote Leave headquarters, sweat pouring from behind his Ronnie Barker glasses and down those chubby cheeks, and called on his fellow Brexiteers to turn up the sunshine.

Leave pessimism and negativity, the Justice Secretary said to those on the Remain side. 'The case for leaving is positive and optimistic.' He beamed at the room. Trust me, I'm the Good News Bunny.

And then Mr Gove compared the European Union to the last days of Rome, before Alaric popped in to rearrange the forum. Stay in the EU, he seemed to be warning, and you'll have to get extra cover against Vandals and Visigoths put on your house insurance.

He threw in a few other collapsing empires, too, to hammer home the point. The Habsburgs, the Ottomans, Russia under Nicholas II ... the EU will go the same way. Vote Remain to be shot by a Bolshevik. Nor was this his only mild hysteria. 'If we vote to stay,' he said, 'we are voting to be a hostage, locked in the boot of a car driven by others to a place and at a pace that we have no control over.' Beware Jihadi Jean-Claude. So much for positivity. Project Fear runs both ways.

It is true, though, that the other lot have been a bit down on Britain's future post-Brexit. The way the Remain camp has been speaking about the apocalypse that will follow a vote to leave – the Channel bubbling with sulphurous pitch and all that – you might wonder why they took the risk of holding a referendum.

In an entertaining passage of his speech, Mr Gove exaggerated the claims of the fear-stirrers to the size of straw giants and then scoffed at them. 'They think that if we left the EU we would not be able to take the train or fly cheaply to European nations,' he said. 'If, by some miracle, we somehow managed to make it to distant Calais or exotic Boulogne we would find that – unique among developed nations – our mobile telephones would no longer work. Or, if we fell ill, we would be barred from all of Europe's hospitals and left to expire unmourned in some foreign field.'

Furthermore, he went on, Remain is claiming that after a

Brexit, Premier League football matches, shorn of all those melo-dramatic Italians and diving Germans, would have to become five-a-side and that it would be 'decades before a single Mr Kipling cake could ever again be sold in France'.

Preposterous, non? A Britain outside Brussels' control, he concluded, was being presented by Remain as 'a North Atlantic North Korea, only without that country's fund of international goodwill'. Mr Gove knows how to turn a phrase. He'd make a great columnist.

21 APRIL
CORBYN RUFFLES FEATHERS AND EARNS THE RIGHT TO CROW

There are few grander birds in the Westminster aviary than the Preaching Bercow, known informally as the Pompous Snipe. This small, grey creature is fond of its own squawk and when riled by a cock or other fowl it likes to draw up to its full 5ft 6in. and utter a screeching rebuke.

Yesterday, this bird (*Orator magniloquus*) was exercised by the whooping noises coming from Michael Ellis during a state-ment on border controls. Mr Ellis is a very loyal backbencher who was given to Theresa May as a pet. When his mistress is in trouble, he likes to honk at top volume.

This upset the Bercow. 'Order, a rather unseemly exchange is going on,' he said. Mr Ellis, he continued, 'always feels compelled to display a level of fealty unequalled by any other member'.

Puffing himself up even further, Mr Bercow added, 'We all know of the fealty bordering on the obsequious that is on evi-dent display from the honourable gentleman on a daily basis.' This grandiloquence is parliamentary code for 'stop being such an arse-kisser and button your trap'.

It was not, though, the most blatant sycophancy on display. That came with the very first question to the Prime Minister, awarded this week by the clerks' tombola to Nigel Adams (Con, Selby and Ainsty).

To be able to say, 'Question one, Mr Speaker' is a privilege. You have the eyes of the House and the viewing public on you and can set the tone for the next half hour before even the Leader of the Opposition has a go. Mr Adams used it to tug his forelock and get in a bit of toadery before the Queen's birthday today.

'When the Prime Minister next has an audience with the Queen,' he said, 'will he pass on my best wishes to our remarkable monarch? Long may she reign.' Yuck.

Up popped Jeremy Corbyn. 'Yeah, whatever,' he said. He wanted to ask about education and the plan to make every school an academy. And you know what? He nailed it. For the first time in seven months as Labour leader, Mr Corbyn won PMQs. He did this very simply by quoting a string of Tories who disagreed with the government policy.

One by one he wheeled them out – the former chairman of the Education Committee; a new MP; a Conservative councillor in David Cameron's own county; the chairman of the 1922 Committee; a former Tory Education Secretary – each one making Mr Cameron look more pained.

Mr Corbyn has finally worked out that the best way to push Mr Cameron on to the back foot is to use his own strength against him. Jezza does ju-jitsu.

The Prime Minister had little response but a limp joke about McDonald's that I won't even bore you with and to suggest that Sadiq Khan (Tooting), the Labour candidate for London Mayor, mixes with terrorists. This enraged the Labour benches, who shouted 'racist' at Mr Cameron with venom. The Speaker saw no need to cry 'order'. Probably too busy preening his plumage.

10 MAY
BACKBENCH BORIS FAILS TO SING AN ODE TO JOY

It was Schuman Day yesterday – a day of celebration across the European Union, so they say in Brussels. I imagine your mantelpiece is groaning with Schuman cards, the last few slices of Schuman cake, with its blue and yellow icing, winking at you from the kitchen. Perhaps you even gathered around the Schuman tree last night and sang the 'Ode to Joy' in memory of the architect of the EU.

Boris Johnson gave his own blast of Beethoven in a conference room in Lambeth. He had not intended to. This was meant to be a serious speech and for thirty-five minutes it was remarkably restrained – tedious, even – but then Boris, in a desire to show how he loves Europe while hating the EU, said that he could sing in German.

'Go on,' the hacks said. 'No, no,' Boris flapped. 'Please,' we asked. 'Well…' And then something stirred inside him. Call it Schuman nature. *'Freude, schöner Götterfunken, Tochter aus Elysium…'*

It had been a muted event up until then. His speech contained some Borisy phrases – 'mere bagatelle', 'supercharged cyclotron' and 'do our hearts pitter-patter' – but the delivery was as flat as his new sensible haircut. Is Boris trying to be a serious politician? Cripes.

It was like watching television in black and white or listening to a jazz saxophonist with socks wedged inside his bell. Something was missing. BoJo had lost his mojo.

A metaphor about negotiating on behalf of the EU being like trying to ride a 28-man pantomime horse fell limply to the floor. He even referred to Europe's trade dispute with America over the production of sheep's milk cheese without making a gag about it being a feta compli.

What caused this deborisification of Brexit's great showman?

Is he feeling listless after leaving City Hall? Before the speech he was seen carrying a mountain of papers into Parliament on his first day as an ex-mayor. As he rummaged for his pass, he sent the contents of his arms and pockets flying. A passing Wes Streeting (Lab, Ilford North) couldn't resist a quip: 'Struggling to cope now you're no longer mayor?' Boris gave him a gorgon's stare.

Perhaps he felt discombobulated by the Prime Minister making a pro-Remain speech earlier that day from the heart of the British Museum: prime Johnson territory. Boris may have felt that he should have been the one declaiming under the gaze of Lord Elgin's pilferings: 'Britons, let us not lose our marbles.'

A line he gave comparing the Leave campaign to the Greeks at Marathon – 'fighting for freedom against an outdated absolutist ideology' – would have soared if delivered amid the greatest hits of Phidias and Praxiteles. Instead it fell flat in a room that looked as if it was previously used for telemarketing.

Last week, he ruled the greatest city on earth; now, he is just a lowly backbencher, a mere pleb in the Westminster forum. It is an understandable anticlimax, but the Brexiteers desperately need Boris to regain his bounce.

19 MAY
POMP AND CIRCUMSTANCE AS CORBYN RISES FOR THE QUEEN

It was fancy-dress day at the House of Lords. The peers had come in their Santa Claus outfits and their wives were arranged on benches behind wearing tiaras and silk gloves that went all the way to the armpit. They did well to survive the downpour outside. The weather for the state opening had taken its cue from the monarch: long to rain over us.

Whatever the collective noun is for law lords (a wiggery?) sat perched on the edge of the woolsack like sailors in a lifeboat, while to the side the Lord Privy Seal held The Cap of Maintenance, from which she would later pull The Loose Change of Necessity with which to pay for The Cuppa of Relief.

Pageantry is wonderful. How can anyone say that Britain suffers under the influence of the Continent when the Queen is escorted into Parliament by a man with such a solid Anglo-Saxon title as Rouge Croix Pursuivant? They were accompanied by Portcullis Pursuivant and Gold Stick in Waiting as well as the York Herald and Richmond Herald. Always nice to see the local papers invited.

The Queen, crowned with 2,868 diamonds, was sparkling, but the speech was not. As Michael Gove, the Lord Chancellor, pulled it from his claret sack, he must have felt guilty, as a gifted writer, that he was about to hand over such bilge.

It plodded from the first sentence. 'Strengthen economy…' 'Working people…' 'Increase life chances…' The Northern Powerhouse got a mention, of course. 'Does this mean Balmoral?' she was tempted to ask.

This was surely the first time that she has ever had to say 'Daesh', too. She pronounced it as if it were what one had to do if running late for the Braemar Games.

If she had been given an honest agenda, the Gracious Address would have said something like, 'My government will spend the summer tearing themselves apart over the European Union referendum, safe in the knowledge that my loyal opposition are an absolute shambles. At some point, my Prime Minister will escape from it all to Ibiza and point at fish for the photographers.'

When the ceremonial was packed away, MPs gathered for the start of a week of debating the flimsy vision that had just been read to them. Jeremy Corbyn began strongly, with kind words about the backbenchers who had proposed and seconded the debate and a string of jokes that actually drew laughter rather than pained expressions.

I have seen every Commons appearance that Mr Corbyn has made since he became Labour leader and this was second only to his excellent offering on the Queen's 90th birthday, despite him taking forty minutes to reply to a fourteen-minute speech. This ardent republican performs best when talking about the Queen. Maybe it's because this is the one subject he has no great enthusiasm for.

25 MAY
DOUBLE-BREASTED ASSASSIN STICKS KNIFE INTO GOVERNOR

You underestimate Jacob Rees-Mogg at your peril. He may seem as fearsome as a snowflake, with his double-breasted pinstripes, Harry Potter spectacles and a voice as rich and British as lemon curd on a crumpet. Yet raise his dander and the honourable member for North East Somerset can turn into an assassin, albeit a very polite one.

Mark Carney, Governor of the Bank of England, had been called before the Treasury Committee to explain why the Bank had warned that Britain faces a recession if we leave the European Union. The Mogg found this rummy. He had already suggested that Captain Carney should drop himself from the Bank of England XI for unsportsmanlike behaviour. Yesterday, the polite assassin stabbed stilettos all the way down the banker's spine.

'Chairman, gentlemen,' he said, nodding at the flunkeys next to Dr Carney. 'Good morning.' These pleasantries done, he reached for his poniard. 'In general elections you do not give a view on parties' economic policies,' he said. 'Why not?'

Dr Carney, that lean, sleek Bagheera, seemed flustered by this. It's against our remit to interfere in general elections, he said, since they are not a 'discrete risk', unlike a vote to leave the EU. After all, what people say in an election doesn't necessarily become their policy in government.

'Sophistry,' The Mogg scoffed. 'There have been specific occasions in the past when opposition policies would have a profound effect on sterling and yet you would ignore those. What's different now?'

Dr Carney tried to talk his way out of it but was cut dead. The Mogg may like flannel when it comes to his pyjamas; he does not appreciate it in Parliament. He took another knife. 'What conversations have you had with the Chancellor in relation to the referendum?' he asked.

Bagheera began to growl. It has all been above board, he said. 'There is no possibility of undue influence coming from the Treasury.'

'There is always a possibility,' The Mogg replied, flashing him a steely stare.

'There. Is. No. Possibility,' Dr Carney snapped back. This was gripping. 'It's very convenient that you're giving out exactly the same propaganda as the Chancellor,' the assassin sniffed. 'I don't accept that at all,' his victim replied. 'This is not a general election.'

'No,' said The Mogg. 'It is much more important than that. Why should anyone trust you to set interest rates now? Call yourselves independent when you can be bought over a Treasury digestif?'

'The only side we have picked,' Dr Carney replied, 'is the pursuit of low, sustainable inflation. We are apolitical, which may be inconvenient for you, but to suggest otherwise is to undermine that.'

'I do suggest otherwise,' The Mogg said. 'And so you undermine that,' Dr Carney repeated. They stared across the room, each daring the other to pounce first.

The Mogg had one more needle to insert. Not a particularly piercing one, but enough to give discomfort. 'What's this I hear', he said, 'about you being asked to have a quiet word with wavering MPs?' Dr Carney laughed. 'No, that is not correct at all,' he said.

The polite assassin was happy to let that one pass, but he gave the banker a final hard stare.

Don't get too attached to your job, it seemed to suggest. We will remember this if my side wins.

28 MAY
UNEASY ALLIANCE FAILS TO LIGHT UP DONCASTER

It takes a lot to impress the *Doncaster Free Press*. Ed Miliband had been rated as the town's fourth most influential person when the MP for Doncaster North was in with a reasonable chance of becoming Prime Minister. Two weeks ago the newspaper demoted Mr Miliband to No. 40 on the Donny Power List.

It might therefore have been better if some other master of the Doncaster universe had been asked to persuade the shoppers on St Sepulchre Gate of the virtues of the EU. Steve Currier of Cooper Lighting, perhaps, who is at No. 39 on the list, or Steve Gill, 'who has really seen Doncaster Sheffield Airport take off' and is at No. 5. Perhaps they were busy.

Labour In for Britain had to make do with Mr Miliband, who arrived with his two fellow Doncaster MPs, Caroline Flint (No. 26) and Rosie Winterton (No. 13). We were also expecting a rare showing from Jeremy Corbyn – only his fourth of the referendum campaign – but as usual the Labour leader was late.

While the crowd milled around, television crews tried to get some vox pops. 'No thanks, lad,' said one councillor. 'Give me a microphone and I'll never stop singing. I know every verse of "On Ilkla Moor Baht 'at".' We did not doubt him.

Eventually Mr Corbyn's rather huge coach arrived. 'All that for one person?' a local said when he was the only one to emerge. 'No wonder the party doesn't have any money.'

The four MPs stood on a platform displaying all the mutual

affection of a Pink Floyd reunion. It is never easy for a former leader to stand in the shadow of his successor, while Ms Flint and Ms Winterton were both placed in the 'hostile' group on Mr Corbyn's ranking of his MPs.

Ms Flint went first and told the crowd that it was thanks to the EU that they can have cheap holidays in the sun. 'Forty years ago the only holiday you could go on was to the seaside in a caravan,' she said. 'Roobish,' shouted a heckler.

Then Mr Miliband. 'Friends,' he began. He always used to begin speeches as if he were Mark Antony at a funeral. Now he felt more like Caesar on the evening of 15 March.

'This campaign has looked too much like an argument between David Cameron and Boris Johnson,' Mr Miliband said. But we have arguments in our party too! 'We want a Labour government as soon as possible, but…' He drifted off, looking across at Mr Corbyn. 'But we need the EU to protect us from the Tories, just in case.'

Then it was Jezza's turn. He gave a toothy grin. 'I've just come from a bio-gas generating plant,' was his opener, nailing the rhetoric like Churchill. He had been to see how they turn vegetables into power. There's a metaphor if ever I saw one.

As he burbled on about the environment and workers' rights, Mr Miliband stared grimly ahead, his dark, brooding eyes burning holes into his leader's back. He must have wanted to be anywhere but there.

7 JUNE
ONCE MORE UNTO THE BLEACH WITH BORIS

Boris Johnson is a man of many parts, especially Shakespearian ones. One day he is a jolly Falstaff, another he is Cassius, eager to stick it to Julius Cameron. More often it's the Fool. Oh, let me play the lion too, he begs.

It was inevitable that the Bard of Brexit would rock up in Stratford-upon-Avon at some point. Instead of a soliloquy at The Swan, however, we were on the outskirts of town in a warehouse full of cleaning products. 'Once more unto the bleach, dear friends,' Boris declared. Or he should have done.

Instead, a speech that promised, like the bottles behind him, to get rid of 99.9 per cent of all Germans from British legislation began with a limp joke about how his surroundings showed that Vote Leave is running a clean campaign. Unlike his hosts, Boris has lacked polish of late.

He tried to liken the referendum to a choice between two products. Most Britons in the Boris Doorstep Challenge, he said, would prefer the lemony zest of Leave to their normal household detergent. The groundlings, patches and rude mechanicals who had been dragged away from putting things in boxes to form an audience applauded politely but, since there were signs in four languages on the walls, not all of them may be keen on Brexit.

Before Boris they were addressed by Gisela Stuart, Labour MP for Edgbaston, a seat once held by Neville Chamberlain. Like her predecessor, she had come from Munich convinced of the need to avoid being dragged into European affairs. In her case she was born there. The immigration controls she seeks would probably have stopped her moving here.

Finally, Michael Gove gave his audition piece, full of alarums and excursions. There is something rotten in the state of Denmark, he warned, and the other EU nations. Remaining in the club would help terrorism and undermine NATO. What was it that Shakespeare's French maid once said? 'Of all base passions, fear is most accursed.'

At the same time, David Cameron was posing at the Oval cricket ground with Harriet Harman (Lab, Camberwell and Peckham), Tim Farron (LD, Westmorland and Lonsdale) and Natalie Bennett in front of a fleet of colourful Minis. The plan to have this rainbow coalition drive off in the cars was scuppered, though, by the Green Party leader insisting on using her folding bike.

It just made me think of *The Italian Job*, another chaotic European adventure. 'You were only supposed to blow the bloody doors off,' the PM has probably shouted at whoever suggested a referendum as the way to unite his party. Perhaps this will all end with the Stronger In battle bus teetering on the edge of a cliff and Croker Cameron saying, "Ang on, lads, I've got a great idea.'

14 JUNE
BROODING BROWN STILL KNOWS HOW TO COMMAND A STAGE

Now is the summer of our discontent made grey and drizzly by this son of manse. We trotted up to Leicester on a soggy afternoon to see an unpopular former ruler, who had made a surprising reappearance in the city after lying forgotten and unmourned since his inglorious fall.

Richard III was found under a council car park. Gordon Brown has been somewhere even more lucrative – the American lecture circuit – but the former Prime Minister has returned to politics in an attempt to persuade voters that it is better for employment if we stay in the EU. A workforce, a workforce, my kingdom for a workforce.

In a half-hour talk at De Montfort University, delivered without notes, Mr Brown showed that, for all his faults, he knows how to make a speech. His words lacked poetry, his views may be debatable and some of the jokes were best before 1989, but after weeks of tedious, cliché-groaning oratory on all sides, it was good to listen to someone with stage presence.

Mr Brown prowled up and down like an old silverback

gorilla, his right hand never leaving his pocket, while the left jabbed and gestured to reinforce his points. The warring Tories just want to swap scarestories, he said. It's time for Labour to start talking positively about what Britain gets out of Brussels.

He pointed to job creation, the environment, workers' rights, security and tackling tax havens as areas where co-operation will be essential. There was even a dash of 1997 rhetoric: 'Europe is tough on terrorism, tough on the causes of terrorism.' The EU had ended 1,000 years of war, he added. 'We have exchanged the sword for the ploughshare,' the clergyman's son said. 'Just think how we can defeat the other great evils of our time.'

Since the audience was mainly students, it seemed odd to begin with a few anecdotes about George Brown, who was Foreign Secretary as recently as 1968. Mr Brown then moved on to those other heroes of the YouTube generation: J. K. (Galbraith, not Rowling), Hayek (Friedrich, not Salma) and Michael Foot. Never mind. His supporting cast may have been antique, but the audience were engaged. Fresh-faced young people in the front row gazed up at the big beast in admiration.

But Mr Brown was supposed to be speaking beyond the room. This was the start of the Labour fightback, taking the referendum campaign to places that the Tories cannot reach, so was it really wise to duck away from any questions about the concerns that working-class communities have about migration? 'It's illegal immigration that's the problem,' he growled, accusing *The Sun* and the BBC of having an 'agenda' in wanting to ask about whether the current migration level is sustainable.

Picking a fight with the most-read tabloid in the country and the state broadcaster is a strange way to reach out. On the bright side, at least, unlike during the 2010 election, he didn't call any voters bigots.

With just over a week to go before the referendum, and having spent some of the campaign on holiday and the rest of it barely visible, the Labour leader was finally persuaded by his party to join a pro-Remain rally. It was very half-hearted.

15 JUNE
THROUGH GRITTED TEETH, CORBYN TRIES
TO SING ABOUT THE EU'S MERITS

It was, to adapt a line by JFK, the greatest assemblage of election-winning talent in the Labour Party since the last time that Peter Mandelson dined alone. The entire shadow Cabinet, most of the national executive and a flying picket of union leaders had come together to plead with Labour voters to support Remain.

They met for a group photo in the foyer of Congress House under the gaze of Jacob Epstein's *Pietà*, a Stalinist stone memorial to fallen comrades. Those who had recently been eager to bury Jeremy Corbyn have agreed to put the needs of the many ahead of the flaws of the one.

As they were being arranged in a carefully planned line-up (Luciana Berger must have known she'd be in the front row, judging by her bright scarlet dress), the press played a game of political Guess Who? 'Is he a man?' Yes. 'Balding?' Yes. 'Glasses?' Yes. 'Beard?' Yes. 'Is it Charlie Falconer?' No, taller. 'Jon Trickett!' A whiff of fish floated in from the canteen next door. 'It's cod in pesto,' a voice said. Or perhaps he said, 'Oh God, it's Peston.' The media aren't dish of the day in these parts.

As Heidi Alexander spoke about the NHS, Mr Corbyn's attention wandered around the room. One of the sweet things about the Labour leader is that he seems blissfully unaware of the cameras that are now always aimed at him. While his colleague was telling us how united the party is on this issue, he seemed to be more interested in something on the ceiling.

'Nobody is more determined to win this referendum than my friend and leader,' Ms Alexander concluded, which didn't say much for the zeal of her colleagues given that Mr Corbyn has already said that his interest in the referendum is no more than 7.5 out of 10.

'We're making the strongest case we can,' Mr Corbyn eventually said. 'It is the Labour position, the trade union position, to remain.' Not the most emphatic personal plea, but he went on to borrow a line that the Queen had made to great effect before the Scottish independence referendum: 'We urge our supporters to think very carefully.'

Will that be enough to convince Labour voters to go with their heads rather than their hearts? Heck, will it convince Mr Corbyn? As the photographers snapped away, I heard Mr Watson mutter, 'Keep smiling, Jeremy.' Nine more days of gritted teeth to go.

Parliament occasionally discussed things other than Brexit. Most of the best work is done in the cross-party select committees, and one of the highlights of this year came when the tetchy businessman Sir Philip Green was grilled by a joint business and work and pensions committee over the collapse of BHS with massive pension liabilities.

16 JUNE
THIN-SKINNED TYCOON TRIES TO AVOID TALK OF BUSINESS

Two hours into Sir Philip Green's grilling a bell rang out. 'Time for a break?' the businessman asked hopefully. 'No, that's prayers,' Frank Field (Lab, Birkenhead), the committee chairman, replied, referring to the start of business in the chamber. 'For me or you?' Sir Philip asked.

He seemed to be a man with a persecution complex. Everyone is against him, especially the press. 'I wish that 1 per cent of what was written about me was true,' he said. Let's give him what he wants, then, but where to start? The moment when he pulled out his chequebook and waved it at the MPs? His claim that he had moved to Monaco for the schooling rather than the tax regime? Or perhaps when, in answering questions from one MP to his right, he suddenly paused, looked to his left and told Richard Fuller (Con, Bedford) to avert his gaze.

'Do you mind not looking at me like that all the time?' Sir Philip said. 'It's disturbing. You just want to stare at me? It's uncomfortable.'

How prickly this supertanned titan of industry was. He later complained about the committee clerk whispering to Mr Fuller. 'I can't cope with this,' he wailed. 'I can,' Mr Fuller replied. Sir Philip also protested at Jeremy Quin (Con, Horsham) putting on his spectacles, moaned that Richard Graham (Con, Gloucester) was bullying him and argued with Iain Wright (Lab, Hartlepool) about whether 27 April was a Wednesday or Thursday. Mr Wright was correct.

Even the plastic cups were against him. As he tried to pour himself a drink, the cup tipped over. Sir Philip bit his lip. 'You seem extraordinarily thin-skinned,' Mr Wright observed.

Sir Philip almost got up and left when Mr Wright suggested it was his ego that made him want to stop someone else from buying BHS. 'That is an insult,' he snapped, gathering his papers together. 'It's disgusting, you should apologise.'

At the start, he had promised to give honest answers. 'I don't tell lies, I'll tell you exactly as it is,' he said. Yet he seemed remarkably sketchy on the details of his business. A man who once drew up a new contract for coat hangers to save BHS money seemed unaware, for instance, of the growing deficit in its pension fund. 'You can't suddenly tell me I'm accountable,' he said.

None of the mistakes were his fault. 'I'm too much of a big boy to blame everyone else,' he said. 'But I could spend the next twenty minutes blaming everyone else.' He looked round, but for some reason the MPs were more keen on questioning him.

On the sale of BHS, his memory was especially deficient. At first he denied ever discussing the possibility of selling it to Mike Ashley, owner of Sports Direct. 'I've got a letter here from Mr Ashley saying you spoke to him,' Mr Wright said.

'Don't bully me,' Sir Philip warned. When he said that they had never discussed it, what he meant was they had spoken on the phone. 'A few conversations,' he clarified.

Poor Sir Philip. All he wanted to talk about was his philanthropy – the knighthood-preservation gambit – and people kept dragging him back to his business. He was like the child in the rhyme. No one likes me, everybody hates me, I think I'll go and eat worms. 'Envy and jealousy are incurable diseases,' he observed. Yes, it is everyone else's fault.

21 JUNE
MUTE CHEERLEADER FINDS THE SHRUGS DON'T WORK

Finally, Jeremy Corbyn came out to play. You would not know that the Labour Party enthusiastically supports Britain staying in the European Union from the limited appearances that their leader has made in the campaign. Last night was his first, and last, outing on television. By the end, a casual observer may still have been unclear whether Labour are all that fussed.

'I am not a lover of the European Union,' Mr Corbyn said during a forty-minute roasting on Sky News. It was pointed out to him that he had voted to leave in 1975 and had voted against the Maastricht and Lisbon treaties. 'Maastricht was about the free market, Lisbon a step in the same direction,' he said. Nasty, Thatcherite beasties.

'So why do you think we should remain now?' Faisal Islam, the host, asked. 'Do you really believe this? Have you had your head turned by François Hollande?' How the French President could have turned Mr Corbyn's head is unclear. Maybe he took him on a tour of Paris's manhole covers. 'My head hasn't been turned by anything,' Mr Corbyn said. 'My head doesn't turn.'

This did not satisfy some in the audience. Mr Corbyn found himself in the rare position of being attacked from the left. 'You are a socialist, you should oppose the EU,' one said. 'But you've just become a member of the establishment.'

'I have not,' Mr Corbyn replied. 'My views are unchanged.' Indeed, his views have remained unchanged for longer than his questioner has been alive.

He tried to claim that he supports Remain because he wants to change the system from within. 'My support is not unconditional,' he added. It was the most tepid argument I have yet heard from anyone on the Remain side. Another person asked how he can achieve his pledge to renationalise the railways when EU rules open them up to competition. Mr Corbyn said he disagreed with those rules and argued that we should just ignore any we dislike.

He then talked up all the things he hates about the EU – the transatlantic trade deal, the handling of the refugee crisis, the collapse of steel – and tried to say that the best way of improving the situation is by employing his own unique powers of persuasion.

Near the end of the session, Mr Corbyn was asked if he would take the blame if Britain votes to leave. 'I won't take the blame,' he said. 'I hope there will be a Remain vote – there may well be – but whatever the result, we've got to work with it. I'll be pursuing the same agenda.'

'So you will definitely be voting to remain?' Mr Islam asked him. Mr Corbyn paused just a shade. 'Yes,' he said. 'I will be there.' As endorsements go, that rang so quietly it would barely be heard by a bat in a belfry. Mr Corbyn has achieved a unique feat: he is the first man to perform the 'Ode to Joy' in mime.

23 JUNE
FARAGE CELEBRATES LAST ORDERS

I suspect that when voting closes, Nigel Farage will celebrate the end of a long campaign with a quiet pint. Followed by eight or nine noisy ones. 'We changed the political agenda,' the UKIP leader declared at his final rally in Westminster, just around the corner from the Marquis of Granby (also known as the work canteen).

He ran through a few favourite tunes for the troops: bashing the EU as a cartel for big business; attacking plans for a European army; calling today's vote 'the people versus the establishment'. He even flashed his passport and demanded the return of the old dark blue British version.

'If the referendum was on joining the EU, we would over-whelmingly reject it,' he said. Passion, always his most effective weapon, was turned right up. 'Most of our supporters will crawl over broken glass to get to the voting booth tomorrow.' It sounded like it would be a messy session in the Marquis of Granby that night.

The speech was prefaced by one of those patriotic videos you only get at UKIP events. It began with Spitfires, naturally, then the Coronation, Stonehenge, a JCB, the Falklands, a black cab, a steam train and Ian Botham at Headingley in 1981. God bless 'em all. But then we saw a rogues' gallery of people who threaten our green and pleasant land: Clegg, Juncker, Merkel. Someone in the audience hissed.

The Kippers are an eccentric but largely amiable bunch. One of them read out a poem he had written. Another was wearing two scrolling dot-matrix screens clipped to his tie, giving instructions to Vote Leave. They made him look like a railway display board. 'People call me The Flasher,' he said proudly. Let us hope it's because of the gadgets.

Earlier, Sir John Major had reminded us of the unique orator that we lost in 1997. 'Let us turn the telescope of introspection around,' the former Prime Minister told an audience in Bristol. 'Remain isn't peddling Project Fear, but Project Information.' If only they had thought of that phrase earlier. The T-shirts they could have sold…

Sir John described the Leave campaign as 'the architects of disarray' and 'the gravediggers of our prosperity', making them sound like prog rock bands. To show that mangled English is universal, Kate Hoey (Lab, Vauxhall), the Brexiteer Labour MP, later referred to Sir John's attack as 'trawling the barrel'.

Meanwhile, Jeremy Corbyn gave his final pro-Remain speech by a Waitrose close to the offices of *The Guardian* in north London. And to think that there are some in his party who complain that the Labour leader hasn't tried hard enough to reach out beyond his core support.

Britain voted to leave the European Union. On a turnout of 72 per cent, more than 17 million (just under 52 per cent) cast their ballot for Brexit. It brought about a change of Prime Minister but not of the Leader of the Opposition, no matter how hard Labour MPs tried.

25 JUNE
BEATEN CAMERON BOWS OUT

The ill-wishers had gathered early outside Johnson Towers. 'Scumbag!' one shouted as the man who would be king emerged from his house. 'Twat!' shouted another. 'Wanker!'

yelled a third. They looked like young voters, but there may have been some members of the Cabinet in there.

Boris Johnson walked down the avenue of yellow-jacketed policemen to his car. This is something he must get used to. In Roman times, the conquering hero would have a slave behind him during his triumph to whisper, 'Remember you are mortal'. Today, they just shout, 'Twat!'

Over in Westminster, Stanley Johnson, paterfamilias of the golden tribe, was wandering among the camera crews wearing a 'Remain for Nature' T-shirt. He had taken the opposing view to his son but was now pushing an optimistic agenda. 'Europe needs us,' he told one broadcaster. 'The broad sunlit uplands lie ahead,' he added.

Boris managed the broad bit when he reached Vote Leave HQ – he has become very stocky – but there was little sunlight. Speaking in a deeper, slower voice than normal, with none of the flights of fancy, he promised not to charge into rash decisions, and pledged to 'take on extremists who play politics with immigration'. Did he not look at his own leaflets?

Michael Gove then spoke in funereal tones about rebuilding this broken nation. 'We should draw on the wisdom of those outside politics,' he said. Would they be the experts he's been so keen to dismiss?

Just after 8 a.m., David and Samantha Cameron walked out. 'The people have voted to leave,' the Prime Minister said. 'Their will must be respected.' He spoke about his achievements in office, but his legacy will now be the end of one political union, perhaps two.

'I fought this campaign in the only way I know how,' Mr Cameron protested. That would be spreading fear about the future and refusing to take part in any debates with his rivals. Well, it had worked in the general election last May.

He promised to steady the ship over the coming weeks, but said it was time for Britain to find a new captain. 'I have spoken to Her Majesty this morning,' he said. And that was that. A dignified, humble and respectful resignation, followed by a slight grimace and a rub of Sam's back as they went back indoors. Nothing in his office became him like the leaving of it.

30 JUNE
LABOUR GHOST BRINGS A CHILL TO THE HOUSE

I see dead people. That can be the only explanation for why I saw Jeremy Corbyn walk into the Commons yesterday and ask some questions of the Prime Minister, while no one sitting in the chamber below seemed to notice or react to the Labour leader.

Normally he gets a few heckles or catcalls from the Tory benches, even if his own MPs have long given up cheering. Yesterday he was simply invisible to everyone. For once, Pete Wishart (SNP, Perth and North Perthshire), who likes to goad the Labour troops for their lack of supportive noise, just couldn't be bothered. Mr Corbyn was a ghost.

He seemed unaware that he had passed to the world beyond. 'The dead only see what they want to see,' said the child in the film *The Sixth Sense*, whose powers I share. 'They don't know they are dead.'

Mr Cameron had arrived a little earlier than usual. He sat down, looked across the table and saw David Anderson (Lab, Blaydon) on the front bench. 'What are you doing there?' the Prime Minister seemed to say to him. 'I'm the new shadow Northern Ireland Secretary,' Mr Anderson replied. 'Oh,' said Mr Cameron. 'Gosh.'

He looked along the bench, trying to find a face that he recognised.

Even Mr Corbyn's loyal lieutenants weren't there. John McDonnell arrived only after the session had started; Diane

Abbott had plonked herself near the exit and Emily Thornberry (Islington South and Finsbury) had chosen to be in a TV studio instead. No one wanted to sit with the dead man.

A couple of minutes later Mr Corbyn walked in. No one made a sound, no one raised a smile. Tom Watson (West Bromwich East), the deputy leader, did not acknowledge him even when Mr Corbyn sat down next to him. Angela Eagle, sitting directly behind but two rows back, seemed to be looking straight through him.

After opening questions from a Lib Dem and a Tory, Mr Corbyn rose. There was the faintest groan, but it could have been someone's stomach rumbling. He asked about the fears that some people have for their jobs. Oh, the irony. Yet David Cameron did not make the obvious crack. Why speak ill of the dead?

For the first four exchanges, Mr Cameron read blandly from his folder. It was only when Mr Corbyn, on his fifth rising, made a dig about the Prime Minister leaving that he got a little riled. 'We must all reflect on our role in the referendum campaign,' Mr Cameron said. 'The right honourable gentleman says he put his back into it – I would hate to see him when he is not trying.'

Mr Corbyn tried a final time and at last the Prime Mnister's passions were stirred. 'I have to say to him, it might be in my party's interests for him to sit there, it is not in the national interest,' he said. 'I would say, for heaven's sake, man, go!' It was still not clear, though, if he had just realised that Mr Corbyn was sitting there or if he were railing, like Lady Macbeth, at a phantasm. 'Out, damn'd Trot! Out, I say!'

Five stood to be Leader of the Conservative Party in succession to David Cameron, but Boris Johnson was not one of them. Michael Gove, who was felt to have stabbed Mr Johnson in the back after

deciding he was unfit to be Prime Minister, was joined by Theresa May,
Andrea Leadsom, Liam Fox and Stephen Crabb. The last withdrew
after allegations were made in The Times of his fondness for sending
inappropriate text messages, while the same front page wounded Mrs
Leadsom after she was taped suggesting that being a mother made her
more qualified to be PM than the childless Mrs May.

6 JULY
THE ELECTION THAT NO TORY WANTED

They bump off their rejects quickly in the Conservative Party. Graham Brady, the chairman of the 1922 Committee and Prince Andrew lookalike, walked into Committee Room 6 at 6.31 p.m. and walked out again at 6.32 having rattled through the results of the ballot. Liam: you are the weakest link, good-bye. After Brexit, Foxit.

As soon as Mr Brady had left, the plotting began again. Where would Dr Fox's sixteen votes go? With Stephen Crabb likely to scuttle off, would Michael Gove or Andrea Leadsom benefit? As for the frontrunner, it's already looking less like Theresa May and more like Theresa Will.

The Home Secretary was an early voter, but not as early as Simon Hoare (Con, North Dorset), who cast his vote for Mr Crabb as soon as the doors were opened. Like Remain supporters in Gibraltar on the night of the referendum, Mr Crabb briefly looked like the runaway winner.

At the other end of the day Gavin Williamson, the Prime Minister's parliamentary aide, sneaked in just before the 6 p.m. deadline, a superstition of his. He refused to say if the boss had voted by proxy, but David Cameron had not popped by.

The atmosphere outside the room was jolly, to the irritation of Labour MPs who walked past. 'It's strange,' Rebecca Harris (Con, Castle Point) said. 'None of us wanted this leadership election, while Labour are desperate to have one.' Robert Syms (Con, Poole) said he kept meeting miserable Labour MPs in the lift who complained that it wasn't fair that the Tories have all the fun.

By 1 p.m. a third of MPs had voted. Mr Gove said it was 'a tough choice, but I've voted for a Scotsman'. Dr Fox's camp put him down as a 'maybe'.

Teams May, Fox and Crabb had badges to hand out, but not every MP wanted to declare their hand. 'I'm keeping silent,' a backbencher said. 'I don't want any more bloody emails about this.' From the candidates? 'No, my constituents.'

Just after 3 p.m., the man who could have been king bounced along the corridor. Mr Johnson was in and out of the room in even less time than he takes over his *Telegraph* column. 'Democracy has been served,' he said. There was not much sadness that he was off the ballot. 'It would have been a bumpy road with Boris,' one said, 'and he fell apart at the first bump.'

Among the odder sights was Victoria Prentis (Con, Banbury) carrying a prosthetic leg. A prop, she said, for the Singing for Syrians charity event next door. Dr Fox should have asked if he could borrow it: he needed all the support he could get.

As the Tories prepared for the next round of their leadership contest, a former Prime Minister made a reappearance after the long-delayed publication of the Chilcot Report into the Iraq War some thirteen years earlier.

7 JULY
BLAIR, THE GREAT ACTOR, TAKES ON A NEW ROLE

Bob Monkhouse observed that the secret to success in show business – and, by extension, politics – is sincerity. 'If you can fake that,' he said, 'you've got it made.' Some feel that Tony

Blair owed all his success to a skill in this area. Perhaps yesterday we saw the actor without his make-up.

'I express more sorrow, regret and apology than you may ever know or can believe,' he said. 'I took this decision with the heaviest of hearts. I know there are those who can never forget or forgive me.'

Speaking before a backdrop of golden wallpaper that made it look as if he were in an Indian restaurant, Mr Blair said that he had no choice but to remove Saddam Hussein by force. Caught between Iraq and a hard place, the Third Way, that trusty ally, had not been an option. The consequences of his decision haunt him every day, he said, but inaction would have done more harm.

It felt sincere. There was something in the way his voice kept breaking, the moments when his haunted eyes took on a thousand-yard stare. This seemed to be a man who has spent a lot of time in the confessional. 'I did my duty,' he said. He will go on saying that to his dying day; he will always believe he was right, but it is driving him mad.

If this was acting, it was a role we have not seen him play before. On the 400th anniversary of Shakespeare's death, the Tories have put on *Julius Caesar* and we had *Much Ado About Nothing* from the Labour Party. Perhaps Mr Blair, a triumphant Henry V in his younger days, was now giving us his King Lear. 'They told me I was everything. 'Tis a lie.'

Lying, however, was one charge he refused to accept. Poor intelligence, bad planning, a lack of a clear strategy for withdrawal were all accepted. The suggestion that he had duped politicians into voting for war was strongly rejected. 'Please, stop saying I'm lying,' he begged at one point in a press conference that went on for almost two hours.

It went unheard by the crowd who had gathered in Parliament Square with banners that read 'Bliar, Bliar' and by those who, like Caroline Lucas, the Green MP, bombarded Twitter with claims that he had lied to Parliament. In fact, Sir John Chilcot stopped short of making that charge.

The truth did not stop politicians, though. 'A House deceived by a fabricated case for war,' said the SNP's Pete Wishart in the Commons. 'The House was misled,' Jeremy Corbyn, the Labour leader, said. David Davis (Con, Haltemprice and Howden) said that it was a 'deception' and that while Sir John 'avoided accusing [Mr Blair] of lying, a lot of the evidence suggests that he did'.

Mark Durkan (SDLP, Foyle) even mocked what should be seen as one of Mr Blair's achievements. 'This is not a day for soundbites,' he said, echoing Mr Blair's comment at the Good Friday Agreement. 'But does the Prime Minister not agree that the hand of history should be feeling someone's collar?' Almost a century ago, contemplating the senseless waste of human life, lions led by donkeys, Kipling wrote in his 'Epitaphs of the War': 'If any question why we died, | Tell them, because our fathers lied.'

What will be Mr Blair's epitaph? Perhaps six words that he wrote in July 2002 to George W. Bush: 'I will be with you, whatever.' It was Mr Bush's 70th birthday yesterday. No one asked Mr Blair what he had given his friend as a present, but the answer was clear: his reputation.

8 JULY
ANDREA LEADSOM AND THE PLEASANTS' REVOLT

———

Some called it a march on Downing Street, but it was more like a gentle stroll into the office. Andrea Leadsom's Barmy Army moved steadily along Millbank yesterday morning, chanting and singing, after hearing their darling's message of sunshine.

It was the Pleasants' Revolt. 'I truly believe we can be the greatest nation on earth,' Mrs Leadsom had told them. 'Prosperity should be our goal, not austerity. Let's banish the pessimists.'

And then a very Tory piece of tummy-rubbing. 'I want a nation where anyone who aims high can achieve their dreams,' she said. Such as junior ministers who think they can become Prime Minister six years after entering the Commons.

'What do we want?' Tim Loughton, MP for East Worthing and Shoreham, shouted as they ambled along to Parliament. 'Leadsom for leader,' came the reply. 'When do we want it?' NOW!

Mrs Leadsom has a soothing personality. During the referendum, she reminded me of the sort of amiable woman you see advertising health insurance or river cruises on daytime television. Or perhaps she might have been a calming pharmacist, one who can make you feel better with a smile and a bottle of linctus. She has something of the Night Nurse about her.

Over in Parliament, Committee Room 7 had opened for the second ballot at 9 a.m. Representatives of Team May and Team Leadsom were engaged in friendly conversation outside but there was no sign of the third horse in the race. In fact, there was no one from Team Gove on 'telling' duty throughout the day. It was as if they had given up. 'It feels like a weak ward in a council election,' a Mayite said. 'Where you don't want to go along to see who is voting in case you find that no one is voting for you.'

Otherwise there was an end-of-term feeling. With only a one-line whip in the Commons, many MPs had taken the opportunity of heading for their constituencies. More than fifty had asked a colleague to vote for them by proxy. Well, they were only electing the next Prime Minister. Nothing major.

By 4 p.m., they had gathered in the room next door for the result, which was declared very briskly by Graham Brady, chairman of the 1922 Committee. Mr Gove fell by the wayside and so Britain will have a female Prime Minister.

Iain Duncan Smith (Con, Chingford and Woodford Green), who knows how capricious party members can be from when he won the leadership in 2001, said that the contest will be very close. 'I reckon I spoke to 30,000 people that summer and lost track of how many events I went to,' he said. 'They are going to find the next two months balls-achingly exhausting.' Fortunately for Mrs May and Mrs Leadsom, aching balls should not be much of a problem.

12 JULY
DARLING BUDDIES OF MAY OUTSQUAWK EAGLE

There they all were outside Parliament, these darling buddies of May, anxious to acclaim their leader-elect. Toady, Lickspittle and Creep, who would have switched allegiance in a blink to Boris Johnson, Andrea Leadsom or Peppa Pig if the prime min isterial lot had fallen their way, yodelled their hardest, while Fawn, Simper and Grovel shot their 'pick me, Miss' gazes at the new boss.

Theresa May's speech was lost in the wind – or was it the sighing of her loving supporters? – but it was irrelevant what she said. Tomorrow evening Mrs May will get the keys to Downing Street. It will be the anniversary, by the way, of Harold Macmillan's Night of the Long Knives in 1962. After a bloody summer, Mrs May is the last one standing.

And where was the Leader of the Opposition at that very moment? Jeremy Corbyn was in a Commons committee room, addressing a meeting of the Cuba Solidarity Campaign. Seriously.

Angela Eagle finally launched her bid to topple him yesterday, but it was shunted down the news agenda by a snap resignation statement from Mrs Leadsom. With the worst of timing, Ms Eagle began to speak twelve minutes after the press had got the half-hour warning email.

'Anyone from the BBC?' Ms Eagle said, looking round the room for Laura Kuenssberg. She'd been there a moment ago but was now on her way back to Westminster. 'BBC anyone?' Ms Eagle repeated. 'No? OK. Robert Peston, where are you?' But ITV's man was dashing along the Embankment. 'Michael Crick?' The chap from Channel 4 had stayed, although Ms Eagle may have regretted calling on him. 'People say you're too gloomy to be leader,' Mr Crick said.

Poor Ms Eagle. This was actually a rather impressive launch, although the pink backdrop, pink jacket and scribbled signature across the banners made it look as if she was hosting a chat show on daytime telly. 'Coming up next on *Angela*, what do you do when someone refuses to leave your party?'

'I'm not a Blairite or a Brownite or a Corbynista,' Ms Eagle said in her deadpan, common-sense Yorkshire way. 'I am my own woman. A strong Labour woman. A practical socialist who wants to get things done.' Labour had been formed to be a voice for working people in government, she said. 'I won't stand back and watch our country become a one-party state.'

None of that seemed to matter, though, when Mrs Leadsom was making a statement at the same time that handed Downing Street to Mrs May. Glum faces surrounded her as Mrs Leadsom admitted that, after a difficult weekend, she had realised she didn't have enough support from MPs to lead her party. That hasn't stopped Mr Corbyn.

Mid-afternoon, David Cameron trotted out of Downing Street and made a very brisk statement, saying effectively that recent events meant that he would now be able to attend the first day of the Lord's Test on Thursday. 'Theresa is strong and competent and…' he burbled.

He left his pocket microphone switched on and a TV audience heard the demob-happy PM hum a few notes as he walked back inside. It sounded like the opening to *Tannhäuser*, if a little quick and slightly off-key. Much like his resignation. As the door closed, Mr Cameron was heard to say 'Right... good' absent-mindedly to himself, as if he were the Earl of Grantham just returned from rogering one of Downton Abbey's maids and not sure of how else to pass the afternoon. That is his future now.

14 JULY
CAMERON GOES BACK TO THE FUTURE

In his beginning was his end. David Cameron left the party leadership the way he had come in, reflecting on the fading promise of youth. 'He was the future once,' a fresh-faced, lip-licking new Tory leader had told Tony Blair on his first appearance at Prime Minister's Questions in 2005. Ten and a bit years on, rueful but surprisingly jolly, Mr Cameron ended his final Wednesday lunchtime tussle by telling MPs, 'I was the future once.'

His hair, like the cheeks of George Osborne beside him, was much thinner and greyer than it had been in 2005. Heck, it was thinner and greyer than it had looked only a month ago. Mr Cameron not only worked for the nation, he may have dyed for it. But image does not matter now; let the bald patch grow.

This was not the time that he had wanted to leave the job, but it was, perhaps, the manner. As the Prime Minister sat down at the end of the half-hour session, the benches behind him rose and applauded long and hard, waving their order papers.

They applauded Mr Cameron on the Labour side, too, more grudgingly on the front bench than on the back, but there was no standing ovation as there had been from the Tories for the outgoing Mr Blair in 2007. A few members of the shadow Cabinet looked across at Jeremy Corbyn, as if willing him to rise, but their leader failed to lead. Not for the first time. Andy Burnham got up just as the applause was dying down, missing his moment yet again.

Mr Corbyn had been pretty churlish at the start of the session. When Mr Cameron began by praising the British winners at Wimbledon, the Labour leader moaned that it would have been 'nice' to congratulate Serena Williams, the American ladies' champion, too.

Mr Corbyn failed to remark on Theresa May being the new Prime Minister. Never mind, she got a loud enough cheer when she entered the chamber during Welsh questions, prompting the Labour backbencher who was speaking at the time to quip, 'I didn't realise I was that popular.'

Most of the leading characters in this soap opera of a political summer were there, although you had to look hard to find them. In the Westminster version of *Where's Wally?*, Angela Eagle sat by the exit, as far from the dispatch box as Mr Corbyn used to sit from previous Labour leaders. Boris Johnson was skulking in the corner, and Michael Gove was seen nodding at the back of the group by the door. Both Tories seemed 'meadowfied', a marvellous Wodehousean word that means somewhere between cowed and sheepish, although by the evening Boris was looking bullish.

Mr Cameron promised that he would still come along on Wednesdays and watch from the backbenches. 'I will be willing you on,' he said. 'I do not just mean the new Prime Minister or the front bench, I mean all of you.' People enter politics for noble reasons, he said, with passion for issues and love for their constituencies. 'You can achieve a lot of things in politics,' he said. 'Nothing is impossible if you put your mind to it.'

And with just a few more words, that was it. As he said when asked about his engagements at the start, 'The diary for the rest of my day is remarkably light.'

15 JULY
CABINET SUFFERS THE DAY OF THE SHORT STILETTOS

Andrea Leadsom bounded into No. 10. 'Good afternoon, Prime Minister,' she said, laying on the jollity. 'How are the children settling in? Oh. Sorry.'

Theresa May pointed at a large sack of manure sweating beside the Cabinet table. 'This is a clue to your new job,' the Prime Minister said. 'Northern Ireland?' Mrs Leadsom ventured. 'Health?' It turned out that she was being handed the environment brief. 'I'm well qualified for that,' Mrs Leadsom said. 'You'll remember I used to be a North Sea fisherman. And I invented wind farms. And then there were those six months I spent playing Badger in *The Wind in the Willows*. It's all in my CV. Oh yes, I love the environment: birds, trees, flowers. Speaking as a Chrysanthemum...'

As Mrs Leadsom was shown out, Mrs May drew a sharpened fingernail down a list of names. Who's next? Speed bumps for Grayling; bin collections for Javid; Scotland for... whoever that Scotsman is. She paused. Why was Karen Bradley written next to culture? 'I said Karren Brady!' Mrs May shouted to a quivering minion. 'The one on the telly who knows about football. Oh, never mind. Culture Secretaries never last long anyway.'

It was all going very well. Mrs May had entered Downing Street on the 54th anniversary of Harold Macmillan's Night of the Long Knives and now she was carrying out the Day of the Short Stilettos. George Osborne had taken one to the goolies the night before. Now a few more scores were being settled. So long, Gove; farewell, Morgan; spend more time with your dating profile, Whitto. Stephen Crabb didn't pay much attention during their chat. He was too busy looking at his phone.

In the Foreign and Commonwealth Office, Boris Johnson

was staring at the globe. 'Where have they put Ceylon?' he asked an aide. 'And can you explain again why I can't say piccaninnies?' Mr Johnson's appointment had surprised many, but not the fans who had gathered outside his house since the referendum to shout 'Eff Off, Boris' at him. They have always believed in him.

20 JULY
FIRST BLOOD TO AMERICA AS BOJO LOSES MOJO

The special relationship has survived its first brush with Boris Johnson. The new Foreign Secretary tried hard not to play the buffoon at his press conference with the US Secretary of State. His tie was done up, his hair was vaguely brushed and when he spoke it was in a slow, steady tone, as if he were commentating on a royal funeral.

The odd solecism aside – I'm sure the recent attempted coup was in Turkey, not Egypt – it was almost statesmanlike. He even negotiated a sentence about Syria that included the words 'dire', 'Daesh' and 'Daraa' without confusing them or cracking a pun.

Fortunately, Mr Johnson has a rich back catalogue for people to pick over and the American press had done their homework. A man called Brad read down the charge sheet of insults that the Foreign Secretary has scattered around the world: Barack Obama hates Britain because he's part-Kenyan, Hillary Clinton resembles a sadistic nurse in a mental hospital, the EU is like Hitler and so on.

With each bullet point Mr Johnson slumped further into his suit, while John Kerry tried hard not to laugh. When Brad suggested that the only interests Mr Johnson represented were his own, the Foreign Secretary could only raise an eyebrow and shake his head wearily.

Finally, Brad reached a pause. 'There is such a rich thesaurus now of things that I have said that, one way or another – through what alchemy I do not know – were somehow misconstrued,' Mr Johnson said. 'It would take me too long to engage in any full-blown itinerary of apology.' These gaffes, he added, were mere '*obiter dicta*' – nugatory piffle.

Fortunately, Mr Kerry rode to his rescue. The American had earlier got a bruised nose after a difference of opinion with the door of 10 Downing Street – Mr Kerry thought it would stay open as he walked through it, the door begged to differ – but he wasn't going to stand by and let his new buddy take all this abuse.

Speaking in a voice so husky that the young David Cameron would have wanted to hug it, Mr Kerry said that he had been talking to the US ambassador in Brussels, who was at Oxford with the young Mr Johnson. 'Oh cripes!' Mr Johnson must have thought, visions of the annual Bullingdon Club smoking concert and rampage flying through his mind.

'He told me that this is a very smart and capable man,' Mr Kerry told the room. 'I can live with that,' Mr Johnson said. Then, as the praise continued, he insisted, 'Phew. You can stop there.' Please stop before he says something embarrassing about the time I debagged a scout.

Mr Kerry left his podium and nudged his friend in the ribs. Then, in a loud stage whisper, he said, 'It's called diplomacy, Boris.' One–zip to the US of A.

21 JULY
'REMIND YOU OF ANYBODY?'

I once knew a Conservative MP who had two photographs beside his bed. One of his wife, the other of the blessed Margaret. The nocturnal presence of Mrs Thatcher – eyes of Caligula, mouth of Marilyn Monroe, as François Mitterrand put it – stiffened his resolve. Or something.

I wonder if there has been a rush of demand from Tory MPs for photos of Theresa May since her debut at Prime Minister's Questions. It was like parliamentary Viagra to her honourable members. I swear that some of them skipped out of the chamber. As for poor Labour, they could only stare at the ceiling and wait for it all to be over as their leader flopped again.

Jeremy Corbyn has such good intentions. He raised serious issues – the price of starter homes, food banks, child poverty, job insecurity – and Mrs May ignored most of them, but PMQs is not about getting answers to questions. In almost a year in the job Mr Corbyn has still not learnt that. It is about showing authority.

His questions are so rambling and lacking in wit, his strategy so unadaptable when offered a chance to attack, that he rarely lands blows. PMQs is a hand-to-hand combat to show that you are strong and your opponent is weak, that your team is confident and the other lot full of doubt. A new leader at the dispatch box should be struggling to make herself heard against a wall of noise. The only noise yesterday came from behind Mrs May.

Her childhood hero was Geoffrey Boycott, the dour England batsman, who accumulated runs selfishly but relentlessly with barely a chance offered to the other side. We assumed that Mrs May would play PMQs the Boycott way: competent, reliable, utterly lacking in sparkle.

Instead she was more like David Gower, that flamboyant left-hander, pulling the first ball she faced to the boundary for four with a twist on an old line of John Major's. 'I have long heard the Labour Party asking what the Conservative Party does for women,' she said. 'Well, it keeps making us Prime Minister.' Twice in a century of women's suffrage is not quite a trend, but it is two more than Labour has had.

Mrs May continued her assault. David Cameron had recently taken to pleading with Mr Corbyn to go for the good of the country. No such reprieve from the new PM. 'I hope we will be having these exchanges for many years to come,' she said. 'YAAAAS!' shouted the Tories. 'URGGHH!' sighed Labour.

Mr Corbyn, sending down what they call 'buffet bowling' – help yourself, madam – got tonked all around the ground. Even when he found a good line of attack, quoting some of Boris Johnson's dubious comments, he was unable to push home an advantage. The Foreign Secretary sat grinning a few places along, manspreading his thighs like some potentate.

Mrs May's best lines went down well. 'He uses the language of austerity – I call it living within our means,' she roared. That's one for the evening news that neatly sums up their philosophical differences. And then there was the moment when Mr Corbyn brought up employment rights. 'I suspect that many members on the opposition benches might be familiar with an unscrupulous boss,' she said, licking her lips as chuckles began.

'A boss who does not listen to his workers, a boss who requires some of his workers to double their workload,' she went on, a reference to there being so few willing to serve in the shadow Cabinet that they have had to double up on briefs.

Then a raised finger, as if she had only just thought of this last point: 'Maybe even a boss who exploits the rules to further his own career.' There was awkward laughter from the frustrated Labour plotters.

And finally the *coup de grâce*. Leaning on to the dispatch box and lowering her voice, Mrs May stared Mr Corbyn in the eyeball. 'Remind him of anybody?' she asked.

She certainly reminded her troops of someone. This was pure, vintage Maggie, sending a whooping thrill of delight along the backbenches. I bet there will have been a few Tory MPs replaying that clip on their iPads in bed last night.

28 JULY
OWEN SMITH CONDUCTS FIRST NIGHT OF THE GLUMS

The annual Labour leadership contest is only in its second year, but it looks like a concept that will run and run. Doubtless in fifty years' time the moderate wing of the Labour Party, all six of them, will still be selecting a challenger to be defeated by a cryogenically frozen Jeremy Corbyn in the by-then traditional September finale known as the Last Night of the Glums.

This year's Glums season opened with 'Mahler's Resignation Symphony No. 2', featuring a choir of 172 disgruntled MPs, followed by 'Franck's Panic Angelicus', Angela's panic growing with each departing member of the audience. Finally, we had Vaughan Williams's 'The Eagle Descending'.

Now the Glums baton has been handed to Owen Smith, a little-known performer from Pontypridd, who tried to inject some passion into the season yesterday with a 'Dies Irae'. It was full of wrath, rattling the rafters of the manufacturing park in Rotherham that he had chosen for his concert.

'We are not contented,' Mr Smith sang in a pleasing Welsh baritone. 'We are frustrated, divided, intolerant and angry. People feel the system is rigged against them.' He was not just talking about the parliamentary Labour Party, it turned out, but the whole country.

Britain is seething with rage, he went on, his face flushed. Anger at bankers, at politicians and at broken promises. To the sound of rumbling timpani, he sang that people want an angry Labour government. 'One angry for them, that feels it in their belly,' he roared.

The present Labour leadership, he added later, are weak and clueless. 'For the last nine months, Jeremy has been wandering round the country saying he wants to end austerity without saying what he puts in its place,' he said. There had not been a single debate in the shadow Cabinet about workers' rights,' he added. 'It's been devoid of ideas.'

Into the void stepped Mr Smith with a list of twenty policies, interesting ones, full of *Sturm und Drang* about how to smash the rich and give their money to the poor. His 'Dies Irae' thundered around the room.

And as the rage grew, Mr Smith began to deviate further from his script, turning this into a *hwyl*. 'We will smash austerity,' he sang. That line seemed to go down well, so he reached for the 'S' word again.

Referring to Theresa May's 'temerity to lecture' Labour on social injustice, he added, 'It pains me that we didn't have the strength and the power and the vitality to smash her back on her heels.'

It was a throwaway remark, a bit of improvisation to show his passion, the sort of comment you often hear on a Welsh rugby field – heels in an anatomical sense, not a leopard print. If he had been talking about a male Prime Minister, it would have been ignored, but we live in a world where smears can go around the world while nuance is tying up its bootlaces. With Mr Smith still on his feet the outrage was growing. The Irator had become the Iratee.

'Did he really say he wants to thump Mrs May?' people were asking. No, he didn't, but don't let that stop Twitter. Within minutes someone had found a cutting from 2010 in which he, rather crassly, compared spending cuts to domestic violence. It was even observed that Owen Smith is an anagram of 'hits women'.

Those new policies were suddenly forgotten; the day was now spent explaining his 'gaffe'. All rather unfair, of course, but that's the Glums for you.

7 SEPTEMBER
CORBYN HITS BUM NOTE IN QUEST FOR COOL BRITANNIA

There is more of Tony Blair in him than Jeremy Corbyn likes to admit. Back in the days of Cool Britannia you couldn't walk down Whitehall without tripping over a Gallagher brother or one of the other acts that had been invited to Downing Street to make Mr Blair feel like Simon Cowell. Now it turns out that Mr Corbyn is also a bit of a groupie, although his musical idols are of an older vintage.

The support of a reggae band who were big in the 1980s could be what decisively tilts the Labour leadership contest to Mr Corbyn. Nothing shows you are ready for government quite like the backing of a group who topped the charts during the miners' strike, or at least the members who stuck around after a bitter schism a few years ago.

Theresa May has the G20 but Mr Corbyn has UB40. Twice as good.

As the band walked out, Mr Corbyn thanked them for their 'incredible endorsement'. 'What an…' – he searched for the right word – '… iconic name you have.'

It was unclear whether he was actually a fan. The band's manager said that this great event in cultural–political history had come about by chance after he met Mr Corbyn in the street. Perhaps Mr Corbyn had misunderstood and was only after some lubricant for his bicycle chain. 'Where's the WD-40 you promised me?' Possibly he thought these men were from the sales team.

As he was photographed sharing a stage with five middle-aged men, someone observed on Twitter that the previous night Mr Corbyn had promised he would never sit on an all-male panel again. Perhaps he will get the backing of The Bangles next week to ensure balance.

Meanwhile, Owen Smith's campaign was trying to find its

own passé endorsement. 'Get me Renée and Renato's agent,' Mr Corbyn's rival shouted. 'What do you mean Renato's dead? How about Musical Youth? Does anyone have an "in" with St Winifred's School Choir?'

Back at the gig, Mr Corbyn was asked to begin with 'a few words' about the arts. The host must not have heard him speak before. That's like asking Pink Floyd to play a quick tune. In words as in politics, Mr Corbyn is for the many, not the few. He rambled on about the importance of music.

'There's creativity in all of us,' he said, looking at a band whose three No. 1 hits were covers of songs by Neil Diamond, Sonny & Cher and Elvis. He told us about the Romanian street band he had seen recently. He also complained about how pub chains are evil because they don't host evenings of Irish music. You seldom find a *bodhrán* at Wetherspoons, he lamented.

Then, remembering that others were sharing the stage with him, he decided to ask some questions. 'Tell me,' he said to the nearest UB40 person, 'do you like classical music?' Mr UB40 seemed nonplussed. 'Occasionally,' he said.

Next came a question from the floor: what can politicians learn from musicians? 'That's easy,' Mr Corbyn said. 'Teamwork. Bands stick together.' There was an awkward silence until Mr Corbyn finally remembered what one of his lackeys had told him about half of UB40 suing the other half over the right to use the name. 'Well, until they fall out,' he added. Then he reminisced for a bit about how he once met Joan Baez.

Eventually, Mr Corbyn meandered back towards the creative process. 'How do you do it?' he asked.

'Oh, we just get in a room and knock something together,' Mr UB40 said. 'We do everything arse backwards.'

Mr Corbyn beamed. Why, that is just how Labour make policy these days. Clearly there is much that he can learn from these chain-lubrication salesmen.

17 SEPTEMBER
FARAGE HANDS OVER THE TWEED MANTLE TO A NEW LEADER

'My goodness,' Diane James said on being named as UKIP's new leader. 'You've handed me quite a mantle.' A tweed one with a velvet collar and leather arm patches. And a pewter tankard behind the bar at the Marquis of Granby. There must be some perks to being Nigel Farage's successor.

She inherits an eccentric tribe. There were lots of three-piece suits and fine moustaches in Bournemouth and 'Land of Hope and Glory' was played at least three times. I heard one Kipper complain that there was not enough choice of real ale. It seems remarkable that such people, some of whom refer to 'my good lady wife', have elected a woman leader long before the Labour Party looks like doing so.

Ms James gave a tummy-tickling speech, full of thanks for those who had elected her and tough-talking about Brexit having to mean Brexit. 'Mrs May, we are the opposition in waiting,' she declared. 'From one grammar school girl to another, stop the faff and get on with it.'

Seats in the hall were reserved well before Mr Farage's farewell speech. The outgoing chairman played his military metaphors in the warm-up act. 'We need to reform the columns of the People's Army and get back in battle order,' he said, calling on members to march with flaming torches on the home of Baroness Wheatcroft, who is leading the opposition in the Lords to implementing Brexit.

After that came a video of the dragons whom St Nigel had skewered, with audience participation. David Cameron (boo!), George Osborne (louder boo!), Christine Lagarde (jeer!), Lib Dems (hiss!), Herman Van Rompuy (a loud chant of 'who are you?'). This was panto for pensioners.

And then the hero himself. 'We did it,' Mr Farage said. 'We changed the course of history. We've brought down the Prime

Minister [cheer!]. And the Chancellor [louder cheer!]. We won the war, but now we must win the peace.'

Barking out his speech, without notes, like an eel salesman at Billingsgate, Mr Farage ran through his CV. How far he had come, he said, since his first by-election, when he beat Screaming Lord Sutch to fourth place by 169 votes. He reflected on his election as an MEP in 1999, when a journalist asked if he would be corrupted by Brussels and start to live a decadent life of long lunches and boozy evenings. 'No,' Farage said. 'I've always lived like that.' And then he relived UKIP's victory in the 2014 European election, a result that pushed Mr Cameron into offering the referendum.

'I have put all of me into this,' Mr Farage said and now he wants to take back control of his lunch hour. He plans to spend the autumn touring Europe, spreading independence to other lands. 'I'm going to start speaking my mind,' he said. For a change. The mantle of leadership may have been passed on but the Farage foghorn will not be silenced.

Diane James lasted just over a fortnight as UKIP leader before handing the mantle back to Nigel Farage. It was taken up by yet another new leader, Paul Nuttall, at the end of November.

22 SEPTEMBER
NO PALME D'OR FOR JEZZA: THE MOVIE

There comes a point in the life of every aspiring Prime Minister when it's time to make a movie with an award-winning director. John Schlesinger, with an Oscar for *Midnight Cowboy*, took John Major kipper-buying in Brixton market and back into Downing Street; Hugh Hudson earned as much critical praise for *Kinnock: The Movie* as he had for *Chariots of Fire*, if not the box-office success; Tony Blair got the Bafta-winning Molly Dineen to burnish his 'normal bloke' credentials by showing him playing football in the park.

Jeremy Corbyn has now followed their example with a film made by Ken Loach, fresh from winning the Palme d'Or. The Labour leadership contest may be in the bag, but Mr Corbyn is working on the struggle ahead. With Loach at the camera, maker of *Kes* and *Cathy Come Home*, he intends to throw the kitchen sink at the government.

My God, it is dull, though. There is no narrative, no direction, no structure. The film, all fifty-nine minutes and thirty-six seconds of it, is essentially two long public meetings with people who complain about their lives, while the leader chews on the arm of his glasses, scribbles in a notebook and agrees, in his usual long-winded way, about how awful it sounds. He takes ninety seconds to answer the first question, about cuts to disability benefits, and says little more than 'government must help disabled people'.

Mr Corbyn does not deal in soundbites. He deals in sound buffets, laying on an all-you-can-eat spread of reheated ideas that have been lying around for ages. It looks great when you are starving but plays havoc with your digestion.

At one point near the end he says this: 'Maybe the worm is turning on the neoliberal agenda and so this is historical justice time.' Eh? Earlier, asked about his foreign policy plans as Prime Minister, he says, 'In the ministerial things that we may well be appointing in the future let's have a minister for disarmament, and a minister for peace as well who is pursuing those things around the world.'

I do not mean to diminish the concerns of those in the film who seem genuinely in despair. 'You are the only person who has ever listened to us,' one says. There is the student considering leaving university after one year because of his poor prospects; the soldier suffering from poorly treated post-traumatic stress disorder; the nurse relying on food banks; the woman on a zero-hours contract.

We should feel angry that society has put them in this position, but also angry that the man they put their faith in is such a mediocrity. Is Mr Corbyn, with his tea, sympathy and waffle about neoliberalism, really the best that the left can do? Yet they love him, dear cuddly Jez. 'When things are bad, you need an old man with a white beard,' one says. 'Jeremy is a sweetie but a very strong sweetie,' says another. Makes him sound more like a sherbet lemon than a statesman.

The best films end with a memorable final line. 'I think this is the beginning of a beautiful friendship'; 'Tomorrow is another day'; 'Well, nobody's perfect'; 'There's no place like home.'

How does *Corbyn: The Movie* end? With this: 'It's been really great to see the hashtag "LezzasForJezza" on Facebook.' *Fin*. Roll credits. I think Ken Loach was better working with kestrels rather than dodos.

Despite 80 per cent of his MPs wanting rid of him, Jeremy Corbyn inevitably was re-elected as Labour leader in a landslide, with 62 per cent of the party's 500,000 members preferring him to Owen Smith. It was announced at their party conference in Liverpool.

27 SEPTEMBER
WACKY MACCA'S MESSAGE OF PEACE WOWS THE CROWD AT CONFERENCE

Macca returned to Liverpool yesterday, the city of his birth, and played a few old favourites for those who had been brought up on the Scab Four. 'Taxman', 'Revolution', 'Three Days A Week', 'Everybody's Got Something to Hide Except Me and Momentum'...

'If you wear red tonight...' John McDonnell, the shadow Chancellor, crooned and the audience pulled out their e-cigarettes, making the air glow faintly with the feeble light of 1,000 socially responsible vaping devices.

This was a mellow Macca, one trying to win people over with a message of love, in contrast to the rowdy gigs he used to play in IRA drinking dens during the 1980s. There was a section when he lashed out at rogue bosses and tax evaders – bang, bang, Macca's silver hammer came down upon Philip Green – but he extended olive branches to those who had drifted away from the group.

To Owen Smith, Caroline Flint, Angela Smith and Jonathan Reynolds, he dedicated 'Come Together' and he almost praised Tony Blair by name – but that would have given peace too much of a chance. Instead he spoke of 'the government elected in 1997' when he paid tribute to the creation of a national minimum wage.

Macca had wondered about winding up with 'Hey Jude' but decided against it. His critics would only accuse him of anti-semitism. Instead he chose to finish with something saccharine. 'In the birthplace of John Lennon, it falls to us,' Macca said, 'to inspire people to imagine.' Imagine no possessions: now there's a slogan with which to woo the swing voters of Middle England. 'You may say I'm a dreamer, but I'm not the only one. There's Jeremy as well. And Diane.' I left before Ms Abbott came on stage to do 'I'd Like to Teach the World to Sing'.

29 SEPTEMBER
FANFARE FOR THE COMMA MAN

An hour after Jeremy Corbyn had finished his second party conference speech as Labour leader, the announcement came over the public address system. 'Attention please: breakdown can now commence.' For many of his MPs it had begun a few days earlier.

Liverpool has been a strange place this week. The mood in the conference centre, largely missing the Momentum groupies, has been flat. Even politicians you would have placed on the left have spoken openly of their gloom at the re-election of Mr Corbyn. Many left town hours before he took to the stage.

This is a pity, since they missed the best speech of his career, which is not saying all that much. It was a relatively good speech in the way Victoria Beckham was relatively Posh Spice. A speech that would earn him a middling GCSE but won't get him into Oxbridge. Or Downing Street.

At least Mr Corbyn has finally learnt what commas do. He paused at the right moments, in the main, and he stopped to take the audience's applause rather than muttering over them.

He even attempted some jokes. It's brave to begin a speech by drawing attention to a time when you've been caught lying, but a reference to Virgin Trains saying there were plenty of empty seats in the packed hall went down well. There was another good joke, if unintended, about those who had stepped into the shadow Cabinet over the summer being the 'future of our party'. The eye fell on the 81-year-old Paul Flynn (Lab, Newport West) and his two briefs.

Mr Corbyn also tried to play the peacemaker with those who had refused to serve, but perhaps he gave away his true feelings about his MPs when he fluffed an attempt to quote the late Jo Cox (the Labour MP for Batley and Spen who was murdered during the referendum campaign). 'We have far more that divi— far more in common with each other than things that divide us,' he said.

They loved him in the hall. One elderly man in front of me gave a couple of wolf-whistles and there were standing ovations when Mr Corbyn criticised the Iraq War and promised to end arms sales. There was room-pleasing policy meat, although the first new announcement – to give councils powers to borrow to build homes – did not come until thirty-five minutes in.

Will it play well beyond his fans, though? Mr Corbyn spoke bullishly about an early election, telling Theresa May to bring it on, but the Tories were barely paying attention. In the past, rebuttals to a Labour leader's speech would have come at the rate of one a paragraph; there were only five tweets from Conservative HQ during his speech. Perhaps they hadn't even bothered to watch. *Find It, Fix It, Flog It* was showing on Channel 4 at the same time and the Tories have got to come up with their own policy ideas for next week.

4 OCTOBER
THE RUNNYMEDE PHIL PERFORMS A MELLOW SET

The Runnymede Phil performed the 'Ode to Post-Brexit Joy' at the Symphony Hall in Birmingham. The Phil is not a large orchestra – just one musician, in fact, who bears a passing resemblance to the Chancellor of the Exchequer – but he took on many roles, banging the drums, blowing his own horns and pulling at the strings like a virtuoso.

It started with a slow movement. Then a slower one. The Runnymede Phil is not noted for being lively. Near the start I detected a snatch of City of London blues – 'I wen' down to the Threadneedle depository, saw my money lying there' – then there was a touch of the Charleston, with a crowd-pleasing reference to Ed Balls's performance on *Strictly*. 'Jeremy Corbyn was asked to go on,' the conductor told the audience in an aside. 'But – wait for it – he's got two left feet.' The sound of a drum roll followed by a cymbal clash echoed around the silent hall.

After that came an *adagio ma non troppo* on a theme of fiscal consolidation and a warning, heralded by rumbling (well, it was nearly lunchtime), that Labour would wreck it. Then back to another extremely slow section about productivity. 'Before you switch off, I know that this doesn't set pulses racing but bear with me,' the conductor said. He doesn't just play all the instruments; he writes his own bad reviews as well.

It was not all pedestrian. There were some familiar leitmotivs drizzled throughout the movements.

The parp of a 'Northern Powerhouse', the trill of a 'long-term economic plan', a fresh arrangement on the phrase 'for the many not the few' and this year's signature theme of 'an X that works for everyone', repeated until you'd got sick of it. The Runnymede Phil was playing all the right notes and most of them were in the right order. It was just not necessarily at a speed at which the audience could be expected to stay awake.

6 OCTOBER
CARPE PM: SEIZE THE MAY!

Here comes old flat top again. Every speech in Birmingham this week was preceded by a snatch of 'Come Together', reinforcing a message of party unity. Yesterday I expected Theresa May to play us the rest of *Abbey Road* in her speech: 'Something', a bit of 'Here Comes the Sun' optimism, then 'You Never Give Me Your Money' and 'Carry That Weight' before, Tories being Tories, ending with 'Her Majesty'.

Instead, the Prime Minister changed the record. She came out to Sam Cooke's civil rights anthem 'A Change is Gonna Come' and repeated the first 'C' word over and over. She may lead the same 330 MPs who were elected seventeen months ago, but this is a new government, with a new mission.

The speech was too long – they always are – and light on policy detail, but it was well structured and the vision and philosophy were clear. Hard work, opportunity, fairness and equality are her watchwords. 'We succeed or fall together,' she said.

She gave as an example of this the Parable of the Staggering Brownlee, citing a British triathlete who stopped to help his brother to complete a race in August even though it would cost him his own victory. It was all very 'Two Little Boys' – 'Did you think I would leave you dying, when there's room on my horse for two?' – but to play Rolf Harris at the party conference would be taking the prisoner rehabilitation agenda too far.

Mrs May had been introduced by a vision in fuchsia. The members love Ruth Davidson and she may soon overtake Boris Johnson as their darling. She sang of Tory victories in Scotland and gave the Labour Party a proper kicking, rejecting Harriet Harman's claim that Mrs May is not a feminist. 'Labour is bathing in its own left-wing sanctimony,' she said. 'Theresa May has done more for women than any pink buses that Labour can launch. She is exactly what a sister looks like.' Kapow.

The Prime Minister kept up the attack, calling Labour divisive, abusive and supporting voices of hate. A fair point, given the death threats written on placards waved outside the hall. Then, in an echo of a lecture she had given to her own tribe many years ago, she added, 'You know what some people call them? The nasty party.'

This was a tanks-on-lawn speech. An attempt to take advantage of Labour's internal chaos and claim the mantle of being the nice guys and the workers' party. 'Seize the day!' were her final words. Carpe PM. If I were a moderate Labour MP, I would be feeling even more gloomy than usual.

26 OCTOBER
NO NOISE POLLUTION FROM ZACAIR

There was no chance of the decibel limits being breached when ZacAir took off from Westminster yesterday lunchtime. The MP for Richmond Park is not one of Parliament's thunderous speakers. He is such an environmentalist that he has replaced the polluting Outrage 2000 engine that many politicians have with an electric motor that emits nothing more than a gentle whine.

Yesterday Mr Goldsmith spoke with all the passion and vim of a vicar in Waitrose who has discovered that they're all out of halloumi. 'Oh, deary me, this is very inconvenient,' he seemed to be sighing. 'I'm so cross about this that I murmur murmur mumble mumble wishy-washy drip drip drip.' There are towels on the floor of my local swimming baths that are less wet. He is so laid-back and flat he would make a pretty good runway himself.

Mr Goldsmith went on to whisper that 'there are so many questions that one could ask I would not know where to begin'. So he didn't try and, after putting his 'absolute opposition on the record', he drifted out of the chamber. Probably for a session with his yoga master.

In order to resign and fight a lethargic by-election against Heathrow expansion, Mr Goldsmith was appointed Crown Steward and Bailiff of the Chiltern Hundreds, one of the two traditional escape routes from the Commons. There is a certain irony in standing down in protest at one massively disruptive infrastructure project only to find yourself nominally in charge of an area that will be cut open by HS2.

Anger was left to other Tories, such as Tania Mathias (Con, Twickenham), whose seat is next door to Richmond Park, or the seldom-seen Adam Afriyie, who was so moved by the threat posed to Windsor that he spoke in the chamber for only the third time this year. One of the previous two occasions was to suck up to the Queen on her 90th birthday. Perhaps his most famous constituent had asked him to stop the planes going over her castle.

Meanwhile, Boris Johnson, whose seat is under the flight path, was telling broadcasters that the runway will never be built. Strange how politicians who think that Britain can unpick forty years of European integration and negotiate trade deals with the rest of the world in just two years are doubtful about whether we can lay down some tarmac by the M4 in a decade.

24 NOVEMBER
CAREFUL DRIVER TAKES ECONOMY FOR A SPIN

Every Chancellor drives the economy in his own style. Gordon Brown was Mr Angry, stabbing at the dashboard, certain of his right of way. George Osborne was Mr Toad, poop-pooping at the pedestrians on the benches opposite.

Yesterday we heard a careful statement from a careful motorist, a man who looks as if he wears string-backed leather driving gloves and has a walnut gear knob in his pristine Jaguar XJ, which goes at up to, but does not exceed, 79 mph on motorways.

So steady and careful was Philip Hammond's speech that there were times when you almost forgot he was there. At one point, perhaps detecting blank faces opposite and a gentle snoring from behind, he ad-libbed some commentary to a list of figures about business rates. 'That's complicated,' he said, 'but it's good news.' A couple of Tories gave a semi-cheer; Labour MPs shrugged.

Beneath the grey exterior, though, beats a powerful engine. A former girlfriend revealed this week that Mr Hammond could be a passionate kisser after half a bottle of sherry. I hear that his permanent secretary has now removed all bottles of Tio Pepe from the Treasury, just in case.

He was the model of respectability yesterday. No risky moves, no hands where they shouldn't be, no tonguing of the nation's erogenous zones. Just a reassuring squeeze of the hand and a gentle spin.

The Budget offered a mixed bag for motorists. A freeze in fuel duty and the promise of more road improvements, but an increase in insurance premium tax. The Chancellor sweetened this by saying that he would clamp down on dodgy compensation claims, but there was little else to give away. Blame the fragile economy since 23 June.

It felt like one of those insurance adverts. 'Has your country been involved in an economic crash that wasn't your fault? Call 0800 BREXIT today and discover how little you're going to get.'

Mr Hammond began with a warm tribute to his predecessor, who was sitting directly behind him, next to Ken Clarke (Con, Rushcliffe). They had been joined by the overambitious Alan Mak (Con, Havant). Two former Chancellors and a future junior minister for teaspoons. Mr Hammond did not feel the pressure of their gaze. He even slipped in an early joke at the expense of Boris Johnson, which Mr Osborne enjoyed.

There would be no rabbits pulled from hats this year, he promised, nor any gimmicks. Unless, that is, you count a £7.6 million grant to do up Wentworth Woodhouse near Rotherham, the largest privately owned mansion in Britain. Is that what you meant about supporting the Northern Powerhouse, George? At the end, as he approached the garage, it seemed as if this gentle spin would end on an emergency brake. 'This is my first autumn statement,' Mr Hammond said. 'It will also be my last.' Ears pricked up. Would there be a twist? There had been rumours of a row.

Instead of his resignation, though, Mr Hammond offered us another joke. 'This will be my last autumn statement,' he explained, 'because I plan to move the Budget from the spring to the autumn.' In case that wasn't funny enough, he added that he was going to replace the Budget with a spring statement.

As MPs on all sides said 'Eh? What?' Mr Hammond pulled the car into his parking space, turned off the engine and removed his leather gloves. 'Textbook drive,' he said to no one in particular.

7 DECEMBER
REMAINERS PUSH THE PANNICK BUTTON

Some want soft, others want hard, but Theresa May finally clarified her position on leaving the EU. 'We should be looking for a red, white and blue Brexit,' she told reporters in Bahrain. 'At last, some good news for Cuba,' a spokesman for Jeremy Corbyn was minded to say.

Things were no clearer in the Supreme Court, where James Eadie, the so-called Treasury Devil, had resumed his argument for why Mrs May can secure a Brexit of many colours without a vote and was making heavy weather of it. Only fifteen minutes in, Lord Sumption, one of the eleven Supremes hearing the appeal, eyeballed the Devil and said, 'You have given two diametrically opposed answers in five minutes to the same question.'

Nothing gets past Lord S, who has the air of a crumpled dilettante with his wild white hair, jazzy ties and the largest personal library in the judiciary (7,000 volumes on the Hundred Years' War alone – and a few Dan Browns for the beach), but a legal brilliance that outshines all but the most cussed online Brexiteer who saw *LA Law* and thinks he's an expert on jurisprudence.

Then we heard briefly from the Advocate General for Scotland, who argued with Lord Clarke over the precise meaning of 'normally', and John Larkin, QC, a flustered Attorney General for Northern Ireland. Mr Larkin, who bears a resemblance to Keith Chegwin (the Brexit-supporting former host of a nude gameshow), kept losing his place and having to restate his argument.

'It's so difficult for you in the short time available,' one Supreme patronisingly told him. 'Which is the bit you should have corrected?' a tetchier one added. Mr Larkin's face glowed. He muttered that he was trying to 'channel the Duke of Wellington'. By getting the boot?

This was all just an amuse-bouche for Lord Pannick, who began his response to the government with the canine gambit. If we listen to them, he said, the 1972 Act that took Britain into Europe would have a lesser status than the 1991 Dangerous Dogs Act. Woof.

He later introduced 'a modus vivendi for lobster fishing in Newfoundland', a reference to a treaty change in 1892 that affected Canadian fishermen and was somehow relevant to Brexit. It was a shellfish motive.

On day one, the Supremes had listened in silence for half an hour as the government began its case. With Lord Pannick, they leapt in from the off. It was like a group of tennis-mad schoolboys who had spotted Andy Murray on a municipal court and run over to ask if they could have a hit with him.

Lord Pannick did not match his name. Unflustered, he batted away all their shots, politely but firmly. He kept using the word 'respectfully' as a form of loaded punctuation, as Quentin Tarantino uses the 'F' word. When Lord Sumption raised some quibble of Mr Eadie's, Lord Pannick replied, 'I respectfully commend my approach.' Back in your box, Eadie.

The essence of his argument was that the EU referendum was merely 'advisory' – for senior ministers had said so – and that if the government had wanted it to have legal force they would have legislated for it. Quoting from Matthew 23:24, he said that Parliament did not intend to 'strain at a gnat and swallow a camel'. No wonder so many Remain-supporting MPs look as if they've got the hump.

2017: STRONG AND STABLE

10 JANUARY
PARROT PM FINDS THAT SQUAWK IS CHEAP

New year, new catchphrase. Or rather an old catchphrase in new clothes. Theresa May had sensed that 'Brexit means Brexit' was getting stale and so, for her first big speech of 2017, she decided to liven it up a little, like a chef trying to cover the rancid taste of some pork that has been in the fridge too long by drowning it in Lea & Perrins.

It was a speech about fairness and equality, 'addressing the everyday injustices that too many people feel', a rebooting of the 'vision' speech that she gave on the day she became Prime Minister. An attempt to define Mayism. And as she was nearing the end, she reached for her favourite riff. 'We must ensure', she said, 'that parity means parity.'

At least I think she said parity. She could have said 'parody means parody', I suppose, but she isn't known for being self-aware. Or perhaps it was even 'parroty means parroty', as in resembling a macaw, all plumage and no meat.

The Prime Minister was rather parroty herself yesterday, with a bright yellow and green scarf around her neck and a script full of phrases, even whole sentences, that she had used before. Her critics were quick to claim that there was little new money or even new policy. Squawk is cheap.

One new phrase was 'shared society', one in which people have ambitions and obligations, where community matters more than self-interest, and there is no glass ceiling keeping people in their place. It was the sort of speech you used to hear from the Labour Party.

As a vicar's daughter, the young Mrs May knows 'All Things Bright and Beautiful' well, but her society would feature less of the rich man in his castle and the poor man at his gate; more of the just-about-managing man in his three-bed semi. It was a plea to Mondeo Man and Worcester Woman to come home to Mother.

Perhaps Mrs May has been influenced by a politician from South America. *The Shared Society* was the title of a manifesto by Alejandro Toledo, President of Peru from 2001 to 2006. The Prime Minister often borrows ideas from Peruvians. Any journalist who has been on the receiving end of one of her hard stares knows that she is a keen student of Paddington Bear.

Gary Gibbon of *Channel 4 News* got the Paddington treatment yesterday when he dared to ask Mrs May about something off-grid. The Prime Minister had hinted in a Sunday interview that she prefers a hard Brexit in which Britain leaves the single market. Since then, Mr Gibbon noted, the pound had gone down. Was it a mistake? Mrs May turned the Paddington dial up to eleven.

'I have been completely clear', she said, 'that Brexit means exactly the same thing I said it meant a couple of months ago.' Which is to say that it means Brexit, of course. No more, no less, no clearer than that.

After Brexit, the subject that seemed to cause the most problems for Theresa May's government was transport, yet Chris 'Failing' Grayling kept the brief for three years. Proof, perhaps, that every Cabinet needs a duffer to make the rest of them feel competent. Here is one of many sketches I wrote about him.

13 JANUARY
DREAMER FOLLOWS THE LINE OF BEAUTY

For many users of our transport network, it would be enough to have a train that runs on time, a bypass where the traffic flows and an aviation policy where decisions are made in months rather than decades. Not for John Hayes (Con, South Holland and The Deepings). That would be too functional. A transport network must be a thing of beauty.

Mr Hayes had set out this theory in a low-key speech a couple of months ago in which the transport minister had railed against 'the cult of ugliness'. Look back at the golden age of steam, he said, at the neogothic majesty of St Pancras and Bristol Temple Meads, or the classical grandeur of Huddersfield station or the old Euston arch, and you see a noble ambition. These were places that made the heart sing.

It was a pleasure to arrive there – even a pleasure to be stuck there waiting for a delayed train. No wonder modern travellers are so miserable, he added, surrounded by all this ghastly and unimaginative concrete. They are suffering from the wrong kind of eaves on the line.

'Philistines wrought monstrous havoc knowingly,' he said. 'Well, now they have met their David.'

We used to have a transport minister called Adonis. He once joked that he had the second least appropriate name in transport after the TransPennine Express. Mr Hayes is no Adonis, in name or physique, bearing a resemblance to one of those cave-dwellers in Tolkien, but he has beauty in his soul. In Transport Questions yesterday, he set out more of his vision for a lovelier Britain.

In a few weeks, he declared, he will produce a design guide for new roads. 'It will dismay all the crass modernists and harsh brutalists,' he said, with evident glee, 'but it will delight all those who believe that our public infrastructure can be stylish and elegant.' What will this involve? More curves on the M1? A softer shade of red for stop lights?

At least there is one aesthete at the department. Chris Grayling, the Transport Secretary, remains as plodding and utilitarian as he was at the justice department. Where Mr Hayes deploys the wisdom of Cicero, Mr Grayling speaks only in ugly Whitehall-approved clichés.

So, when asked about the awful state of commuter rail, Mr Grayling said that he wants to create 'a franchise that works for all the passengers'. Yuck. He uses words like 'amelioration' when Mr Hayes would reach for something more poetic.

Not that Labour had many weapons to fire at him when they are funded so heavily by the transport unions. Andy McDonald (Middlesbrough), the shadow Transport Secretary, accused Mr Grayling of playing party politics with train services into London by not agreeing to let Sadiq Khan take them over, but the charge fell limply to the floor in a week when millions of Londoners were so inconvenienced by a Tube strike that Mr McDonald and his leader refused to condemn.

'I cannot believe what I have just heard,' Mr Grayling said, affecting outrage with his hands on his hips like Frankie Howerd. 'I will not take him seriously until I hear him condemning the strikes.' Fat chance. So, the pressing issue of late-running trains and crowded platforms was shunted into a siding for another day. Still, at least if Mr Hayes has his way commuters might get to look at a nice Doric pediment or a frieze above the jam-packed concourse while they wait for the delayed 8.23.

18 JANUARY
ALL WHITE ON THE NIGHT FOR TUNGSTEN THERESA

We had been promised a red, white and blue Brexit but the colour scheme for Theresa May's big speech was monochrome.

A white lectern, white backdrop, white blouse, perhaps even a few white lies.

It reminded me of the Yasmina Reza play *Art*, which has just been revived in the West End. Three men argue over their interpretation of a white canvas. The one who paid a fortune for it sees detail and nuance, even vibrant colours, that the others cannot. They bluff, argue and fall out. Can three friends – never mind twenty-eight – ever get on when they cannot agree on what they are looking at?

For Mrs May, the lines that she has drawn upon her white canvas are quite clear. She has a twelve-point plan, a dodeca-hedron of diplomacy. Twelve, note, not ten: a decimal negoti-ating stance sounds awfully continental. This will have caused much discussion in Downing Street.

'Can you find me a couple more bullet points, Tarquin? The PM wants to beef it up to twelve. Yeah, she thinks it sounds more British. Will play well in the rural seats where they don't like it metric.'

If the dignitaries in the grand gallery of Lancaster House wanted a reminder of our past they had only to look to either side of the stage, at the huge portraits of men in silly wigs hang-ing on the walls, or up at the impressive golden ceiling. Mrs May's whitewashed backdrop tried to mask Old Britain's gilt complex.

This was where Margaret Thatcher had given her 'Europe Open for Business' speech in 1988, in which she had sung the praises of the single market, now ditched by Mrs May. It was where Malaya, South Africa and Rhodesia had pushed for in-dependence from Britain.

Now Mrs May was setting Britain itself free against a white wall that seemed to glow ever brighter under the camera lights, while the enormous room gave her voice an echo. Is this what purgatory will be like? A radiant waiting room in which a bossy angel explains your options: be good and it's up, up, up to a glorious nirvana for all; be bad and you're going down to devil-town.

Mrs May tried to be emollient at first. The room was full of EU ambassadors and it is good diplomacy to start with an armful of compliments. This is not a rejection of the values we share, she said. We still love you. We just can't stand living with you any more.

Then came her dodecahedron of diplomacy, followed by the threats, first at those who had been pushing Mrs May for more detail. 'This is not a game,' she said. 'Every stray word, every hyped-up media report is going to make it harder for us.' She had already held the press in a windowless, WiFi-free basement room for ninety minutes before the speech. It will be the Tower next for any irritants.

Then the threats to the EU27. Do not punish us because we dare to leave, she said. Do not be petty, do not endanger your own people's economic success just to stick one to Blighty. You need our spies, you need our military, you need the protection of our nuclear weapons. Any tricks and you're on your own against Vlad. After six months of evasion and obfuscation, finally we had a glimpse of a Prime Minister with a backbone. Europe remembers the determination of one Iron Lady. Was this the first outing of the Tungsten Theresa?

We now cross the Atlantic briefly for the inauguration of the 45th US President.

21 JANUARY
TRUMP TIME

God blesses those who are humble, for they will inherit the earth, said the Rev. Samuel Rodriguez, reading from the Sermon on the Mount. Well, it's always good to start off with a joke, and Donald J. Trump tried hard not to smirk. He failed.

'I am so, so very humble,' he thought as the start of his presidency drew near. 'No one is more humble than me, of that there can be no doubt. I am, in fact, the humblest President there has been.'

As half of America prayed for Bobby Ewing to walk out of the shower and reveal that the past few months had all been a dream, the President-elect walked on to the stage at the Capitol, mouthing 'thank you' at the cameras and sticking his thumbs up. The age of the reality-show President was here.

First, some ceremonial. A choir from Missouri sang about welcoming strangers from overseas to their new land. That didn't quite fit with Mr Trump's immigration policy. The chairman of the inauguration committee damned the choir with faint praise. 'They practise two blocks from my home so it was easy to get them,' he said.

Then it was Trump Time. It had been briefed that he would borrow from the great inaugural speeches of the past and give them a personal twist. 'Better angels of our nature? I tell you, my angels will be so much better than Lincoln's. They are the best. Come here, Tammy, let them see what a cute lil' angel you are.'

Or perhaps a riff on Kennedy: 'Ask not what your country can do for you but how much of a deal you can screw out of your competitors.'

Instead, the speech was all Trump: belligerent, bombastic, nothing in moderation. Not enough political speeches contain the phrase 'eradicate from the face of the earth' as his did. He started with a gracious nod to his predecessor but quickly got into his main theme of bashing the enemies of those who had elected him: elites, foreign companies, immigrants.

Pointing his finger straight at the camera, as if he were about to fire some hapless advertising executive on *The Apprentice*, he declared, 'The people are the rulers of this nation.' Even though almost three million more of them had voted for the other candidate than for him.

There was little attempt to heal the divisions in America, though he did claim that he was swearing an 'oath of allegiance to all Americans' and he reminded them that whatever their skin colour they all bled the same red blood. For some reason that felt more sinister than was probably intended.

As he reached the end of what was effectively a rehashed campaign speech, rain began to fall. Hillary Clinton could be seen through a transparent umbrella, stony-faced. At once, the spin began from the podium. 'In the Bible, rain is a sign of God's blessing,' Franklin Graham, the preacher, said. Plenty of others were wondering if now was the time to buy shares in arks.

27 JANUARY
AT 137 WORDS, THE LONG GOODBYE IS TOO SHORT FOR SOME

The bill laid before Parliament yesterday that will enable Britain to begin two years of well-I-ought-to-be-off-ing and attempting to find its coat is a mere 137 words long. Half the length of the Gettysburg Address and twice the Lord's Prayer. You don't need many words to achieve big things.

Strip away all the padding about 'the Queen's most Excellent Majesty' and the 'Lords Spiritual and Temporal' and it comes down to twenty-three words that matter, which will be allocated five days of debate in the Commons before it is sent to the afore-mentioned LS&T. For many MPs, that is nowhere near enough.

Angela Eagle said she was astonished at how little time was being given to it. 'It's a two-clause bill,' David Lidington, Leader of the Commons, explained. Chuka Umunna (Lab, Streatham) said voices like his were being 'muzzled'. Mr Lidington could only repeat that Parliament had already voted for Article 50 to be triggered by the end of March and that this bill was simply the means to do so.

Ben Bradshaw (Lab, Exeter) called it a 'contempt of Parliament', Chris Leslie said Parliament was being gagged. Mr Lidington replied that this was 'synthetic rage'. Mr Leslie said that Parliament spent forty-one days debating the Maastricht Treaty but that was a 260-page document, not two short paragraphs, much of it waffle.

It is not as if Brexit has been hiding shyly on the outskirts of the dance floor for the past six months, desperate for someone's invitation to have a twirl. Barely a week goes by without David Davis, Mr Brexit, being asked about it in the House.

It has taken its toll on his voice. Mr Davis sounded like he had developed an eighty-a-day habit when he took Brexit Questions in the morning. 'It's just wear and tear,' he told MPs. 'Not emotion.'

It would be understandable if he had shredded his larynx in frustration. On Tuesday he had doggedly defended the government's decision not to publish a White Paper on Brexit, despite personally thinking that there should be one. On Wednesday the Prime Minister announced a change of mind. 'It is nice to be able to agree with myself from six months ago,' Mr Davis wryly remarked.

Pushed yesterday by Sir Keir Starmer (Lab, Holborn and St Pancras), his shadow, to commit to briefing the Commons every two months on how the Brexit negotiations were going, Mr Davis looked like a convict who has been let off with community service.

'In the past five months I have done five statements, ten debates and appeared in front of a number of select committees,' he said. 'Two months is a rather unambitious aim.' Rest assured, there are many millions of words still to be spouted in Parliament on this subject.

28 JANUARY
RATTLE OF BONE CHINA PUTS MR TOAD ON BEST BEHAVIOUR

What had Theresa May done to him in the Oval Office? This was not the Mr Toad of legend. We expected bluster and bravado; the trademark trumpeting; 'Poop poop' and all that. Instead we saw an awkward, almost humble, Toad. A Toad on his very best behaviour. He was indeed an altered Toad.

'It is so great an honour,' Donald Trump said at the start of their press conference. 'The special relationship is one of the great forces in history. Great days lie ahead for our two countries.' And he looked as if he meant it.

Perhaps it was a mother thing. He seemed especially proud to boast that Mama Trump had been born in Scotland. 'Stornoway,' he added. 'Serious Scotland.' Mrs May had doubtless just been singing the praises of the Hebrides. The Scottish quaich, or drinking cup, that she had given as a gift was filled to the brim with nostalgia.

Or maybe it was the Queen that did it. The strongest item in the diplomatic arsenal is tea at the palace. Foreign leaders go gooey at the prospect of a slice of Battenberg. Mrs May has rattled the bone china earlier than expected in their relationship. A state visit will be held this year. Weaponise the Windsors! This is the time for Downton diplomacy.

Nostalgia can be deployed both ways, of course. Their first set piece for the cameras was in front of the bust of Winston Churchill, given to President Johnson in 1965 and now restored to the Oval Office after President Obama had, according to some excitable fellows, decided to insult Britain by moving it to a table outside his private office where he could see it every day. What a snub.

'This is the original, folks,' Mr Trump crowed. 'It's a great honour to have Winston Churchill back.' The President is known for his appreciation of a fine bust.

After their confab, they came out for the press conference. Mrs May praised her host on his 'stunning election victory' – the Toad's face puffed up with pride – and spoke about shared interests, especially in defence. 'Very nicely stated,' Mr Trump replied.

The American press didn't care much about the special relationship. Their two questions were on Russia and Mexico, not about Mr Trump's plans to import more Marmite.

Laura Kuenssberg avoided trade too. The BBC's political editor wasn't interested in their mutual cooing; she wanted to know where they had disagreed. 'And do you think the President listened?' she asked. Mr Trump coughed. 'We'll see what she says,' Kuenssberg told him.

And the BBC went on, listing Mr Trump's policy positions on torture, Russia, banning Muslims from coming to America and abortion. 'For many people in Britain those sound like alarming beliefs,' she said, bluntly but politely.

Mr Trump turned to his guest. 'This was your choice of question?' he said. 'There goes that relationship.' The audience laughed, a little edgily, assuming it was a joke but not totally sure. Mr Trump seemed happy to move on and Mrs May gave no indication that she had raised any of these distasteful subjects. That's diplomacy for you.

Then more cooing and we were done. One of Mr Trump's final acts was to express a common bond with the PM. 'I'm a people person,' he said. 'I think you are too, Theresa.' It seemed like the beginning of a beautiful friendship.

1 FEBRUARY
MEMORIES OF MOULES FRITES SPARK MELANCHOLY

Torn between principle and pragmatism, Sir Keir Starmer looked as if he was going to burst into tears as he announced

Labour's support for triggering Article 50. His heart said no, his head said go. 'This is a short and simple bill,' he said, 'but for the Labour Party this is a very difficult bill.'

Awkward laughter broke out opposite and Sir Keir paused, his eyes glistening. 'I ask that members be courteous as I try to set out our position in very difficult circumstances,' he said. It felt like a reluctant eulogy. He'd come neither to bury Brexit nor to praise it.

Labour loves the European Union, he said. The optimism, the collaboration, the junkets, the *moules frites*. They had campaigned 'passionately' to stay in, but it was not enough. 'We failed. We lost. But we are democrats.' And with two thirds of Labour MPs in seats that voted to leave, the path ahead was clear.

He proceeded awkwardly, stumbling, distracted by every attempted intervention. Was this really a Queen's Counsel? He resembled a child walking into the sea for his first swim, terrified of getting out of his depth, halting at every wave that wetted his shorts.

David Davis, in his opening remarks for the government, had said that the bill presented a simple question: 'Do we trust the people or not?' To Ken Clarke the answer was equally simple: of course we bloody don't. Unlike Sir Keir, the former Chancellor of the Exchequer was happy to tell democracy to go soak its head. 'No sensible country has referendums,' he said. He had not wanted an EU referendum so he had no problem with ignoring it. As he fairly pointed out, his Eurosceptic friends on the Tory benches would not have meekly accepted a result that went the other way.

He spoke for seventeen minutes without notes about how his party had shifted position, not him, and on how the Brexiteers had followed a rabbit down a hole into a trading wonderland. 'No doubt somewhere a hatter is holding a tea party,' he said. It seemed like a valedictory and its conclusion was greeted with applause from the Labour rebels. Sir Keir just looked even sadder.

9 FEBRUARY
LETTUCE CRISIS BAD NEWS FOR GARDINER

Salad days in the House of Lords as peers discussed the lettuce crisis. Salad is a subject that has much in common with the Brexit debate: namely, are you leaf or romaine? Delightfully, the government minister who had been sent to answer questions on it was called Lord Gardiner of Kimble.

'There are news reports of empty shelves in supermarkets,' said Baroness Jones of Whitchurch, a Labour peer. 'The crisis is expected to last until the spring.' This was too much for Lord Tebbit. 'To describe a shortage of lettuces in the supermarket as a crisis', the old polecat snarled, 'shows a lack of understanding of the meaning of the words.'

The debate was scheduled to last only seven minutes – not much of an allotment for the Gardiner to work with – but he was eager to quash talk of mayhem in the salad aisle. 'The only shortage will be of iceberg lettuce,' Lord Gardiner said. 'There is a wonderful variety called cos, which is even better.' He knew this because he had performed a cos-benefit analysis.

10 FEBRUARY
MPS ENJOY A SING-SONG, IF NOT FROM THE SAME HYMN SHEET

Britain may be marching out of the European Union, twenty five years to the week after the signing of the Maastricht Treaty, but the band of the Brussels fusiliers will not go away without a tune. Beethoven is not ready to roll over quite yet.

As MPs voted on the third reading of the Brexit Bill on Wednesday night, members of the SNP began to whistle, hum and then sing the 'Ode to Joy' before they were told to shush by the Deputy Speaker. Yesterday, Paul Flynn gave his own interpretation of Ludwig van.

His fist pounding out a rhythm, though the words were declaimed rather than sung, the Labour MP for Newport West delivered the first few lines of the choral movement of Beethoven's Ninth, making a small mark in Commons history. It's the first time that *Götterfunken* and *feuertrunken* have appeared in Hansard.

Mr Flynn then skipped ahead to the end of the first verse: '*Alle Menschen werden Brüder* – all men will be brothers.' It is, he said, the 'essence of the European ideal'.

He was heard in respectful, if slightly amused, silence. It was his 82nd birthday – 'the midpoint of his parliamentary career', said the Speaker – and if you can't go in for some götterfunkery on such an occasion, when can you? It was a pity, though, that Mr Flynn and the SNP's 'Ode to Joy' recital was not met with a defiant volley of English music from the Brexiteers, like the duel between the French singing '*La Marseillaise*' and the Germans belting out '*Die Wacht am Rhein*' in *Casablanca*. We could have had Peter Bone and John Redwood (Con, Wokingham) tum-te-tumming the theme from *The Archers*, perhaps, or a bit of Elgar from Sir Gerald Howarth, who is always keen to give us his pomp and circumstance.

David Lidington, Leader of the Commons, said it was right for a Welshman to highlight the importance of peace through singing. He then reminded members that the parliamentary choir can be found stretching their vocal cords in the Westminster crypt every Monday evening. It is the one place where you will find the brexiteering Bernard Jenkin singing from the same hymn sheet as the SNP's Eilidh Whiteford (Banff and Buchan).

The Commons was in a musical mood. The second question of the day was about brass bands. Matt Hancock (Con, West Suffolk), the culture minister, parped away about Arts Council funding and tax relief for trombones. He normally likes to blow his own trumpet, but Mr Hancock told MPs that the highest he had risen in the brass band world as a lad was second cornet. 'I want to bang the drum for brass bands,' he added. How multi-talented he is.

The only MP who wasn't allowed to show off her musical talents was Labour's Lyn Brown, who yodelled away like one of the less reticent Valkyries at Amber Rudd as the Home Secretary spoke about refugees. Mr Speaker told her to pipe down, suggesting that as MP for West Ham she might find it more therapeutic to blow bubbles instead.

22 FEBRUARY
MACRON EST MAGNIFIQUE, MAIS IL N'EST PAS LE BLAIR

Westminster had a touch of Gallic Blair about it last night as Emmanuel Macron, the young French centrist, addressed a rally of 3,500 adoring fans. With the National Front on the rise in his country and the conservative François Fillon's presidential campaign in trouble over his financial dealings, Macron wants to offer a third way to those who fear that Le Pen is mightier than la fraude.

Here in France's sixth biggest city – more than 200,000 French people live in London – a young and noisy crowd, all waving their tricolours and EU stars, gave Mr Macron the rock-star treatment. 'It's wonderful to be here,' he said at the beginning. 'Here, in a city that is home to so many great authors. Such as Boris Johnson!' A joke? Or perhaps *grand auteur* has a ruder second meaning that I never learnt at school.

The mention of our Foreign Secretary so early in the piece drew jeers and the odd hiss, not all of it from Nick Clegg who was sitting in the front row. Mr Macron called on them to shush, though. 'Don't boo or hiss at my rallies,' he said. 'That is for people without hope.'

THE WEAK ARE A LONG TIME IN POLITICS

Yes, he also sees himself as the Amiens Obama. This was a trademark hopey-changey speech from a fresh-faced candidate. Lots of sunlit uplands here and brighter tomorrows there. Or that was what I could make out from the beams on the faces of his young fans. They had that glow you often see in the presence of a new political messiah.

My masters at school, I will be honest, had not properly prepared me for the task of following an hour-long speech in rapid French. Mr Macron did not ask for directions to *la gare* once, for example.

Nor did he invite anyone in the audience to come to *une boum chez lui ce week-end*. He didn't even say '*zut*' or '*bof*'. One wondered if he was French at all.

Ten years ago he married his French teacher, who is twenty-four years his senior, which may explain some of these rudimentary gaps in his knowledge. Too much sitting at the back of class sighing at madame and writing poetry rather than learning such essentials as '*le oiseau est dans l'arbre*'. Still, he struggled by and with the help of a friendly interpreter so did I.

'My project is anti-establishment,' Mr Macron said. 'I will help the middle and lower classes to reach as high as possible.' Opportunity was a word that came up a lot. For his struggling countrymen and, of course, for himself. At thirty-nine, though, and with only two years of frontline political experience, is Mr Macron too callow for the top job? 'I reject accusations of political immaturity or inexperience,' he said. 'Their experiences in politics are also their failures.' It was bold and ballsy and the audience loved it.

Boys who went further with their French at school than I did had one sentence drilled into them for exams. '*On ne peut pas nier que, sur le plan economique, la politique de l'autruche est vouée à l'échec*,' they were taught. 'One cannot deny that, on an economic level, the policy of an ostrich is doomed to failure.'

Useful, you'll agree. 'Say that in your oral and they'll be dead impressed with you,' Mr Jenkinson would tell his A-level class.

I didn't catch whether Mr Macron also deployed this phrase, since he spoke too quickly for my pen (the one belonging to my aunt) but the essence was there. He will not stick his head in the sand at this time of crisis. 'We must build a new France or submit to our fate,' he said in a stirring conclusion. But what were his actual policies? The manifesto, he said, is coming soon. *C'est magnifique, mais ce n'est pas le Blair.*

25 FEBRUARY
MARSHAL CORBYN FIGHTS ON AFTER TWO SETBACKS

In the cold light of the morning after two difficult by-elections, Jeremy Corbyn could have thrown in the towel. Instead, he was filled with the spirit of Marshal Foch, the French general, who sent back a message to HQ during the Battle of the Marne in 1914: 'My centre is giving way, my right is retreating, situation excellent. I am attacking.'

Mr Corbyn is not known as a military historian, but the French commander seems to be his role model. Indeed, those passing by the committee room where the parliamentary Labour Party has its Monday meetings often hear a cry from within of 'For Foch's sake, Jeremy, do something'.

The loss of one small seat in Cumbria that had been held by the Tories as recently as 1935 could be brushed away as a mere communications issue. Mr Corbyn told a gathering in London that 'our message was not enough' in Copeland. They had delivered leaflets saying that babies would die or be born with brain damage if the Conservatives won the by-election and had paid for a front-page advert in the local paper that declared the poll as 'a matter of life and death'. The swing to the

Tories was almost 7 per cent. That will teach Labour for being too timid.

Stoke-on-Trent, though, why that was a famous victory. 'Many were predicting that we couldn't hold Stoke,' Mr Corbyn said. 'We did.' It is always hard for opposition parties to win a by-election in a seat that they have held for only eighty-two years, barely long enough to form a ground operation, when the government has been in power for seven years, the economy is creaking, the NHS is in crisis and the other main challenger has been exposed as a fantasist.

Against such odds few in the media had expected Labour even to be on the first page of the results list, or so Mr Corbyn suggested, but there it was, triumphantly at the top, within 30 per cent of the share of the vote that it had got during those dark days of 1997. A magnificent win.

Yet curiously the 'corporate-controlled media', as Mr Corbyn affectionately puts it, did not agree that this had been a success. They thought it was rather disappointing. 'Do you ever look in the mirror and think, "Could the problem be me?"' one television reporter asked. 'No,' Mr Corbyn replied. 'Why not?' There came no reply, save, 'Thanks for your question.'

This skirmish out of the way, Marshal Corbyn gathered his troops and headed for Stoke to inspect the scene of his triumph. Naturally, his intended train was cancelled. When he finally arrived, he came under immediate shelling from Michael Crick of *Channel 4 News*, who asked him fourteen times if he would stand down.

Yet still Mr Corbyn pressed on. 'I was elected to lead this party,' he said. 'I am proud to lead this party. We will continue our campaigning work … and we will win.' You almost had to admire his defiance. After all, this approach worked for Foch in the end, although it took an awful lot of bloody, muddy trench warfare before he got there.

3 MARCH
MINISTER PUTS GLOSS ON PALACE PAINT JOB

There was rejoicing in Buckingham Palace. The Queen can do up her bathroom at last. 'Get on the blower to Farrow & Ball, Philee,' she trilled. 'See if they've got any tins of Distempered Corgi left – and some Equerry's Breath for the writing room, I think. Parliament's come good with the readies.'

If only all pensioners in need of a maintenance grant for their council house could get the nod so quickly. The seventh delegated legislation committee met in room nine of the Palace of Westminster at 11.30 a.m. to discuss whether to give the Queen an extra £370 million for the restoration of her London residence. By 11.43 the cheque was in the post.

It took longer for the king in the A. A. Milne poem to get some butter for the royal slice of bread than it did for Parliament to nod through a 66 per cent rise in the sovereign grant over the next decade. The decorators will move in after Easter and the faint whiff of turpentine will soon hang over the Serpentine.

The deal had already been done, of course. The royal trustees, who include the Prime Minister and the Chancellor, had worked out what is needed to stop the Queen's London residence from falling down last year. Parliament just had to give the cheque a rubber stamp. Sixteen MPs were sent along by the whips to wield it; only five of them even bothered to speak.

Simon Kirby (Con, Brighton Kemptown), a Treasury minister, opened the debate. A dapper but whimsical fellow, who speaks a bit like Peter Cook's philosopher E. L. Wisty, Mr Kirby was not having the best of mornings. It emerged before play began that his experience of running Juice FM and a couple of nightclubs in Brighton had proved less useful than the Prime Minister had expected when it comes to dealing with the City of London's fears about Brexit. His responsibility for financial services had been gently removed from his in-tray. The royal refurb was more on his level.

'It's an important historic property,' he said. 'One of London's top tourist attractions, but it requires urgent attention, otherwise it faces severe risk of fire, flood or safety incidents.' He reassured MPs that guards would still be changed and colours would still be trooped during the restoration and that when it is all done the place will be able to host an extra 110 events a year. MPs, mindful of their invitations to garden parties, could hardly refuse.

However, Peter Dowd (Lab, Bootle), the new shadow Chief Secretary to the Treasury, made a token grumble. 'We are in an age of austerity,' he protested. 'I'm not over the moon about this but we will not be making any objection.' He can start getting measured for his morning suit.

Tommy Sheppard (SNP, Edinburgh East) was the sole voice of protest. He wanted the whole House of Commons to debate the issue. 'Yeah, yeah, whatever,' muttered the Tories opposite who had been chatting between themselves. After a debate lasting eleven minutes, it was put to a vote and passed easily, with only Mr Sheppard and George Kerevan (SNP, East Lothian) choosing to withhold the grant.

'No garden party invites for you,' mocked Michael Fabricant as he left. When it comes to finding money for the royals, there will always be more support for a canapé than a 'cannae pay'.

8 MARCH
OH! OH! LORDS HAVE A PLEASURABLE TIME

One of the oddities in the House of Lords, even more curious than the phrase 'adjournment during pleasure' (which is essentially a lunch break but sounds like a scene from *Caligula*),

is how Hansard records consternation: 'Noble Lords: Oh!'
It conveys everything from raised voices and red faces to the
smelling salts being passed along the bishops' bench.

There were quite a few 'Oh!'s yesterday as the Lords' turn
with the Brexit Bill came to an end, three during Lord Forsyth
of Drumlean's turn alone. The former Scottish Secretary must
have had a stiffener during his pleasure time, for he came out
swinging after lunch.

He was in no mood to play nicely with the Europhiles. An
attempted intervention by Viscount Hailsham was given an
elbow to the groin – 'Oh!' said the Noble Lords – while a legal
point by Lord Pannick was met with a growl of 'we know what
he is up to' – 'Oh!' – and a grumble about 'clever lawyers'.

The biggest 'Oh!' came when Lord Heseltine, on a rare visit,
had a pop. 'I have the utmost respect for my noble friend,'
Lord Forsyth said (always a sign of impending insult), 'but this
is not the moment to grab the mace and challenge the authority of the Commons.'

'Oh!' they gasped, getting the reference to Hezza's moment
of infamy back in 1976. Lord Heseltine sat there growling, his
arms folded, his face like thunder. I would not have fancied
the chances of any passing Alsatian, Hezza's squeezable stress
toy of choice.

We had a couple of 'Oh!'s in the morning, too, notably when
Lord Newby, Leader of the Lib Dems, suggested that our European 'friends and neighbours' would negotiate with Britain 'in
good faith'. This 'Oh!' was more an 'Oh!' of hilarity than anger.
Lord Howard of Lympne, the former Tory leader, gave a loud
chuckle that said, 'Have you ever met a Frenchman?'

Lord Newby, who despite his name has been a member of
the House for twenty years, had tabled an amendment wanting
a fresh referendum at the end of the negotiations. Lord Roba-
than wondered what would happen if the second referendum
backed Remain. 'Best of three?' he offered.

Lord Newby gave a weary look. Obviously there would not be a third referendum, it seemed to say, since the people would get it right next time. Lord Cormack made a fair point in reply: what makes you think that after two years of rancorous negotiation our European friends would want us back?

9 MARCH
CHANCELLOR'S COMEDY ROUTINE HAS A WEALTH OF MATERIAL

It was cabaret hour in Westminster and a former DJ from Brentwood was making his debut in stand-up comedy. 'Ladies and gentlemen,' rolled Lindsay Hoyle, the Deputy Speaker, in his rich Bolton working men's club voice, 'our next act has gone down a storm on the Runnymede Rotary circuit but today is his first Budget speech. Please give applause and a wave of the order paper for Philip "Chuckles" Hammond.'

His fans clapped and cheered. Chuckles took a sip of water. His eyes passed over the joke at the top of the first sheet – 'Hear about the constipated Chancellor? He couldn't budget!' – which he had crossed out as being too crude for a lunchtime crowd, and he hit them with some self-deprecation.

'This is the last spring Budget,' he said. 'Twenty-four years ago Norman Lamont also presented what was billed as "the last spring Budget". He reported on an economy that was growing faster than any in the G7.' A pause. 'And ten weeks later he was sacked! Wish me luck.'

That was quickly followed by more self-mockery, tackling his renown for being dry. 'I turn now to OBR forecasts,' Chuckles said. 'This is the spreadsheet bit, but bear with me because I have a reputation to defend.' And I swear he gave a wink.

Even the awkward customers opposite liked that. Two rows behind him, George Osborne, a previous darling of the Budget spotlight, beamed in benediction. His own style of humour was more cruel, but times had moved on. Mr Hammond began to expand his repertoire: a joke about Ed Balls here, a dig at Jean-Claude Juncker there.

Then a sequence aimed at his critics. 'Under the last Labour government, corporation tax was 28 per cent,' he said. 'By the way, they don't call it the "last" Labour government for nothing!' Those opposite looked glum as more jokes about Jeremy Corbyn followed. 'Driverless cars, eh? That's a technology the Labour Party knows about. I tell you: Mr Corbyn is so far down a black hole that even Stephen Hawking has disowned him.'

Mr Corbyn looked cross. He had not realised this was a comedy club. The routine he planned to perform next was a lecture on the evils of capitalism. It was light on jokes.

By now, a confident Mr Hammond had roped in his boss. 'I've got three ones here about women,' he said, 'but the PM has already told you two of them.' He gave her a kick. 'Well, it is International Women's Day!' said Mrs May. Ho ho.

There was even a pantomime routine. Hammond: 'We're going to invest in schools.' Labour MPs: 'Oh no, you won't!' Hammond: 'Oh yes, we will!' But the joke they were all discussing later was the one about self-employed workers and national insurance contributions.

'NIC NIC!' he shouted. 'Who's there?' came the reply. 'Philip.' 'Philip who?' 'Philip the coffers, we're running a bit low!' There was laughter on his side but a lot of confused Labour faces opposite. They didn't find it funny. 'No, seriously, folks,' he added. 'Hand over your money.'

The critics suggested this went too far – his agents had promised he wouldn't do a NIC, NIC joke – but Mr Osborne loved it. As he left, he gave a thumbs-up. Always leave them wanting more, the former Chancellor would have told him. But not as much as you want from them.

10 MARCH
THE SIGHS HAVE IT IN EMPTY HOUSE

Productivity was low, interest rates were falling and unemployment was nearing dangerous levels. It is fair to say that day two of the Budget debate had not excited the Commons. While Philip Hammond was touring the studios explaining why manifesto pledges now have the lifespan of a hamster, MPs were debating the detail of his statement. Well, a handful of them were.

Yards of unoccupied green leather stretched in every direction. Only six Tory backbenchers showed up, plus a Lib Dem, a couple of Scots and a dozen from Labour. Few wanted to defend the Budget; not many could be bothered to attack it.

At least they were paying vague attention as John McDonnell began to slice it apart. The shadow Chancellor had complained in the morning about Labour MPs being discourteous and looking at their phones while Jeremy Corbyn was replying to the Budget, but Mr McDonnell is quietly effective. While his leader is all sound and fury, like a bullied supply teacher trying and failing to make himself heard, the shadow Chancellor deals more in sadness than anger. A sigh is often more audible than a shriek. He sounded almost disappointed that the Budget was unravelling.

There is often a touch of the 1960s East End gangland associate about Mr McDonnell. Someone who may not have run with the Krays but who perhaps assisted with their bookkeeping. 'Nice little economy you've got here, guv. It would be a pity if it accidentally fell over the edge of a cliff.'

Yesterday, he was more like a disapproving bank manager. 'I really expected you to look after your money better than this.'

It was only halfway through his speech that I saw Mr Corbyn sitting beside him. The leader had shimmered in unnoticed. Or had he been there all along? He puts the shadow into shadow Cabinet. It reminded me of the Hughes Mearns poem: 'Yesterday, upon the stair | I met a man who wasn't there! | He wasn't there again today | I wish, I wish he'd go away.'

16 MARCH
CORBYN HITS ALL THE WRONG NOTES

It was a bad day for the government, the sort of day that normally ends with the Prime Minister being given the epithet 'embattled', the Chancellor becoming 'beleaguered' and 'friends of' an ambitious minister giving helpful briefings to the press in which they say 'of course we have full confidence in Theresa but…'

Politics stopped working normally a while ago. The Tories will probably be twenty-three points ahead in the next poll. This is what happens when the Leader of the Opposition has the charisma of Albert Steptoe and the intellectual dexterity of a cinnamon whirl.

A Prime Minister's Questions in which the PM admits to a U-turn on a key policy (the reform of national insurance contributions) should not end with her own side smiling and laughing. On the Ides of March, with Julius Theresa wearing a target upon her back, the Islington Brutus plunged a dagger into his own left testicle.

To be fair to Jeremy Corbyn, he was given only twenty-three minutes' notice of the U-turn. He was probably signing a few apples at the time or arranging a rally in aid of Peruvian basketweavers. Not much time to think up any questions on the government's embarrassment, let alone the full six.

Mr Corbyn used 641 words in his half-dozen turns yesterday but asked only four questions, two weak ones in the same outing and one in a request to wish the world a happy St Patrick's Day on Friday. A contentious topic, of course. Mrs May was perplexed. She had entered the chamber prepared for a roasting and instead got a Guinness advert.

After a second question-free stint from Mr Corbyn she witheringly told him, 'I don't think the honourable gentleman has got the hang of this. He is supposed to ask me a question.'

Labour MPs looked forlorn. Tom Blenkinsop (Lab, Middlesbrough South and East Cleveland) tweeted a video of Ronny Rosenthal missing an open goal for Liverpool in 1992. It was worse than that. Mr Corbyn's clunking display was like a concert pianist sitting down to play Rachmaninov's Second in the Albert Hall and finding that he has an oven glove taped to each hand.

A first appearance now follows for Paul Nuttall, one of the many leaders of UKIP, who made claims on his CV that did not turn out to be entirely accurate.

28 MARCH
UKIP REFUSE TO ENGAGE WITH BREXIT

Professor Sir Paul Nuttall VC gave a lecture on Brexit yesterday at County Hall, so of course I trotted along. It's not every day that you get to hear a Nobel laureate speak, especially the morning after he scored the winning goal at Wembley.

Some people unfairly tease the UKIP leader – or His Grace as he likes to be called – for the embellishments on his CV that have come to light. Slapdash assistants are to blame, not Wing Commander Nuttall. His PhD is still on ice, he admits, and he never played professional football. His entry for Eurovision came bottom but one, not dead last.

None of those claims, however, are half as incredible as the one that UKIP launched yesterday. 'We don't want Article 50 to be triggered,' said Gerard Batten, their Brexit spokesman, sending two dozen jaws crashing to the floor.

What? Had things gone completely *Through the Looking Glass*? Are UKIP now the Lib Dems? Was the referendum all just one big joke? Not quite. It turned out that Mr Batten (as in 'down the hatches'?) is opposed to Article 50 because it involves negotiating with the enemy.

'It's a trap,' he said. Two years of jaw-jaw will just allow the EU to work out how to do us over. 'It will be out of the dark forest of the EU and into the quicksand.' Britain should leave right now.

Mr Nuttall then stepped forward to explain, generously, that UKIP will give Theresa May the benefit of the doubt over this Article 50 nonsense for now. 'We will be the guard dogs of Brexit,' he said. Grrrr.

He added that UKIP will use six tests to decide how Brexit is going. I assumed these would be Trent Bridge, Lord's, Edgbaston, Old Trafford, Headingley and the Oval, all cricket grounds where Mr Nuttall has scored a century – but he meant real empirical tests with numbers and everything. Tests on laws, trade, migration, money and timetabling, and 'the maritime test', which sounded like Trafalgar 2.0.

'We will keep breathing down the Prime Minister's neck,' Mr Nuttall added. I just hope that they stock up on extra-strong mints.

At the end, however, the cameras were all pointing in the opposite direction, at the batrachoidal figure over my shoulder. 'Give us one of your smiley faces,' the paparazzi shouted at Nigel Farage, which was like asking George Osborne to try looking smug.

For once, Mr Farage was not for gurning. 'I don't pull those faces so much now that I've stopped drinking,' the former UKIP leader said. What? Nige off the booze? It would be like the Pope becoming a Buddhist or Jeremy Clarkson a vegan.

'No, no, I'm not teetotal,' he protested, aware of what this could do to his image. He's just had a spell of relative restraint – one man's cutting down is another man's binge – and is looking very healthy for it. Glowing skin, bright eyes and trim round the tummy.

'That's more due to me not having to be in meetings all the time than giving up alcohol,' he insisted. Nonetheless, I expect the Marquis of Granby to issue a profits warning if this continues.

Under Article 50 of the Lisbon Treaty, a country that wishes to leave the EU will have a two-year period for negotiating the terms of its withdrawal. Theresa May chose to trigger this countdown on 29 March 2017.

30 MARCH
AT LAST, THE END OF THE BEGINNING

It was, as Nigel Evans (Con, Ribble Valley) noted, 'a red, white and blue letter day'. Many of his Conservative colleagues had dressed for the occasion. Sir Gerald Howarth wore a tie bearing a portrait of Elgar; Victoria Borwick (Con, Kensington) had an Alice band, with bow, in the colours of the Union Jack; while Andrea Leadsom came as the flag itself: blue suit, red top and two stripes of gleaming white teeth when she smiled, which was often.

If you were a Remainer, this must have felt like the Last Night of the Voms. Theresa May's statement presented a land of hope and Tories. Owen Paterson (Con, North Shropshire) performed a fantasia on old sea shanties, while Jacob Rees-Mogg gave a solo from *Merrie England*, saying that Mrs May would be a new Gloriana if she could defeat the European armada. *Gaudeamus!*

There was an awful lot of bobbing up and down, too, as for almost three hours 113 backbench MPs asked different questions of the Prime Minister. Or, in the case of the Scottish National-ists, the same question twenty-nine times. 'I know,' Mrs May said, 'that this is a day of celebration for some and disappoint-ment for others.' A clarion Scottish voice replied, 'And anger for us.' Angus Robertson (SNP, Moray), their leader, was shaking his head so hard that one feared that it would fly off.

Scotland, they kept pointing out, had voted to remain in the EU. 'So did my constituency,' Mrs May retorted, which really upset them. 'Scotland is a country, not a constituency of England,' Alex Salmond roared. 'It is a constituent... nation,' Mrs May replied, mischievously.

At least some Remainers were jolly. 'Now, more than ever, the world needs the liberal, democratic values of Europe,' Mrs May said. The comma and lower-casing did not translate. Tim Farron, the Lib Dem leader, nodded and winked, while Tom Brake pumped his fist.

'This day, of all days,' Mr Farron said later, 'the Liberal Dem-ocrats will not roll over, as the official opposition have done.' It was just a pity that only three of his party's nine MPs had joined him in the chamber. What to say about Labour? That's probably enough.

The triggering of Article 50 is not, of course, the end, but it is, perhaps, the end of the beginning. Or, as Henry Kelly used to say halfway through each episode of *Going for Gold*, the 1980s quiz that did more for European unity than Junck-er, Delors and all the Kinnocks, 'It's time for the first round proper.' Hands on the plunger, David Davis, the category is agriculture: play or pass?

A few minutes away, Nigel Farage was holding court outside a pub, a pint of beer in one paw and a copy of the Article 50 letter in the other. The former UKIP leader looked very happy. One passer-by threw a pain au chocolat at him. An especially apt protest. Rich, flaky and lacking in substance, Mr Farage avoided the pastry and carried on crowing.

19 APRIL
SNAP! MAY PLAYS HER JOKER

Theresa May is not one of life's snappers, apart from when a lackey irritates her. She certainly has no snap to her actions. The Prime Minister is the sort of woman who, when playing cards with a child, will turn over the six of diamonds beside the six of clubs and then consider for a while the chance that one of them might be a nine before eventually stretching out a hand and saying 'pair'. She no more snaps than she crackles or pops.

Yet out she came to the lectern yesterday almost ten minutes ahead of schedule – a snap statement on a snap election – and announced that Britain is off to the polls again. She may have used the word 'reluctant' twice but there was steel in her voice and ice in her eyes.

It was, as everything is these days, about Brexit. 'There should be unity in Westminster but instead there is division,' Mrs May said. Labour, Lib Dems, the SNP, the 'unelected Lords' have been getting in her way. How dare opposition parties oppose? Why can't we have a system like that nice Mr Erdoğan is after in Turkey?

The news must have surprised the Cabinet. 'Pleasant Easter, Theresa?' someone will have asked as they gathered at 9.30 a.m. 'Oh, you know,' the PM replied. 'Went walking with Philip in Snowdonia, church on Sunday, did a few bits and bobs in the constituency and – oh yes, nearly forgot – I decided that we ought to have an election.'

It was presented later as a communal decision. 'I have just chaired a meeting of the Cabinet where we agreed that the government should call a general election,' Mrs May said, as if the subject had come up under AOB and she had gone with the mood of the room, but this 'we' was of the royal variety. It was the most first-person singular 'we' heard in Downing Street since Margaret Thatcher became a grandmother.

So this is what a brisk hike in the foothills of Cadair Idris does to you. Clears the head, focuses the mind. Makes you forget all those times you said 'no way, uh-uh, not gonna happen' when people said that an early election made sense.

None of us in the press pack had any inkling. At 9.12 a.m. there was an email from the press office saying daily briefings were returning to normal and then half an hour later a PS: Mrs May to make a statement outside No. 10 at 11.15 a.m.

What could it be? Were we about to go to war? Had Boris pressed that big red button that says, 'Do not push'? Was it Northern Ireland? Or Scotland? Was Larry the Cat unwell? Perhaps Larry wanted to become a dog. All seemed unlikely but no more so than a snap election. Mrs May does not snap.

26 APRIL
MP MAKES HER MAIDEN SPEECH A SWANSONG

Parliament is full of strange birds: common loons, thieving magpies, a multitude of tits. Gannets, boobies, bustards and lots of spotted shags. The air on the backbenches is filled at question time with grouse and quail. There is even the odd wise owl. But yesterday, for the first and perhaps the last time, the Commons heard the song of the Copeland swan.

Trudy Harrison won her seat at a by-election in February, the first Tory to represent that part of Cumbria since 1935, but she had played an ostrich role for two months. Keep your head down, learn the ropes, there's plenty of time to make a mark.

And then Theresa May called a snap election and suddenly there was a risk of Ms Harrison's entire Commons career being a non-speaking role. When the Prime Minister decided to go to the country last week, Ms Harrison's maiden speech was still in her drafts folder and the tally of questions against her name was as round as a duck's egg.

There was a chance that she could end up being less of a parliamentary force than Sir Isaac Newton, whose only contribution to a Commons debate was to complain about a draught and ask if someone could shut the window.

Who wants to play the third spear-bearer? Ms Harrison had nothing to show for her time in the House. But yesterday she delivered. After two months of ducking, she turned out to be a swan. And if this was her first and final performance, as swan-songs traditionally are, it was a fine way to go.

Most days I mock politicians. Most days they deserve it. Many of them are vain, pompous, verbose and tribal or, worse, bland and sycophantic. Or are those just the ones who catch our eye? There are lots of noble public servants – in all parties – who work hard, not seeking the limelight. Many good MPs, a lot of them Labour, will not return after next week through no fault of their own. They deserve thanks; they will get raspberries.

Ms Harrison seems to realise the fleeting nature of her trade. She devoted the first 400 words of her speech to her predecessor, Labour's Jamie Reed. He had served Copeland, she said, 'with great talent and dedication, a proud supporter of our local industry'. She even gave him the credit for her taking an interest in politics. Some years ago she had attended a Westminster debate that he had called about her local struggling school. 'I saw the positive impact that MPs could have and the powerful influence of their support, even in remote areas which I had previously felt would never be anyone's political priority.'

She did not need to praise a politician from a rival party,

but she was right to. And on she went: talking, as MPs often do in their maiden speech, about the delights of her constituency with charm and eloquence. She spoke of her three most famous constituents – Peter Rabbit, Squirrel Nutkin and Mrs Tiggy-Winkle – and the views of Scafell that she had from her childhood bedroom window.

She also said how much it meant to her four teenage daughters that she was the woman who tipped the balance between the number of women MPs there has ever been – 456 – and the number of men there are now in the Commons.

Most importantly, though, she did not use her speech as a party political broadcast. Aside from one 'Northern Powerhouse' there were no clichés. No 'a country that works for everyone', nor a peep of Mrs May's new buzzword, 'stable', which makes me think of something you shut after the horse has bolted. It was sincere, passionate and personal. And if it included a groaner of a pun – 'land of Copeland glory' – she at least had the awareness to grimace.

If this proves to have been her only song in the Commons, it just showed up how many MPs waste their more frequently exercised voices. As Coleridge wrote, 'Swans sing before they die – 'twere no bad thing | Should certain persons die before they sing.'

1 MAY

STRONG AND STABLE, MAY PLAYS A STRAIGHT BAT

It says something for the banal, risk-averse election campaign Downing Street is anxious to run that the most interesting news from the Conservatives was that David Cameron has a new shed. Or a stable, as Sir Lynton Crosby would prefer us to describe it. A strong stable that works for everyone, especially former Prime Ministers with £25,000 to spend on a hut painted in Farrow & Ball's finest.

While Mr Cameron's most difficult decision yesterday was which artisan cheese to eat while pretending to work on his memoirs in the shed, his successor was trying to explain why people should vote for the Conservatives in what she called 'the most important election the country's faced in my lifetime' while avoiding anything that hinted at a concrete reason for doing so.

'No slogans,' Andrew Marr instructed Theresa May at the start of their interview on BBC One. 'Stronganstableleadership,' she replied, straight away. Then, in case we had missed it, she added, 'Stronganstablegovernment.' Marr looked at her. 'Right,' he sighed. It was a word that he would repeat often, almost as often as Mrs May said 'stronganstable', to convey the weary recognition that he wasn't getting an answer to this question either.

It is, of course, a valid strategy and one that will probably work. Geoffrey Boycott, the Prime Minister's childhood hero, had the reasonable view that you can't be caught out if you don't hit the ball in the air. Mrs May bats in the same way. Nothing flash, nothing risky. A nudge here, a nurdle there and thirty-seven not out by stumps. So long as she faces only the gentle non-turning lobs of Jeremy Corbyn, she has little to fear.

'People might think that this is robotic,' Marr observed as the Prime Minister played out another run-free over. 'Ummm, whirrrr,' the Maybot said, searching her programmed vocabulary for something new. 'Take this country forwards. Deliver on Brexit. Best deal for Britain.'

'Right,' said Marr and he tried another tack. 'We have nurses going to food banks,' he said. 'That must be wrong.' Mrs May looked confused. 'There are many complex reasons why people go to food banks,' she said, sounding briefly like

Margaret Thatcher without the warmth. Mrs May offered a solution: 'We can only get better public sector pay with stronganstablegovernment.'

'Right,' Marr said again. He then tried her on education spending, followed by Brexit, which he called '*l'éléphant dans la chambre*' in case Emmanuel Macron was watching. 'Right, right,' he said a moment or two after starting down each of those tracks. At one point, Marr tried something existential. 'Do you ever pause and wonder if you've got it wrong?' he asked.

It got an icy glare. 'We need to get Brexit right,' she said, 'and so we need strongan...' Yes, yes, we get it.

The Prime Minister did give him two straight answers. 'I'm not in a different galaxy,' Mrs May said emphatically, when told that some in Brussels feel she doesn't live on Planet Earth. She should have continued by saying, with Margo Leadbetter indignation, 'I live in Sonning.'

She also answered a question about whether gay sex is a sin with an immediate and rather fierce 'no' that suggested that she had been practising. One imagined the rehearsal in the car on the way to the studio. 'Perhaps I could tell him that we want stronganstablesex?' she may have asked Sir Lynton. 'Steady on, Sheila,' he would have replied. 'It's breakfast telly. We need to turn their minds, not their stomachs.'

3 MAY
ABBOTT FOUND TO BE FUZZY ABOUT POLICE DETAILS

It was, to be fair to Diane Abbott, a stinker of a question. How could the shadow Home Secretary have anticipated, when she went on LBC to announce Labour's plans for more police officers, that Nick Ferrari would set such fiendish conundrums as 'how many' and 'how much will they cost'? Who did he think she was, Carol bloody Vorderman?

Ms Abbott clearly had a large pile of briefing notes on the desk in front of her, for you could hear frantic shuffling as she made a search for these opaque pieces of trivia, but the Labour research department must have armed her with information that they thought would be more useful when asked about the police. A potted history of the Orgreave and Hillsborough inquiries, perhaps, or what happened in the latest series of *Line of Duty*.

Ferrari, though, wanted to know how many extra police officers Labour planned to create. 'Ten thousand,' Ms Abbott told him. 'And how much would 10,000 police officers cost?' Ferrari replied. 'Well, er, um, we believe it will be about £300,000,' Ms Abbott said. She was out by a factor of 1,000, which was probably written in tiny italics above a chart, but for some reason an alarm bell did not ring in her head. Thousands, millions, it's all just zeros.

The broadcaster looked at the numbers he had just scribbled on his pad. '£300,000 for 10,000 police officers?' Ferrari asked. 'What are you paying them?' For a second, Ms Abbott may have wondered if he had assumed she meant £300,000 each. Then the penny dropped and she started to flick through her notes.

'They will cost,' she said. Flick, flick. 'They will … it will cost, erm.' Flick, flick. 'About £80 million.' Ah yes, that sounds more like a proper amount to spend. Or is it too much? 'That's recruiting 25,000 extra police officers a year,' she said, plucking a further 15,000 bobbies out of thin air. Then she added, 'At least.'

Ferrari was less terrified of numbers than the shadow Home Secretary. Ignoring this rapid inflation in the police force, he patiently explained that if you divide £80 million by 10,000 it comes out at £8,000 each. Never mind moving into the Home Office, Ms Abbott has a future in the human resources department of Sports Direct.

There was a baffled silence at Ms Abbott's end of the phone line, then more energetic flicking. It sounded as if she were removing her shoes and socks so that she could count on her toes as well as her fingers. I expected her suddenly to blurt out, 'Twelve trillion and five!' 'Has this been thought through?' Ferrari said, killing her with gentleness. 'Of course it has,' Ms Abbott said indignantly. 'Look, we anticipate recruiting 250,000 policemen...'

'Two hundred and fifty thousand policemen?' Ferrari asked, agog. 'And women,' Ms Abbott added quickly, not wanting him to make fun of her. Gender politics was not his concern. He wondered how she had gone from 10,000 police officers to 250,000. 'No, I mean 2,000,' she said. 'And perhaps 250. You said 250,000, not me.' Did she not realise this was being recorded?

6 MAY
JUNCKER SPEAKS WITH FORKED TONGUE

Jean-Claude Juncker strode up to the lectern, looked in bewilderment at the bottle of mineral water placed in front of him ('Who gave me this poison?') and fired a shell across the Channel at Theresa May.

'*Buongiorno, cari amici,*' the president of the European Commission began, for his address was being given at a conference in Florence. Then he slipped into English to explain how he would continue. 'Setting aside Luxembourgish, because only a few people are able to understand it,' he said, 'I am agitated between English and French but I have made my choice.'

'I will express myself in French because, slowly but surely, English is losing importance in Europe.'

Crikey! Or, as Mr Juncker would put it in an attempt to ingratiate himself with *les grenouilles, sacré bleu*! He is free to speak whatever language he wants, of course, but to express it in such a way was rather pointed, especially as English is spoken by twice as many EU citizens as French. I wonder how the Irish will have taken it?

So much for the recent warning by Donald Tusk, president of the European Council, that Brexit negotiations will be impossible if the participants are 'emotional', a state that Mr Juncker is often accused of being in (see also: 'tired').

The president went on to explain, in French, that this would be 'just a chat, not a real speech' (ignore that 'State of the Union' on the front of the lectern) and after a blether about how much he likes Florence – 'you get lots of sunshine here' – he reached his main theme, which was how magnificent the EU is.

'We never discuss the successes of the EU, only its short-comings,' he said. 'The further we travel from Europe the more enthusiasm we see for it.' Why, the tribes of the Amazon basin speak in awe of the principles of subsidiarity and the Clean Sky Joint Undertaking.

The euro, he went on, was up there with the printing press as one of the greatest European inventions. And if you think that financial union is great, he added, just you wait for the fun of ever closer military union.

Despite all this, he sighed, 'our British friends' want to leave. 'This is a tragedy.' Then he tried to be a diplomat. 'Of course we will negotiate with our British friends in full transparency,' he said, while standing in front of an advert for the conference sponsor, the *Frankfurter Allgemeine Zeitung*, the newspaper that recently printed a partisan leaked report on Mr Juncker's latest dinner in Downing Street. And they say that irony is an English weapon.

9 MAY

TORIES UNVEIL THEIR BEE-LIST CANDIDATES

The Conservatives are no longer a party. They have become a hive, a collective of drones all devoted to the dominant queen. Individual identity has been renounced, the old brand has been buried, all must bow down before the nourishing mother. They are not Conservatives, but Theresa May's Team.

'Looking forward to campaigning as Theresa May's local candidate,' one of them loyally tweeted after winning selection on Friday. Not as the Tory candidate or, God forbid, a sentient being in his own right, but as a servant of the queen bee. 'Zzzz-trong,' they buzz. 'And zzzztable.' Over and over.

Eighty of these drones gathered in Harrow to receive benediction from the queen. Eager first-timers and try-again bee-listers rubbed wings with senior Tory drones such as Michael Gove, David Lidington and Damian Green (Con, Ashford). No Boris Johnson, though, who represents the next-door constituency. The queen does not like competition.

They took their seats in front of seven giant banners that read 'Theresa May's Team'. If you looked very closely you could just make out the word 'Conservatives', almost hidden at the bottom. The Prime Minister's name clearly outstrips the party brand in focus groups.

Yesterday, the queen bee was anxious to exhort her drones not to be complacent. 'I need a strong team,' she told them. 'Leave no stone unturned. No street unwalked down. No door unknocked.'

Every vote for Mrs May will strengthen her position with Europe, she said. Emmanuel Macron had won a big victory in France. 'I need an equal mandate,' she said. 'A strong mandate to take a strong position.'

'Zzzztrong,' agreed the drones.

'And zzzztable.'

This felt like cult worship, or perhaps a Greek tragedy with the candidates forming a monotonous chorus around the leading lady. After the French staged a novel twist on *Oedipus Rex* – the politician who married his mother overcoming the one who killed her father – Mrs May has taken the star role in her own drama. A new take on a famous play by Euripides: *Medeoca*.

While Medeoca, the wronged and vengeful queen, spoke of needing to destroy her enemies at home and in Europe, the chorus found a new line, borrowed from another Greek playwright, and croaked over and over: 'Brexit effects, coact coact.' Such choreographed hubris seldom ends well, but unless Jeremy Corbyn can arrange a deus ex machina it looks like she will get away with it.

17 MAY
YES! YES! YES! CORBYN'S STIMULUS PACKAGE THRILLS FAITHFUL

Jeremy Corbyn walked out to huge applause in Bradford, gave a toothy grin, saluted Harold Wilson and then waved the Little Red Book with which he intends to take Britain back to the 1970s, an era that some of his comrades, such as the transport union chief in the front row with the shoulder-length peroxide hair of a prog rocker, never really left.

'For the many, not the few' may be an election catchphrase of Tony Blair but there was little of New Labour in the manifesto's 124 pages – and the audience loved it. When the BBC asked at the end if Mr Corbyn could clarify that he wants higher taxes, higher spending and more borrowing, a woman sitting behind me clapped and squealed, 'Yes! Yes, Yes, Yes!' Mr Corbyn had certainly tickled her erogenous zones with his £50 billion tax plan.

The Labour leader did not dispute the charge. He revelled in his mission to tax and renationalise. A former official of the National Union of Students punched the air when the leader announced £11 billion of tax rises to ensure free university education, while the biggest cheer came for his pledge to renationalise the railways. Mr Corbyn's call to 'take back control of our water' was, ironically, one of the few policies that hadn't leaked.

Mr Corbyn is enjoying this campaign. He was among fans, of course, and unreserved unquestioning adoration can lift the spirits, but he is winning the battle of ideas – in terms of quantity, at least – and he showed genuine pride each time he waggled his manifesto.

This is undoubtedly his baby, which will suit the less enthusiastic members of his team just fine. It will be his victory or his defeat, implausible though the second option seemed to his acolytes.

In the Q&A a man wearing a Lenin cap and a large walrus moustache asked, 'What can be done about this shockingly biased media?' He turned out to be on the editorial staff of the *Morning Star*, the one untainted paper. A few minutes later the man from the *Daily Mirror*, that defender of the establishment, suggested politely that the leader's polling was still on life support and got roundly booed. 'Told you so,' shouted the *Morning Star*. 'We love you, Jeremy,' a woman added.

Mr Corbyn insisted that this wasn't a cult but it gave him a chance to define what his premiership would mean. 'I see leadership as not being about dictating but about listening and understanding,' he said, 'and ensuring that our party's policies reflect reality.'

He would speak up for those with 'frustration, thwarted ambition and anger'. Leadership, he concluded, is about showing compassion rather than strength. They were the words of a

decent man; the voters will decide whether they were the words
of a Prime Minister.

19 MAY

NO I IN TEAM, BUT THIS ONE BEGINS AND ENDS WITH TM

If we had any doubt that we are in a presidential election rather
than a parliamentary one it was removed right at the start of
the event in Halifax. After a video of suitably diverse voters
parroting 'I'm standing with Theresa May', the Prime Minister
walked out and announced, 'I launch today my manifesto for
Britain's future.' My manifesto. Not my party's or my government's. Mine, all mine. The Maynifesto.

The Cabinet were arranged in rows before her, the men all
wearing mandatory blue ties, but they were mute assistants,
winged monkeys to serve their mistress's bidding – the ones
who lack the hearts, brains and courage to negotiate with Brussels. The Wizard of Oz, also known as Sir Lynton Crosby, has it
all worked out. There may be no I in team but this one begins
and ends with TM.

The document she presented was called 'Forward, Together',
but it will be in strict flying formation behind the leader. The
only photograph in the document's eighty-four pages was of
the Prime Minister, standing in front of a giant poster that said
'Theresa May'. Every chapter began with bullet points headed
'Theresa May's Conservatives will…'

Mrs May had drunk her Sunny Delight that morning. She
kept stretching up on her toes as she delivered her speech, phys-
ically demonstrating her belief in 'a country that stands tall in
the world'. Someone must have told her that she can look a bit
cold, for she slathered on the charm, beaming awkwardly as
she spoke of her 'vision for Britain'.

She also tried to woo the media through their stomachs. After bacon sandwiches the day before, cakes had been laid on for those who had boarded the 7.05 a.m. from King's Cross, although one might question whether millionaire's shortbread sends out the egalitarian image intended.

No one could remember the Conservatives launching an election manifesto in the north before. John Major, in 1992, and David Cameron, in 2015, had been thought bold in deploying their plans for government from Brighton and Swindon respectively. Yet here was Mrs May, in a Yorkshire seat held by Labour for forty-nine of the past fifty-three years, kicking for goal from way beyond the usual Tory comfort zone. She probably feels she can slot them over from her own half these days.

Her party should win Halifax. A Labour majority of 11,000 in 1997 is now below 500 and the activists in the room enjoyed her rather nebulous talk of aspiration and the Great Meritocracy (her capitals). Other local seats are firmly in the Tory sights, like Dewsbury, which the Tories have won twice in the past ninety-nine years, and Wakefield, held by Labour since 1932.

This may be a presidential campaign, but May seemed reluctant to claim the title deeds. 'There is no Mayism, there is good solid Conservatism,' she insisted. Yet this remains a one-woman show. 'Join me on this journey, strengthen my hand,' she exhorted the audience at the end of her speech.

'Let us all go forward together.' It was more of a command than an invitation.

23 MAY
TORYTANIC'S SKIPPER IS JUST ABOUT MANAGING

Strong and stable, Theresa May kept saying at the start of this campaign. I suppose that's what the White Star Line's PR department said in 1912, too. The unsinkable RMS *Torytanic* survived its brush with a BBC iceberg yesterday but it was a rough night just the same. Smashed glass all over the captain's table.

This is the problem with making a voyage all about an unremarkable skipper. It only takes one big storm and a wobbly performance from the bridge to have people looking green about the gills. The *Torytanic* had set off with talk of a record crossing but some passengers may now just be relieved to reach port on 9 June.

Mrs May repeated her mantra to Andrew Neil last night that the election comes down to whether she or Jeremy Corbyn should negotiate a Brexit deal with the EU. It remains a fairly strong line, although that is like saying that Victoria Beckham would be a better replacement No. 8 for the Lions rugby squad in New Zealand than Nicholas Parsons.

We should send Neil to Brussels instead. The BBC interviewer gave Mrs May an uncomfortable time. No party leader likes to be told repeatedly that her policies are 'half-baked and uncosted', as Neil did, but she stuck to her lines and tried not to show how flimsy they were. It was not a smooth ride – like taking speedhumps on a unicycle – but she kept going.

'This must be the first time that a party has broken a manifesto policy before the election,' Neil scoffed of her jink on social care funding. Mrs May replied that governments face challenges and she is trying to fix things. It was not a U-turn but a clarification.

Mrs May has modelled her style on Geoffrey Boycott, the Yorkshire barnacle: self-preservation and risk-avoidance are everything. It seems she shares his habit of running out teammates, too. 'Yes, no, wait, sorry!' Jeremy Hunt, Damian Green and David Gauke had all defended her at the weekend and were now back in the pavilion feeling rather silly.

Neil moved on to NHS funding and asked how she would pay for the extra £8 billion promised. 'When I go round the country, people want to know if we're going to have a strong economy,' she replied. 'Yes, but where is the extra money coming from?' Neil pressed. 'Well, if you look at our record, we put record sums into the NHS,' she replied. 'Our economic credibility isn't in doubt.'

'Your ability to answer this question may be in doubt,' Neil added, giving her a third attempt. Followed by a fourth, fifth and sixth. Then she ducked questions about immigration, winter fuel payments, the deficit and national insurance.

'It's really about Brexit negotiations and who you want sitting round that table,' Mrs May repeated. 'That's a point you've made,' Neil replied. 'Because it's very important,' the PM said.

This was not a complete disaster for her but nor was it all that convincing. Perhaps the best that can be said is that Mrs May finished the interview closer to those voters whom she regards as her core support. She, too, was 'just about managing'.

31 MAY

CORBYN FAILS MATHS TEST BUT HE DOES MAKE GOOD JAM

Radio 4 offered its listeners something new just before 10.30 a.m. when a candidate to be Prime Minister was castrated live on air. After an interview that went so badly even Diane Abbott would have winced, Jeremy Corbyn's testicles were served up to him on a plate, sizzling. That will teach him to take *Woman's Hour* lightly.

Mr Corbyn had been in trouble from the start. Emma Barnett asked why he had announced a policy about childcare on the day that he was on her show, with Mumsnet to follow. 'Do you think childcare is just a women's issue?' she asked. 'Er, no,' yelped Mr Corbyn. 'Of course it's not just a women's institute, er, issue.' A revealing slip. This was not the *Jam and Jerusalem* interview he had expected.

'No,' Barnett snapped, her thermostat falling rapidly. 'The idea of a "women's vote" is a myth. We care about the economy – so how much will it cost to provide childcare for 1.3 million children?' Mr Corbyn sniffed. Then sighed. He looked at the tiny notepad beside him. 'Er, it will cost, er,' he said. 'It will obviously cost… a lot. We accept that.'

'I presume you have the figures?' 'Yes,' he replied, too defensively. 'I do. It does cost… a lot.'

He flicked aimlessly through the manifesto. Then his phone went ping. 'In a moment,' he said.

'You don't know it,' Barnett scoffed. 'You're holding your manifesto, you've got an iPad, you've had a phone call and you don't know what it costs… Hopefully someone's emailing it to you.'

With Mr Corbyn displaying more flounder than a Grimsby fishmonger, Barnett asked, with patronising kindness, 'Would you like to know how much your policy is going to cost, Mr Corbyn?' He gave an exasperated sigh. The Corbynista online army went into meltdown and attacked Barnett. Imagine their glee when they discovered that she was Jewish. Misogyny and antisemitism rained down. Oddly, they had liked her last week when, in the words of The Canary, their house website, Barnett 'repeatedly skewered' a leading Tory.

Mr Corbyn was much better on the soft upholstery of *The One Show*: relaxed, charming, even self-aware. Asked why he only got two Es in his A levels, Mr Corbyn explained that he wrote over-long answers and didn't finish the papers in time. Some things do not change.

He spoke with evident glee about his childhood, his love of trains, poetry and manhole covers, his allotment ('the wonders of planting beans'). Someone should give him a BBC Four series – the new Michael Portillo! He even gave the presenters some of his homemade jam. He came across as a very likeable grandfather. Fortunately, no one asked about policy. In any case, as he explained: there's 'no difference' between being a Prime Minister and an activist. Says it all.

1 JUNE

NO FAIRYTALE AS DOPEY AND QUEASY BICKER

This election hasn't gone to plan for Queen Theresa. For several weeks she had been asking her adviser, 'Lynton, Lynton, on the wall, who is the strongest and most stable of them all?' And each time the reply came back, 'Why, you are, your majesty.'

No longer. The polling mirror has become misty. There may not be an obvious Snow White in the kingdom to replace her but rather than risk her reputation in a BBC debate last night, Queen Theresa went off to a cheese festival while seven dwarfs argued about the state of the nation on telly.

Dopey, Creepy, Queasy, Crappy, Dreadful, Lumpy and Jock took it in turns to shout over the top of each other in an attempt to win votes. It was as lively and enlightening as a pub lock-in after the beer's run out.

Jeremy Corbyn decided to show up at the last moment, in an attempt either to draw Queen Theresa out of hiding or to shame her for not doing so, but as the evening went on the Labour leader seemed to go missing himself. Unwilling to play the shouty game, he looked like a man in need of a buzzer so that he could get a word in.

He made a bright start, however, taking the attack to Amber Rudd, the Prime Minister's stand-in, early on. 'Have you ever been to a food bank?' he asked. 'Have you seen people sleeping around stations?' Ms Rudd gave him a tickle with her withering stick. 'Jeremy, Jeremy,' she sighed. 'I know there is no extra payment you don't want to add, no tax you don't want to rise.' She also gave his magic money tree a watering. 'It's easy to talk about how to spend money; much harder about how to raise it in the first place. This is people's hard-earned money.'

Caroline Lucas, the Greens' demi-leader, spoke of wanting the right to have sex in all twenty-seven EU countries. Well, you can't fault a girl for having ambition. Leanne Wood, of Plaid Cymru, and UKIP's Paul Nuttall couldn't hide their mutual dislike – 'We all know men like you,' Ms Wood shivered – while Angus Robertson, for the SNP, just wanted to talk of Scottish independence. Ms Rudd came a-withering again. 'I know that there is no referendum result that he will accept,' she said.

Tim Farron was the enigma. At the start he was like the presenter of one of those daytime television adverts that you find on a low-audience satellite station. 'Has your country been in an accident when it wasn't your fault? Dial 0800 SECOND-REF today and see what you could save.'

As the debate went on, though, his eagerness and ability to get a word in began to work. He was a bit too keen to turn every area of policy into an anecdote but the folksy charm was refreshing. One attack on Mrs May particularly hit the mark: 'If you want to lead the people, you have to like them and spend time among them.'

In his conclusion, Mr Farron observed that the PM hadn't bothered to ask for the electorate's vote so why should they bother to give it? 'Go and watch *Bake Off* instead,' he suggested. That sounded like much more fun.

8 JUNE
SHORT-SIGHTED ELECTION CAMPAIGN ENDS IN DOUBLE VISION

Theresa May has a nightmare; Jeremy Corbyn a dream. They feature the same scene. Mrs May in Downing Street announcing that she has just tendered her resignation at the palace, while the cameras show Mr Corbyn cycling down the Mall, El Gato's head sticking out of the basket, on his way to become the Queen's fourteenth Prime Minister.

This vision dictated their final day of campaigning. In Norwich in the morning, Mrs May repeated her mantras: strong and stable leadership, seize the opportunity of Brexit, reignite the British spirit. In the front row, Chloe Smith, seeking re-election in Norwich North, simpered and nodded as if this was the wisdom of Confucius. It was light on policy, deliberately so. The Tory message is all about who is fit to be Prime Minister.

In a spartan room on an industrial estate, Mrs May addressed a huddle of 100 activists. The placards said 'Standing up for Britain', and so we were. Someone had forgotten to order the chairs. Or perhaps they just wanted to ensure a standing ovation. I wasn't the only one after a safe seat. She ran through her platitudes, mentioned Mr Corbyn as Prime Minister, grimaced for the cameras and then left by private jet for the next stage-managed event.

Mr Corbyn, on the other hand, was scattering policies like confetti as he visited constituencies from Glasgow to Islington. There is no logic to the route he has taken during this campaign. While Mrs May has largely visited Labour seats with the sort of majority that would fall on a good night for the Tories, Mr Corbyn has flitted from Labour stronghold to Tory marginal. I caught up with him in the early evening on a shopping street in Watford, a seat he has now visited twice. This should not be in play for Labour: Richard Harrington, a junior pensions minister, has a majority of almost 10,000.

One visit by Mr Corbyn would be optimism; two seems a waste of time. But he told the crowd of about 500 that Harold Wilson had won it in 1964 and he intends to do the same. He did not mention, for some reason, that Tony Blair also won it in 1997.

This was the eighty-eighth rally of a tiring campaign – think of all the time off in lieu he will take if he becomes Prime Minister – but the 68-year-old is not flagging. He ran through almost all the policies in his manifesto, which he has waved as often as Nigel Farage waggled his passport in the referendum, and told the crowd that he would talk tough to Donald Trump about climate change. Oh, to be a fly on the Downing Street wall for that chat.

It had the pleasant hippy festival feeling you get at many Corbyn events. Lots of Doc Martens, dogs and purple hair. An old man wandered around dispensing choc ices at random. A metaphor for the Labour manifesto: have what you like, it's all free! Hope was in the air, but is this really a PM-in-waiting? At least no one can say this time that they don't have a choice.

The general election did not quite go as Theresa May had hoped. Having been twenty-one points ahead in the opinion polls before the publication of her manifesto, the Conservatives lost thirteen seats and, with them, their majority. Labour, with only 262 MPs, were unable to form their own coalition government, so Mrs May limped on with a confidence and supply agreement with the Democratic Unionist Party in Northern Ireland. Not very strong or stable. Nick Timothy and Fiona Hill, her joint chiefs of staff, were blamed and resigned.

10 JUNE
THE MORNING AFTER THE NIGHTMARE BEFORE

Theresa May spread out the map of Northern Ireland on the Cabinet table. 'So let me see if I've got this right,' she said to Nickanfi, her double-headed chief adviser. 'The green bits are held by Sinn Féin?' Nickanfi nodded and hissed a little. 'And the reddish areas belong to our new friends and allies,

the DUP, on whom our stronganstable leadership depends?'
Another nod.

Then Mrs May saw a large blue area on the map. 'And I suppose this is where all the Conservative MPs are to be found?'
Nickanfi cleared their throats. 'Not quite, Prime Minister,'
they said. 'That's Lough Neagh.'

It had been a long and difficult night for Mrs May. She had
been surprised by the exit poll showing her short of a majority.
'But I am stronganstable,' she protested. 'The numbers must
be wrong. Nickanfi, ring the BBC and demand that they add
another fifty to our tally.'

At her count in Maidenhead the paranoia grew. Was that tall
man with the bucket on his head actually Philip Hammond,
mocking her? That would be beyond the pail. She won her seat
comfortably enough but it was clear that the rest of the party
had let her down. They had not been stronganstable. She was
surrounded by weaklings and fools.

Mrs May paid particular attention to the count in Hastings.
There had been rumblings that she would have to go for this.
How could she continue after fighting an election on the question of strong leadership and losing seats? When Amber Rudd
clung on, Mrs May told Nickanfi to send the Home Secretary
a message. 'Tell her "well done" and to go out and resign on my
behalf in the morning.'

In the end, the sacrifice was not needed. The red bits of
Northern Ireland agreed to lend a hand. Mrs May went to
the palace to tell the Queen that she was stronganstable. 'I am
determined to go on and on,' she declared. 'You certainly do,'
Prince Philip grumbled.

In the car on the way back, Mrs May asked Nickanfi for
a speech. 'The one marked "contrite and humble"?' Nickanfi
suggested. 'No,' Mrs May barked. 'Give me the "whopping
majority" one.'

And so she delivered a speech that gave no indication of

the events of the previous night. It oozed stronganstable. 'I will now form a government that can provide certainty and lead Britain forward,' she said. 'We must fulfil the promise of Brexit.'

In Brussels, Michel Barnier was wheezing like Muttley, while Jean-Claude Juncker opened a bottle of chilled schadenfreude. Mrs May had taken seven weeks to disintegrate a 24-point poll lead; this renegotiation was going to be fun. 'Tell her she can take as long as she needs,' Mr Barnier told an aide. 'But remind her that the clock is ticking.'

At the *Evening Standard*, George Osborne took a break from flicking V signs at the television to tell his comment editor to up the snark a shade in the leading article. He was going to enjoy tucking into a dish of revenge for lunch, served cold with lashings of May-on-her-knees.

The Prime Minister, however, did not appear humiliated. Trying to affect an Elizabeth-at-Tilbury look, she promised to deliver a brighter Brexity future. 'That is what the people voted for last June,' she said. What they voted for the day before had already been disregarded.

14 JUNE
NOT DEAD YET

See, the conquering hero comes! Or at least the chap who didn't preside over a Labour wipeout as predicted. Jeremy Corbyn entered the Commons to a standing ovation. From Canterbury to Chester, from Plymouth to Peterborough and from the People's Republic of High St Ken., politicians rose from their death beds to cheer him to the rafters.

You would almost have thought that he had won the election rather than fallen sixty-four MPs short of a majority. The Labour benches had that look you see among Scottish rugby fans after losing the Calcutta Cup by less than a converted try. Success is relative and they are entitled to enjoy it.

Plenty – journalists to the fore – thought that Mr Corbyn was toast. Instead, he is barely warmed focaccia.

22 JUNE
ENTER THE DRAGON, DASHES OUT THE QUEEN

It's the heralds and pursuivants I felt most sorry for as the Queen opened Parliament. When else does a Rouge Dragon get to be pursuived by a Portcullis, egged on by Maltravers Herald Extraordinary? They had all been given the day off for this dressed-down, semi-casual state opening, along with such royal hangers-on as the Lady of the Bedchamber and Gold Stick in Waiting. All surplus to requirements this year, as was the Master of the Horse, who was doubtless hoofing it to Ascot.

The Queen was anxious to join him. 'I've got your goat, Ma'am,' purred David Lidington, the Lord Chancellor, as he handed over the vellum. 'You're telling me, sonny,' the monarch's expression seemed to be saying. She flicked through the thin speech as if it were one of those programmes you get in a provincial theatre that consist largely of adverts for estate agents.

'Oh well, at least we'll be done with this swiftly,' she sighed to the work experience kid sitting next to her. It was Bring Your Heir to Work Day. Normally, the Queen would have been accompanied by her husband, but Prince Charles had come instead to pick up experience in reading out tripe while straddling the grammatical and constitutional line between sounding disinterested and uninterested.

This may have been a depomped ceremony, but everything is relative. Yeomen with bouncing plumes still marched along the Royal Gallery; there was parping brass at the monarch's arrival; and the Leader of the Lords carried forth on a stick the Cap of Maintenance. Up in the gallery we reached for our Biros of Whimsy to scribble upon the Notepads of Irreverence.

The crown, too heavy for the Queen on such a hot day, had been sent ahead in a separate car and was sitting there on a cushion. The royal head was instead covered with what appeared to be the flag of the European Union: a blue floral number with a circle of yellow dots. You can take the girl out of Saxe-Coburg-Gotha... The speech was delivered in only nine minutes, the Queen reaching the post at quite a gallop. There was racing to be enjoyed after all.

Later, in the Commons, John Bercow began by reminding MPs to behave with civility and courtesy to each other. An optimistic entreaty. They were soon baying and barracking, particularly when Jeremy Corbyn claimed that he led a government in waiting. Theresa May congratulated the Labour leader on coming 'a good second' in the election: 'Better than the pundits predicted and many of his own MPs hoped for.'

Mr Corbyn reverted to his normal Commons performance: moany, preachy and long-winded. It provoked a point of order from Jacob Rees-Mogg, who observed that Mr Corbyn was still speaking ten minutes after he had said 'in conclusion' and wondered if he had misled the House. The Queen took less time over her entire speech than Mr Corbyn did on his summing-up. Perhaps he's just not a racing man.

1 SEPTEMBER
MON DIEU! DEL BOY GETS LOST IN TRANSLATION

The monthly press conference that David Davis and Michel Barnier hold at the end of each round of Brexit negotiations is starting to resemble a game show, one in which the audience have to guess how the talks have gone from two completely contrasting descriptions.

'We're not making much progress,' sighed Mr Barnier with all the enthusiasm of a Frenchman who has ordered the cheese trolley at the end of lunch and been given a choice of Babybel and La Vache qui rit. 'Time is passing quickly.'

'*Au contraire, mon bonnet de douche*,' riposted Mr Davis, the Del Boy of the privy council. 'In fact, we are making concrete progress.' This just made me think – perhaps because the Brexit Secretary has the look of an East End boxing promoter – of someone in Blue Circle boots being pushed off the Isle of Dogs and progressing to the bottom of the Thames.

Mr Barnier was unconvinced. He kept talking about the 'legal obligations' that Britain has to the EU, which appear to be low on Mr Davis's list of priorities. 'It's all about creating trust,' the Frenchman said. 'There are still areas where we need to build trust.'

The relationship between Britain and the EU, as a former secretary of the English Rugby Football Union once said about his nation and the Welsh, is based on trust and understanding: 'They don't trust us and we can't understand them.' Well, what does the EU expect when Mr Barnier keeps slipping between French and English without the need to reach for his *Larousse*? His press conferences are properly bilingual. '*Lundi, j'ai dit à David*, "I am concerned",' Mr Barnier said at the start of his statement, before veering off into his native tongue for a bit to talk about the orders he has been given by the European Parliament and then slipping easily back into English to warn of 'consequences'.

Mr Davis did not seem flustered. He flicked out his translation earpiece with a gesture that seemed to say '*mangetout, ma crêpe suzette*' and set about explaining that it is the EU that needs to buck up its ideas. 'We want a deep and special relationship,' he said. 'But we'll only get that through flexibility.'

He was rather keen on the 'F' word. Several times, the Brexit Secretary argued that Britain is being more 'flexible' than the

EU. It can only be a matter of time before a new portmanteau is born – Brexible: the act of working such contortions that you can't tell your *culus* from your *cubitus*, as Jacob Rees-Mogg would say.

From their body language it seems that Mr Barnier regards his counterpart as a right pain in the *culus*. 'You appear to be angry,' a journalist told him. 'I have shown the calm of a mountaineer,' Mr Barnier said, implying that he is more on-piste than piste-off. 'If I get angry it will be very obvious, I can assure you.' He then accused Britain of showing 'a sort of nostalgia' with its have-cake-and-eat-it approach to EU benefits.

'It's just a belief in the free market, *mon vieux parapluie*,' Mr Davis replied, all sweetness and innocence. He had the cheeky look of someone who intends to see just how far he can push this relaxed mountaineer towards an avalanche at their monthly summit meetings, but whose chalets will end up being crushed by it?

7 SEPTEMBER
CRAPPY MEAL DIET LEAVES CORBYN FEELING WEAK

Jeremy Corbyn shuffled up to the front of the McCommons queue, where the bored woman behind the desk gave him a look of barely disguised contempt. 'Wotchoowant?' she asked him, one painted claw poised over her keyboard.

'A Sunny Meal please,' Mr Corbyn replied. 'Something nutritious and warming. I want an end to zero-hours contracts, action on corporate greed and a side order of onion rings. I'm lovin' it.'

'Sorry, mate, we're fresh out of Sunny Meals,' Theresa May replied, flicking dust off the solitary star on her name badge. All her enthusiasm for the job had gone. On the wall, an

Employee of the Month certificate, dated July 2016, was starting to look dog-eared.

'I can do you a Crappy Meal,' she said. 'Or how about some Whoppers?' Mr Corbyn looked queasy. 'I think everyone had enough whoppers during May and June,' he said. 'Anyway, I'm a vegan now. Sort of. Are you sure you can't get me an energy price cap and some higher wages for nurses?'

Mrs May sighed. 'Now look here: you say you want all these things but where are they coming from? Remember when my lot took over McCommons from your people? There was nothing left in the deepfreeze. That was only seven years ago. You can hardly expect us to have restocked it by now. So don't blame us, look at yourself.'

Yes, Wednesday lunchtime in McCommons is as unappetising as it was before the recess. Mrs May still blames everything on the previous Labour administration and Mr Corbyn still wants to fill his tray and get someone else to pay for it. Your menu choice is Mrs May's small fries or a pile of Corbyn fritters.

Yesterday, Mr Corbyn suggested that Mrs May could raid the bonuses of corporate fatcats to provide a few scraps for striking fast-food workers. Mrs May didn't have an answer to that so she complained about Mr Corbyn's policy on nuclear submarines instead. 'He talks about manifestos and people going back on their word,' she said. 'The Labour manifesto included a commitment to support Trident and yet he's been telling people in private that he doesn't agree with it.'

Mr Corbyn looked bewildered. 'I listened very carefully to what she said on this occasion,' he said, 'and I'm struggling to see the connection between what she just said and McDonald's.'

He had a point. Or is our nuclear deterrent so unreliable that we're just going to fire stale burger baps at North Korea instead? Then Mrs May did her usual trick of reeling off boiler-plate platitudes about income tax cuts, employment figures and the need to balance the books. There was no fizz about her and it was even boring her colleagues. Philip Hammond suddenly threw back his head and gave an almighty yawn.

Not a good look for television but a McCommons diet can leave you with a dreadful lethargy these days. It's not even fast food. The noon session, which should take thirty minutes, dragged on until 12.48 p.m. By the end, even the vegans were desperate for some proper meat.

18 SEPTEMBER
THE NAME'S CABLE. SIR VINCE CABLE. DOUBLE-OH NO!

Always expect the unexpected with Boris Johnson. Even so, it was a surprise to see him on the Bournemouth seafront, outside the Liberal Democrat conference, waving an EU flag and singing about how he is going to cancel Brexit.

It was an impersonator, but quite a good one. Blond mane, Falstaffian belly, all gollies and cripes. He should stay away from Westminster lest Michael Gove use him as a pincushion. 'Now I'm the king of the jungle, the Foreign Secretary,' he sang, imitating King Louie in *The Jungle Book*. 'You'll see it's true-oooo that a fake like me-hee-hee could talk our way back into the EU.'

Never let it be said that the Lib Dems aren't serious. Pseudo-Boris had led a few dozen Eurofanatics on a march and was now serenading them beside the pier while waving a puppet Theresa May. His fans held EU flags and wore berets and badges saying things like 'bollox to Brexit'. Someone was wearing a Kate Middleton mask. All charmingly loopy. All very Lib Dem.

I left Boris on the seafront, now performing a version of Miley Cyrus's 'Wrecking Ball' – 'All I wanted was to break Dave's balls' – and returned to the conference where Sir Vince

Cable was taking questions from members. Outside the auditorium a sign warned that 'smoke, pyrotechnics, strobe lighting and lasers' may feature. Alas, a broken promise. No smoke, nor even all that much hot air. It was a sleepy session.

The first questioner was Doreen from Newcastle, who wondered what the new leader would do about airport expansion. Another member then recalled a joyous afternoon when Sir Vince had come to their garden party in Hounslow and they hadn't heard a word he said because of the aircraft.

Sir Vince ended by telling them that he is not the mild undertaker he appears to be. 'I love danger,' he said. 'The one thing I miss most from being in the Cabinet is the adrenaline rush I got from visiting car companies and being allowed to drive their fastest cars.' Chairing a Lib Dem subcommittee on wind power just doesn't match up to taking an Aston Martin DB9 for a spin at 150 mph.

He is a demon on skis too. The Lib Dem answer to James Bond – a man whom all parish councillors want to be and all accountants want between their balance sheets – took up skiing at sixty-three and is addicted. 'I've done the red runs, but I want to try a black run,' he said to gasps. Having reached the summit at seventy-four, it is all downhill from here for Sir Vince, one way or another.

23 SEPTEMBER
TECHNICOLOUR BACKDROP SOON FADES TO GREY

In one of the most beautiful cities in Europe – a place where, as Henry James wrote, 'everything seems to be coloured with a mild violet, like diluted wine' – a grey woman stood in front of a grey backdrop and gave a monochrome speech about Brexit.

Theresa May had gone to Florence in search of a metaphor. 'It was here that the Renaissance began,' she said near the start of her speech. The rebirth of European civilisation and, by implication, the whole faltering Brexit process.

By the banks of the Arno (coincidentally, what 48 per cent of the country screamed on the morning after the referendum), Mrs May wanted to invoke a vision of a bright, colourful and creative future. Let Brexit make Michelangelos of everybody! All we need is imagination.

'The eyes of the world are on us,' she said. Yet, for all that the world knew she could have been speaking in a Westminster office rather than beside the church of Santa Maria Novella. The Prime Minister stood before a screen painted in a dull shade that I think Farrow & Ball call Think Tank Guff and spoke in similar tones. There is no beauty in Mrs May's art; no subtlety about her brushwork.

'It is good to be here at a critical time,' she began, throwing in the word 'critical' twice more in the next minute. Feeling the criticism, perhaps. In the front row, her Chancellor, Foreign Secretary and Brexit Secretary stared straight ahead. Then some more platitudes: 'defining moment', 'vibrant debate', 'beginning a new chapter'.

The next few years are going to be an 'exciting time', she went on. Or perhaps that was a typo. Maybe she meant to say 'exiting time' for Britain is definitely leaving, she wanted to assure us of that; she just couldn't say when. The solitary piece of news was that she would like a two-year transition period before Brexit becomes total. A bit of breathing space, but no second thoughts.

Our relationship with the EU has become like a failed marriage where one partner wants to leave but can't afford to do so. Mrs May's speech was the equivalent of suggesting that we sleep in separate bedrooms and make our own meal plans. The slogan on her lectern said 'shared history, shared challenges, shared future' but at some point we will need to divide the CDs and decide who is responsible for the dog.

It was a generous speech in many ways. An 'it's me, not you' explanation for the impending divorce. 'The United Kingdom has never totally felt at home in the European Union,' she admitted. A bit later she added that the EU didn't want this divorce at all.

Well, they might if they have to listen to any more of her tedious speeches. On and on she went for some 5,000 words, most of them management waffle. 'Co-operation and partnership ... respectful of the challenges ... dynamic arrangements ... our fundamentals are strong.' Mrs May saps all the fun out of fundamentals. I'm sure that she read the same page three times.

One thing seemed clear: there has not been much progress in many areas. 'Ireland', she said, 'has unique issues.' And she will definitely do something about them. At some point. Then on to the rights of EU citizens to stay in Britain. 'We love you,' she said. 'Why, we even have Italians in Maidenhead.' Mrs May promised to sort out their status 'quickly', a mere six months after saying it would be her top priority. No wonder she wants more time. Renaissances don't happen overnight.

26 SEPTEMBER
BOOF! THORNBERRY SOCKS BORIS WHERE IT HURTS

Same tune, different words. As the shadow Foreign Secretary ended a rollicking speech from the platform yesterday morning, one that mocked Boris Johnson's sex life, called Theresa May a coward and laid into Donald Trump, a familiar chant began to roll across the hall. 'Ohhh, Em-i-ly Thorrrrrn-bree.' Jeremy, she's stolen your anthem.

This was a speech worthy of a song. Ms Thornberry has all the subtlety of a rhino playing Rachmaninov, but there is

something magnificent about her. She reminds me in tempera-
ment (it would be ungallant to say in appearance) of Miss Piggy.
In an instant she can switch from flirtatious eyelash-fluttering
to – BOOF! – clouting you like an All Blacks forward who has
spotted that the referee is looking the other way.

She certainly laid out her opposite number. Noting, in a
gentle purr, that there are now no Tory MPs in Brighton, she
said, 'There is no seat we can't win, no Tory we can't bin.' Then
she invited the audience to come on a bombing mission with
her. 'Let's go to Hastings and end the ambitions of Amber
Rudd,' she said. 'Let's go to Chingford and send Iain Duncan
Smith to the jobcentre. And then let's go to Uxbridge…'

Yes, her primary target was now in the sights. Poor Boris,
she faux-lamented. He's upset because people keep blaming
him for Brexit being a mess. Then the purr turned into a snarl.
Well, you're going to own this one, buster. 'I know that Boris
doesn't like paternity tests but he might need one for Brexit,'
Miss Piggy jeered. SOCK! 'It must have been that wild night
you had with Michael Gove.' CLUNK! 'I've calculated your
maintenance payments – it's going to be £350 million a week.'
KAPOW! Ms Thornberry's speeches should always be accompanied by *Batman*-style sound effects.

Then she moved on to Mrs May and her plea for the EU
to be more creative in its approach to Brexit. 'Hey, I've got a
creative idea,' Ms Thornberry said, her voice now back to resembling the Cadbury's Caramel bunny. She raised one finger,
then her eyebrows, gave a smile, and changed personality once
more. 'Step aside, love,' she growled. (I may have made up
the last word but it was in the tone.) 'Let the grown-ups take
charge.'

On she went. Donald Trump is a 'rogue dictator' – ZAMM!
– and Mrs May was a disgrace for walking hand in hand with
him. 'Supine, sycophantic, spineless,' she said, each word spat
out. BOSH!

Labour, of course, would be different. 'We will set a new standard for Britain and be a shining example to the world,' she said, all sweetness again, raising her eyes to heaven. It was brazen, it was shameless, it was utterly wonderful.

Poor Sir Keir Starmer, who had to follow that. The shadow Brexit Secretary always looks perplexed and on the verge of tears, like Stan Laurel. 'That's another fine mess the country's got into.'

He speaks slowly and stiffly, as if he has just realised that he left a hanger in his shirt, with long pauses, giving the audience time to mull over such zinging phrases as 'the government's policy is constructive ambiguity'. While Ms Thornberry provided a buzz, Sir Keir was verbal Valium. No one sang at the end. No one ever sings after his speeches.

28 SEPTEMBER
CORBYN SINGS A PLEASING TUNE OUT OF TIME

We learnt something new about Jeremy Corbyn yesterday. He can't keep time. As his conference speech in Brighton ended and 'Power to the People' was played, I watched the Labour leader clapping with the audience and saw that he was constantly a beat behind the rhythm, following when he should be leading. That figures.

Up until then, Mr Corbyn had been perfectly synchronised with his tribe. There is seldom such a tight connection between speaker and audience. They were rapt, even though his speech had little meat to it. Every point received 5,000 nods; every full stop demanded 5,000 pairs of clapping hands. The last time so many people were fed on such meagre rations it involved loaves and fishes.

Mr Corbyn got a three-minute standing ovation just for walking into the hall. They stamped and they clapped and they waved their Corbyn scarves, all the while singing his anthem: 'Ohhhh, Je-re-my Corrrr-byn.' It was like going to the darts at Ally Pally, only without the benefit of being drunk.

He would have delighted them if he had simply read out a menu from one of the fish and chip restaurants along the seafront. 'Comrades, I would like the haddock.' YEAH! 'And some mushy peas.' WOO! 'And let me be very clear: I would like a pickled onion as well.' WE LOVE YOU, JEREMY!

To be fair to Mr Corbyn. I have heard a lot of his speeches over the past two years and many of them have been badly written and poorly delivered. Yesterday, he made the best twenty-minute speech of his career. It was just a pity about the hour that followed.

It began with a bit of Labour history – the local shop girl who had gone on, via a trade union, to sit in the Cabinet – then praised all those who had helped to achieve a better-than-expected election result and taunted the Tories. He wounded them with the weapons they had used against him: 'coalition of chaos', 'magic money tree', 'strong and stable'. There were some good lines, nicely delivered, and he was rightly applauded.

Behind him on the stage were thirty new MPs, many of whom had not expected to be there. As a delegate had said earlier in the conference, with Corbynite optimism, 'If we can win Canterbury, we can get world peace.' He gave a wave to his shadow Cabinet in the audience – 'It's OK, you can wave back,' he told them – and then he sang 'Happy Birthday' to Diane Abbott. There was so much love in the room.

It is a pity that he didn't stop there. Mr Corbyn has learnt how to speak in short sentences; he still needs to learn how to give a short speech. Yesterday's was 25 per cent longer than either of his first two conference speeches. I was surprised to discover that it was still light on leaving the hall. Or perhaps it was now October.

30 SEPTEMBER
UKIP TURN TO BOLTON TO TAME THE CRAZY GANG

As Torquay's most famous Spanish waiter would say: we know naahthing. UKIP unveiled its next former leader on the English Riviera and everyone had expected that it would be a straight fight between Peter Whittle, the former London mayoral candidate, and Anne Marie Waters, an anti-Islam activist who was described by one of her colleagues as the 'Joan of Arc of neo-fascists'.

There were other colourful candidates, such as the one who had claimed that a gay donkey tried to rape his horse or the one who wants to spend £1 billion on mining the asteroid belt. Instead, surprisingly, the party members went for a former Liberal Democrat. Nothing is predictable these days.

Henry Bolton was not high on anyone's radar, though he was said to be Nigel Farage's favourite. He has the sort of ultra normal name you find used as a pseudonym in a spy novel. Some wondered if he actually was Mr Farage in disguise, using this as a way to take back his party.

Mr Bolton represented the Lib Dems in the 2005 general election against Philip Hammond, but that handicap was overcome by being a former captain in the Army, a police officer who received an award for bravery and by having an OBE. They do like their medals in UKIP.

He gave a short and well-received speech, promising that protecting Brexit will be his 'core task'. His party, however, now dwindles in the polls, almost falling within the margin of error not to exist at all.

Mr Bolton said that 'there is no greater calling' than to be leader of UKIP. Then, realising that he was being watched by a bishop, he corrected himself and said that perhaps there was one greater.

Michael Nazir-Ali, the former Bishop of Rochester, had

given the conference an enjoyable half-hour sermon, although I had wondered whether his presence was down to a typo on a memo, in the expectation that Ms Waters, the purple Le Pen, would win. A Nazi rally, rather than a Nazir-Ali.

His Grace told the audience that not all men are created equal. 'I can bowl with either arm,' he said, proudly, then showed them. 'That's got me into sides I didn't deserve to get in.' He also passed comment on UKIP's new lion logo, which he likened to Aslan. 'He isn't safe, but he's good,' he quoted from *The Lion, the Witch and the Wardrobe*. Let us hope that Mr Bolton is both the safe option for UKIP and a good one.

2 OCTOBER
TORY CONFERENCE FALLS FOR THE QUEEN OVER THE BORDER

In bars and restaurants around Manchester, many a delegate and MP raised a glass last night and drank a toast to the Queen Over the Border. Ruth Davidson, the young pretender, had given them a conference speech full of passion, wit and purpose that few will match.

She insists her only aim is to be First Minister of Scotland. She would rather be Theresa May's champion than her rival. Yet with one brief speech Ms Davidson jump-started a conference that had been flatlining. No wonder they dream in Westminster of Bonnie Princess Ruthie riding to the rescue.

After Ms Davidson's speech there was a buzz around the hall. Beforehand, only a zz. Poor Sajid Javid is like Piriton in human form. The Communities Secretary was listened to in such silence you could almost hear the beads of sweat as they fell from his glistening head.

The audience had already endured a chairman's bumbling from Patrick McLoughlin (Con, West Derbyshire), a robotic address from Damian Green and a less than sizzling one from Justine Greening (Con, Putney). Mr Javid was now like the glass of wine too many over Sunday lunch, sending them off for forty winks. At one point he delivered a good rhetorical line about home ownership – normally catnip to Tories – that received no reaction at all. He paused, wondering why they had not applauded, before trudging on. In the end he started clapping himself, just to encourage them.

Fortunately Ms Davidson bounded on, full of energy, and changed the tone. 'It's great to be here in Manchester,' she said. 'Or as I call it, the Southern Powerhouse.' They sat up at that.

Then a good joke about the party winning just one MP in the 2015 election. 'We were still outgunned by those sodding pandas,' she said, in reference to the pair of Chinese bears in Edinburgh Zoo.

Not many MPs risk a 'sodding' in public. They fear upsetting the older members. But it shows Ms Davidson's down-to-earth, no-nonsense appeal. The party can surely take someone saying sodding in its stride now.

She spoke of the twelve gains made in Scotland this year – 'The pandas are going to have to go some to catch up now!' – and told her party to shake off the idea that they are losers just because they had not won. 'Jeremy Corbyn is not a shoo-in to No. 10 just because Glastonbury chanted his name to the White Stripes,' she said. 'Folks, he hasnae even won a raffle.'

Ms Davidson is used to taking on cult figures. She poked fun at Nicola Sturgeon, with her branded merchandise and speeches in stadiums, and said that celebrity soon fades. 'People tire of being offered free unicorns.'

And then we got a section that was less fun but more

important as she explained what the Tories are for. They were little more than bullet points: 'show working people we have their back'; 'be a party of home-building'; 'welcome those who have settled here'; 'stay united as a country'. But they showed purpose. Short and simple works.

'These are the things I believe in and I know you believe in them too,' she concluded. It sounded awfully like a manifesto for a leadership bid. But for now Ms Davidson remains the Queen Over the Border, the leader many want but cannot have.

3 OCTOBER
HAIL SUPERMOGG, THE ABLATIVE ABSOLUTE MAN

Look, up there. Is it a banker? Is it a stockbroker? No, it's SuperMogg, defender of truth, justice and the British way of doing things.

Mild of manner, stiff of upper lip, double-breasted of suit, the Clark Kent of Somerset conservatism may not look like much on the outside but he seems to be the right's answer to Corbyn populism. A man armed not with a Little Red Book but a Kennedy's *Latin Primer*. Labour members for some reason call their messiah 'the absolute boy'; the Tories now have their ablative absolute man.

And woe betide any ruffian, hooligan or ill-kempt yahoo, as he might put it, who gets in his way. A few tried yesterday at the start of his luncheon fringe event in Manchester Town Hall. The room was packed, a few hundred sitting and a good hundred standing, and Jacob Rees-Mogg seemed surprised by the ovation as he took his seat at a table on which stood an icon of the Blessed Margaret Thatcher. 'Oh, do stop, please, it's embarrassing,' he muttered, not very convincingly.

Then the protest started. A handful at the back began to

chant and wave banners that said 'Tories Out'. Before security could move in, SuperMogg took control. 'Ladies and gentlemen,' he told them. 'Let us have a proper debate.' And then he came down from the stage to speak to his foes directly. 'Hello, what would you like to ask me?' he said. Politeness can be such a deadly weapon.

The rude mechanicals seemed surprised. 'You're a despicable person,' one said. 'What do you disagree with me about?' SuperMogg said, as calmly as a surgeon advising a patient. 'Everything,' was the reply.

And so they chatted for a bit. When SuperMogg tried to argue that employment was the best route out of poverty, he was again told that he was despicable. 'Let's leave my despicability to one side for a moment,' he said. After a bit more of this, he ended by saying, 'Well, very nice to have met you,' before security carted off the protester.

On with the fringe, where The Mogg said that Britain needed to be more generous in the Brexit talks. 'Let's not faff around negotiating over security matters, we're not that sort of nation,' he said. He called for immediate clarity on the right of immigrants to remain. 'How lucky we are that millions of brave souls come to this country to work hard.' And he said that he was prepared to cut a good trade deal to maintain his cellar's access to good French claret.

'You, perhaps, may prefer Parmesan cheese,' he told the delegates.

But this generosity, he went on, must come with 'a titanium-plated backbone'. No giving Brussels an easy ride. They need us more than we need them. In his third fringe later in the day he would explain that negotiations are a quid pro quo. 'They want more quids, we are concerned about the pro quo.'

He also praised Boris Johnson for his 'panache, verve and vigour', complained that some people are 'Eeyorish' and demanded 'a Brexit in our image'. That must mean a double-breasted Brexit with a sharp parting and shoes so shiny that Nanny deserves an extra shilling.

They lapped it up and applauded lustily. All three events were rammed to the gunwales, with dozens turned away. The second was so full and clammy that a woman fainted. SuperMogg was quickly at her side with a cold compress, which almost made her swoon again. He is a cult hero. It would be *infra dig.* for The Mogg to have his own rock song, as Mr Corbyn does, but perhaps he will get a Gregorian chant.

Some will say this is ridiculous, and they may be right, but at least he injected some colour into this drab festival. The BBC coverage of proceedings in the hall says 'Live: Conservative Party Conference.' They really should add 'Barely'.

4 OCTOBER
LET ME PLAY THE LION TOO, ROARS BORIS FROM HIS BOTTOM

Boris Johnson is a man used to falling asleep on the job and waking up looking like an ass, so it was no surprise that the image conjured at the end of his conference speech was that of Bottom in *A Midsummer Night's Dream.*

'The people are the lion,' he told the conference hall. 'It is up to us now – in the traditional genial and self-deprecating way of the British – to let that lion roar.' And by implication, he intends to be the golden-maned head of the pride, for this speech by the Foreign Secretary, which only occasionally touched on foreign affairs, was inevitably seen as a leadership bid.

'Oh, let me play the lion too,' Bottom pleads. 'I will roar, that I will do any man's heart good to hear me.' To which Quince, representing Tory HQ, replies, 'And you should do it too terribly, you would fright the duchess and the ladies that they would shriek. And that were enough to hang us all.' Perhaps that was why Mr Johnson's voice faltered a little at his final line, roaring the last words as gently as a sucking dove. He did not want to scare the audience; he wanted to remind them that he is a big beast. The big beast.

If only he had delivered a speech to match that mantle. It was a curiously flat performance with little meat to it, odd given all the hoo-hah and soup-stirring from Mr Johnson in the build-up to this conference. It felt as if he had just scribbled down a few notes on a pad in the lift after being told that he had to ditch 80 per cent of his material. A neutered, toothless lion.

He opened with a joke about how many jobs George Osborne now has, which had been nicked from David Gauke's speech the day before, then had a long section on Jeremy Corbyn being a leftie that featured a joke about his love of Venezuela – 'I call him Caracas!' – nicked from his own back catalogue.

The rest was a lot of flim-flam, with a few lines that appeared to carry a deeper inference. 'I'm not saying that everyone loves us or completely follows our sense of humour, though a lot more than you might think,' he said, speaking of Britain but using 'we' in the royal sense it seemed.

And when he called Sir Alan Duncan 'that Mount Rushmore of wisdom' was it perhaps a subtle suggestion that his deputy, who was rude about Brexit voters recently, has several faces? If so, does that make Boris a dodecahedron? While he thinks he is Lord of the Jungle, others see him as the Lying King.

There were lots of traditional Borisisms, of course. Few politicians use words such as 'syncretic', 'dubitation', 'murrain', 'voletrousered' or 'manifestation of the Heisenberg uncertainty principle', as he did. Even fewer get a laugh for it, but these weren't the belly laughs he normally expects.

The first proper cheer did not come until a long way in, when he said that the new Mayor of London wasn't a patch on the last guy, almost as if that memory of former glories gave them a chance to shout for the old, absent Boris. At the end he got an ovation, but not an especially long one, not like he has in the past. The party still loves the old lion but they were not sure why.

5 OCTOBER
SOME PMS DO 'AVE 'EM

At least it was memorable. So many speeches in this conference season have been dismal, with leaden phrases and banal paragraphs vaguely linked together and instantly forgotten before the speaker has left the stage. It will take a long time for the memory of Theresa May's speech to fade.

It had started well enough, with an apology for an uninspiring election campaign that had been, as she said, 'too scripted', but what happened next was certainly not in the script.

RoboMay somehow turned into Frank Spencer. Gradually, painfully, everything collapsed around her. It started with the stuntman. To call him a comedian, his preferred title, would be like calling Boris Johnson a diplomat. Just as Mrs May had begun a section criticising Labour, this pillock came up to the stage and offered her a mock P45.

Mrs May handled this interruption well. Barely breaking her stride, she plucked it from his fingers, like a teacher who has caught boys passing a magazine, and gave him a look that said 'you can have this back at the end of term'. There was then a disturbingly long pause before security reached this numbskull and bundled him out.

Mrs May had lost her rhythm, but she had not lost the room. If anything, this man did more to unite the Conservative Party than any platform speech this week. Alas, she then lost her voice. Those whom the gods wish to destroy they first make croaky. Five minutes earlier, Mrs May had promised to be a 'voice for the voiceless'. Now she was joining their number. She developed a cough that would not shift. After a few glugs of water failed to clear it, she had no option but to stop altogether.

'The test of a leader is how you respond when tough times come upon you,' she would say near the end of her speech. Or, as Churchill never said, when going through hell, keep going. Someone kindly stood to start an ovation, which carried on for as long as she needed to regain her voice, helped by a lozenge from Philip Hammond. This led to that rarity, a joke by Mrs May. 'I hope you all noticed the Chancellor giving something away free,' she ad-libbed. She's not bad off script.

It was only a brief remedy. Her voice dried again, the cough returned, the water had no effect. So she tried another joke – 'shows how good the Chancellor's cough sweet is' – and ploughed on. She would not be beaten by laryngitis. And then letters started to fall off the screen behind her. First an F from 'for' then an E from 'everyone'. Would the floor open next? The Prime Minister might have hoped so.

This speech was titled 'Renewing the British Dream'. For Mrs May it must have seemed like a nightmare. She is in danger of becoming like Gordon Brown or John Major, when everything she touches turns to grot, yet there was something admirably unbeatable about her.

It may be the cough that carries her off, but Mrs May kept going. If she was crying inside, she was unflappable on the surface. It reminded me of the joke about the Kipling poem. If you can keep your head, when all about you are losing theirs and blaming it on you... you probably haven't realised the gravity of the situation.

13 OCTOBER
BREXIT NEGOTIATORS FACE A KNOTTY PROBLEM

Like two sloths wrestling in treacle, David Davis and Michel Barnier continue to make slow progress. At their latest press conference, the EU's chief negotiator admitted that they have reached a deadlock. Five months in and they have barely agreed on which font to use for the lunch menus.

The negotiation is moving at a rate of knots. Gordian knots. Every few weeks, they come together in Brussels and, like the Phrygian princes in the legend, scratch their chins about how to undo the tangled mess of citizens' rights, Ireland and our bill for checking out of the EU.

The more they look at it, the more loops and hooks and impossibilities they see. How we need a modern Alexander (no, not you, Danny) to stride in and cut this knot in two.

What goes on in that negotiating room? 'We have explored some creative solutions,' Mr Davis said enigmatically. He made it sound as if our team have been practising origami, making paper aeroplanes to throw across the table in boredom. If Mr Barnier can't come up with something lively next month, Team Davis may start a Mexican wave.

Mr Davis implied that his counterpart's hands have been tied by orders from the twenty-seven EU leaders. 'I hope they give him the means to explore ways forward,' the Brexit Secretary said. Mr Barnier denied that his mandate was restrictive. 'I would call it "precise",' he said. The EU negotiator is very keen on using the right terminology. He admitted that he dislikes the word 'concession'. Our hope of a good deal may lie in Roget's Thesaurus. If he won't offer concessions, perhaps he might go for modifications, adjustments or, in extremis, sops.

Both men played with their glasses during the press

conference, taking them off, putting them on, twisting them in their fingers. At one point, when Mr Davis said that 'no deal' was a real option, Mr Barnier was so distressed that he put an arm of his glasses in his mouth. 'No deal, that will be a very bad deal, *hein*?' he said.

Mr Davis still appears the more relaxed, though he is less cocky than before and gets tetchy when people ask why more progress has not been made. 'I am not going to conduct the negotiation on this podium,' he growled at one reporter.

For a long time he has had the air of an A-level student who will start revising at some point but only after he has colour-coded his reading list. Now he has a slight look of panic, as if realising how close the start of his exams is.

People say that much of the wrangling is over money. Perhaps they are still quibbling over who should have paid for their lunch in July. 'Split it down the middle, Michel, my old mucker?' offers Mr David. 'Ah, *non*,' Mr Barnier replies. 'I only 'ad the sparkling water and no dessert.'

The EU would like Britain to put its offer of a financial settlement in writing rather than just dropping hints and winks. Theresa May is reluctant to do so because of all the trouble it will cause her with the Eurosceptic wing of her party.

'Look, the backbenchers are getting restless,' Mr Davis must have told Mr Barnier. 'Bernard Jenkin is never off the radio. Bill Cash has got that look in his eye that sends Cabinet ministers dashing into traffic to avoid a conversation. And Jacob bloody Rees-Mogg is more popular than Maggie. Just cut us some slack on this.'

If this impasse continues, Mrs May will have no option but to deploy the one weapon left in her armoury that all the other leaders fear. She should send them a Christmas card showing Boris Johnson on the steps of Downing Street and the message, 'Do you really want him instead of me?'

2 NOVEMBER
BORIS TAKES OFF ON A FLYING BUTTRESS

More than a year had passed since Boris Johnson last gave an account of himself to the Foreign Affairs Select Committee and he was keen to let them know how busy he had been. 'I realise you've been chafing at the bit to hear me,' the Foreign Secretary boasted, before going off on a canter around the world. 'I've been to fifty-two countries!' he boasted. 'On a 36-year-old plane!' Oh, the things I have seen and the people I have shaken hands with and in some regrettable instances offended.

Eventually, after six minutes of totting up the air miles, Mr Johnson drew breath and Tom Tugendhat (Con, Tonbridge and Malling), the committee chairman, tried to bring him back to ground. 'Could we perhaps move away from the written statement that was prepared for you,' he suggested, 'and on to the question that was asked? We've only got two hours.'

'I wrote it myself!' Mr Johnson protested but never mind. He was game to give this strange concept of knowing where he is going a lap around the block. Ask away!

How about life after Brexit? What will our relationship with the EU be like? Mr Johnson searched for a metaphor and found it in the folder marked 'Medieval Architecture'. 'We want to be a flying buttress!' he said. Twenty eyebrows suddenly hit the ceiling round the table. 'Yes, a buttress,' Mr Johnson went on. 'Supportive of the EU kirk but not particularly fussy about exactly how the masonry interlocks.'

Nor had he finished with the metaphor. 'Imagine a flying buttress,' he said, 'supportive, contiguous, adjacent, useful – but not integrated.'

I began to wonder whether he actually meant the buttress, since that is surely part of the EU's – I mean the kirk's – structure. Perhaps the pub across the road from the kirk would have been a better image, supporting the congregation but not under the control of Bishop Juncker.

Mr Tugendhat made a stab at interpreting what the Foreign Secretary was on about. 'So you're saying that the buttress is British,' he said, 'but the Mass being said inside is in French or German?' Close, but not quite. Mr Johnson informed them that they now speak jolly good English on the Continent.

I do not want to give the impression, however, that the whole two hours was taken up with trifles like buttresses. In discussing trade deals, for instance, Mr Johnson reached into the metaphor file marked 'Homer' and said we would be like Paris choosing between Hera, Aphrodite and Artemis. (He meant to say Athena, but even good Boris can nod, as the Romans say.) 'And you're Paris?' a puzzled Mr Tugendhat asked. 'No, the United Kingdom is,' Mr Johnson said. 'But do you have a golden apple?' pressed the chairman. 'We want to be friendly with all three,' Mr Johnson explained.

'That's not how it ended up,' said Mr Tugendhat, who knows his *Iliad*. Let us hope that we do not spend the next ten years fighting over Brexit just because Boris misremembered his classical myths.

22 NOVEMBER
ALL THE WORLD'S A STAGE FOR ODD COUPLE

This is a tale of two ministers in the same department, both Old Etonians and authors, but that's where similarities stop. One is bearish and chaotic, using the hurricane force of his personality to win arguments; the other is lean and donnish, softly spoken and precise, less in need of showing off. They are like Felix and Oscar, the Odd Couple of the Foreign Office.

Boris Johnson was in a bouncy mood at departmental questions. The Foreign Secretary had probably had a plateful of kedgeree before. From the off, he was throwing out superlatives. 'DELIGHTED,' he said, when asked about next year's Commonweath summit.

'AMBITIOUS. GRRRRREAT.' Everything was sunshine and, for once, gaffe-free. He may have got up a few Labour noses by referring to Burma not Myanmar, but what's in a name? Burrrrma is a far more pleasing, booming, sort of word.

He played a full part in the session even when not on his feet. When Tom Tugendhat suggested the government lacks a policy on Iran, Mr Johnson wrinkled his nose and let out a 'pah!' When James Gray (Con, North Wiltshire) asked about wildlife in the Antarctic, Mr Johnson gave him a thumbs-up as if to say, 'I watched *Blue Planet* too!'

He gives his folder a good workout at question time, flicking through like Paddington hunting in his hat for a lost marmalade sandwich. Occasionally he will run a paw through his hair in bemusement that something is not there. 'Why can't I find anything on Abyssinia?' Rory Stewart (Con, Penrith and the Border) is the opposite. This swot does his homework. The Africa minister's folder sat unopened as he took questions on ten countries.

Africa covers more turf than it used to. As well as Egypt, Sudan and Somaliland, he travelled to India, Pakistan, Syria, Qatar, Bangladesh, Trinidad and Cambodia. He was not noticeably uninformed. He speaks well off the cuff, aptly since he shows a couple of inches below the jacket sleeve, like Prince Charles, whose children he once tutored.

Mr Stewart is as scrawny as Mr Johnson is upholstered. While his boss slouches, jacket open, he sits smartly with his back perpendicular. He pronounces places differently to those who have not trekked across Asia. It's 'Bungladesh' and 'Keshmir', which I assume is how locals say it. When Bob Blackman (Con, Harrow East) asked how Pakistan is running Badakhshan, he replied that Badakhshan is in Afghanistan. 'I think he means Balochistan,' he said gently.

In short, Mr Stewart seems bright, informed, careful and conscientious. Is he sure he is cut out for politics?

28 NOVEMBER
FRESH RECRUIT SURVIVES EARLY SKIRMISH

Gavin Williamson is such a raw recruit as Defence Secretary that I expected his first appearance at the dispatch box to be laced with practical jokes from those who resented his field promotion from subaltern to chief of the general staff. 'Could he tell the House how many cans of elbow grease are held by the navy?' might cause panic if asked with sufficient authority.

This was only the second time that Mr Williamson had ever spoken at Defence Questions – and the first for almost five years. His voice had not been heard in any Commons debate since 2015, when he spoke on the subject of hedgehog conservation before heading into the dark burrows of the Chief Whip's office. From protecting Mrs Tiggy-Winkle to handling the renewal of Trident is like asking a Trappist monk to perform our next Eurovision entry.

Mr Williamson looked nervous. He perhaps needed Cronus, his tarantula, but creepy-crawlies aren't encouraged on the front bench these days. That, after all, is how Mr Williamson had won his promotion. Sir Michael Fallon was not in the chamber, by the way.

The day started with an outbreak of warbling as MPs celebrated the royal engagement. Michael Ellis, the unguent deputy Leader of the House, led the lowing. I suspect Mr Ellis has already ordered his commemorative tiepin for the wedding.

Mr Williamson then rose to take his first question, from the Scottish Nationalists. He deflected it well but No. 2 was a stinker. The splendidly named Bambos Charalambous (Lab, Enfield Southgate) wanted to know about his discussions with the Chancellor in regard to defence funding. The new recruit leant gingerly on the dispatch box as if it might contain a bomb and paused a little too long before going into no man's land. 'I have ... regular meetings with the Chancellor,' he said. 'As yet, I have not had a formal meeting with him but I am very much looking forward to doing so.'

Nia Griffith (Lab, Llanelli), his Labour shadow, was aghast. Did he really not make any representations to the Chancellor before the Budget? Mr Williamson gave her a pained look, as if to say, 'I've only been in the job for three weeks and I spent half of that trying to get my permanent secretary some striped paint and half-inch holes.'

Labour may want to rush into things, he replied, but he will not. Mr Williamson would rather take his time and work out how much a glass hammer costs before asking the Chancellor to buy a job lot.

'It is a little bit rich', he added, 'to be lectured about defence spending by the party that is led by a man who does not even believe in the British Army.'

Mr Williamson speaks with a nasal sneer that makes him sound like a supercilious caretaker in a school drama. A man in need of a brown jacket and broom and a set of regulations to enforce. He pronounces the first letter of HMS as 'haitch', too, which may cause shudders in the Admiralty, used to the honeyed tones of Sir Michael.

However, his first tour of duty passed without disaster. Existing enemies were kept at bay and no new ones were picked up. The Tory backbenchers are mutinous and would have preferred that Tobias Ellwood (Con, Bournemouth East), his deputy, had got the job, but they weren't prepared to spoil the commanding officer's first sortie. Some battles can wait for another day.

12 DECEMBER
BREXIT BINGO FAILS TO STIR THE HOUSE

Harold Wilson's observation on the lengthening effect that the air in Westminster has on the passage of time was demonstrated again when Theresa May gave the Commons an update on Brexit. A week ago it was being whispered that the Prime Minister had as much chance of making it unscathed past Christmas as a tray of pigs in blankets; yesterday she cruised through her statement with barely a sniffy comment from either flank of her party.

Ken Clarke got the eulogies rolling by describing her deal as 'a triumph'. Mrs May looked round and raised a hand at him as if to say, 'That's quite enough, Ken, you don't need to say any more.' The veteran Europhile did not ruffle her feathers.

On the other wing, Iain Duncan Smith added his congratulations on securing 'an improved agreement which many thought would not be feasible' and all along the Tory spectrum, from the pinkish Anna Soubry (Con, Broxtowe) to the deep blue Sir Bill Cash, MPs spoke of unity in the party. She even got likened by Robert Halfon (Con, Harlow) to Zebedee, the bouncy fellow in *The Magic Roundabout*. Mrs May is not really the boinging type but she had put the Tories in an upbeat mood.

There was also apparent harmony on a well-stocked front bench, helped by the absence of the feuding Chancellor and

Defence Secretary, who were probably settling their differences by wrestling in front of a log fire like Oliver Reed and Alan Bates in *Women in Love*.

The statement itself was trademark May babble, which the Labour backbenchers seemed to acknowledge with a game of Brexit bingo. Every time the Prime Minister delivered one of her banalities, there was an ironic cheer from members of the party opposite. 'Deep and special partnership' (TICK!) ... 'Smooth and orderly exit' (DRINK!) ... 'Nothing is agreed until everything is agreed' (HOUSE!).

They had little to celebrate in their own leader's response. Jeremy Corbyn plodded along, moaning about the 'posturing, delays and disarray'. He insisted that Labour respected the result of the referendum but asked for the planned exit date of 29 March 2019 to be put back.

Mrs May, who had Jeremy Hunt whispering in her ear through much of Mr Corbyn's set, found the Labour leader especially amusing on the subject of regulatory alignment. Claiming that the Labour Party has had twelve different positions on Brexit, she observed that Mr Corbyn 'cannot even reach alignment with himself'.

Nick Boles (Con, Grantham and Stamford) then told the Prime Minister that she had turned in 'a performance worthy of Geoffrey Boycott', which would not be taken as a compliment by everybody, but she accepted it as one. Mrs May had certainly played an innings noted more for its length and obduracy than any memorable shots.

There is a lesson from history, however, that she should heed. Fifty years ago, Boycott played an unbeaten innings of 246 at Headingley, his highest Test score, but took far too long over it. There was one turgid period when he failed to score a run for forty-five minutes. Some sessions in Brussels these past six months have felt almost as productive. The selectors responded by dropping Boycott for the next match. Perhaps Mrs May should start playing some strokes in her second innings.

More than a year of government defeats and backbench rebellions began with an amendment tabled by Dominic Grieve, the former Attorney General, demanding that Parliament should have a meaningful vote on the Prime Minister's Brexit deal. With eleven Tory MPs voting against their party, it passed 309–305. Theresa May would come to look at losing margins like that as a good night.

15 DECEMBER
THIRSTY SIR EDWARD DRINKS CHARDONNFREUDE

On the morning after the rebellion, Anna Soubry seemed to be as popular on the Tory benches as King Herod in Mothercare. The Commons day began at 9.30 a.m. with departmental questions on Brexit, as if we've not heard enough on that subject lately, and yard after yard of empty green leather separated the chief mutineer from any other MP.

None of the Tory loyalists wanted to be seen near her, perhaps fearing a ticking off from the whips, and none of her fellow rebels had come out to play at this ungodly hour until Sarah Wollaston sloped in half an hour late. This was not, Ms Soubry emphasised, because they had been toasting their victory on the Brexit Bill into the small hours.

'Nobody on [our] benches who voted against the government took any pleasure in that,' she said, which earned a sarcastic comment from a distant colleague, inaudible to the press gallery. 'Nobody drank champagne,' Ms Soubry snapped. 'Let me just nail down that rumour.'

There may have been a photograph circulating of her and others sitting in a bar in front of a couple of green bottles after the vote, but it was clearly just white wine, not Dom Pérignon, and she may have stuck to lemonade.

Ms Soubry said that the government could have avoided the embarrassment of defeat by speaking to the rebels earlier in the week. David Davis just sighed and mumbled incomprehensibly, which he did for most of the session.

He appeared, as Barry Sheerman (Lab, Huddersfield) noted, to be less 'bright-eyed and bushy-tailed' than normal. The swagger had vanished. Mr Davis explained that he was suffering from a migratory cold. 'It is having a transition period of its own in my head,' he said. His frontbench team were also going through the motions yesterday, like bored children forced to perform in a nativity play.

You know the story well by now: some time ago, Theresa May had been visited by an angel, who bore a resemblance to the chairman of the 1922 Committee, and told that she had been chosen to deliver a Brexit, even though she had not campaigned for it. The blessed May recently produced an infant Brexit in a stable (not quite as strong a stable as she had hoped for), surrounded by bleating sheep and braying asses. It was meanly wrapped in impact assessments and in the library of the Commons laid. And that was where the tidings of comfort and joy ended. Three unwise men – Mr Davis, Steve Baker (Con, Wycombe) and Robin Walker (Con, Worcester) – arrived yesterday but had no gifts to bestow.

It took Sir Edward Leigh to remind MPs of the true message of Christmas, the one that Ms Soubry had been so keen to distance herself from earlier: that this is a time for getting sloshed. The Tory MP for Gainsborough informed the House that there are more than 42,000 bottles of booze lurking in the cellars of the EU. He demanded that Britain receive its 'fair share' of these riches after Brexit.

'Don't leave it for Mr Juncker to enjoy,' he thundered. Why should we remain in hock to the Germans? I bet they even have a word in Berlin for taking pleasure in denying Sir Edward his favourite vintage: Chardonnfreude.

At last, Sir Edward has found the hill, or lake, on which he is prepared to die. As the referendum motto of the Brexiteers almost put it: Vote Leave, Take Cointreau!

20 DECEMBER
PEERS SAMPLE MULLED WHINES AND REFLECT
ON MEANING OF EXISTENCE

Down at the red end of Parliament, turkeys were voting for Christmas. Or at least gobbling about it. It is rare that the House of Lords sits before lunch on a Tuesday, but they had to begin early to fit in the ninety-six peers who wished to speak on a matter of the utmost importance: themselves.

Specifically, they were discussing how many of them should continue to enjoy what a Lib Dem peer this year described as 'the best daycare centre for the elderly in London'. Lord Burns had led an inquiry that recommended cutting the number of peers from 830 to 600, using a 'two out, one in' system, and introducing a fifteen-year term limit. His proposals received a lot of support, albeit for many it was in the spirit of St Augustine: 'Lord, make us fewer – but not yet.'

Lord Forsyth of Drumlean, for instance, had not slogged his way up to the pinnacle of Scottish Secretary under John Major in order to give up his peerage after a mere eighteen years. Margaret Thatcher had once prodded him in the chest and told him to view his presence in the Lords like the ravens at the Tower. Obedient to her command, Lord Forsyth seldom goes home. He called on others to show such duty.

Lord Hain, a relative newbie after only two years there

(unlike Lord Newby, a Lib Dem, who has been a peer since 1997), said that the number was an embarrassment but not of their own making. 'We did not fill this House to bursting, Prime Ministers did,' he pleaded. 'Though we all agreed with their immense wisdom in choosing each of us.' Tony Blair and David Cameron, who created 619 peerages between them, must have been exceptionally wise.

Some wanted an age limit rather than a term limit. Bishops have to retire at seventy, for instance, though the presence in the chamber of the former Bishops of London and Oxford and a former Archbishop, all translated from lords spiritual to lords temporal after they got their *Nunc dimittis*, shows that there is often a way to stay in the place.

Lord Steel of Aikwood argued for compulsory retirement at eighty. 'That seems generous,' the 79-year-old former Liberal leader said. To those who observed that this would mean putting Lord Lawson of Blaby, eighty-five, out to pasture, Lord Steel replied, 'So what? There is nothing to stop him going on the airwaves or writing to the newspapers.'

Baroness Boothroyd, however, would be a great loss. Now eighty-eight, her hair still magnificent, her voice still dripping with Yorkshire common sense, if less piercing than in her Madame Speaker days, she said that she 'may be decrepit' but she won't be quitting yet. 'I shall go when the time comes, but I shall not go alone,' she warned. 'I intend to take others with me.' And she is damned if she will retire to make way for party hacks or donors.

Lord Selkirk of Douglas, a mere seventy-five, also wondered if eighty was a low threshold. He remarked that Lord Renton had died at the age of ninety-nine after sixty-two years in Parliament, when 'old age was beginning to creep up on him'. Lord Selkirk suggested that perhaps a cut-off date of 100 might be better. You don't want the place full of youngsters like him.

2018: THE ZOMBIE PARLIAMENT SHUFFLES ON

9 JANUARY
RESHUFFLE TURNS INTO A CAT FIGHT

Larry the Cat refused to budge. Theresa May had wanted to move the Downing Street old-timer from his perch on the radiator beside the front door. His kill rate is below target and most of the day he just wants to sleep. It was time to bring in some fresh fur. But Larry would not shift. In the battle of PM and puss, there would be only one winner.

Lest anyone think that Mrs May had spent an hour fruitlessly trying to sack a grumpy feline, she gave him a new title: minister for social mousing. Larry spent the rest of the day ordering new business cards; the Downing Street mice threw a party.

This set the tone for the rest of the day as Mrs May's reshuffle became more of a rebranding exercise. Ministers came and ministers went and generally it was the same people, just clutching an order form for new headed notepaper. It was the Night of the Prolonged Lives.

It had been briefed that Mrs May would appoint a minister for 'no deal'. What this actually meant was that none of her ministers would accept the deal she offered. The one person who left against her will chose to resign rather than move to the job that Mrs May intended.

Jeremy Hunt, it was decided after ninety minutes in triage, can still wear his NHS badge but will add a second one that says 'and social care'. Sajid Javid now has 'housing' as part of his title, to go with communities and local government, though it was already part of his job. Apparently it shows that the government takes housing seriously, although the potential change in acronym from CLG to HoCoLoGo made it sound like a West End nightclub.

Greg Clark (Con, Tunbridge Wells) was also in with the PM for ages, perhaps arguing that 'governance and exports' should be added to business, energy and industry in his title. Mrs May was tempted. If any member deserved to be Secretary of State for Beige it is the tepid Mr Clark. Even he talked the PM round. There are trade unions more adept at dismissing their colleagues than Mrs May.

For about thirty-seven seconds in the morning, Chris Grayling was apparently party chairman, a role that requires charisma, strategic vision and superb motivational skills. These are suits in which he holds only low cards. The lofty Mr Grayling's only possible qualification for the job would have been if someone had placed the rather dusty *Tory Guide to Winning Elections* on a high shelf and no one else could reach it.

Eventually, the affable Brandon Lewis (Con, Great Yarmouth) was named chairman and 'minister without porfolio'. A few minutes later, the announcement was removed from Twitter, then reposted. Another mistake? No, someone at Tory HQ just couldn't spell portfolio. You can see why the place needs a new broom.

Late in the day, Mr Grayling got the summons and was told that, after making a mess of the transport brief, he would, you guessed it, be staying on as Transport Secretary. I'm just surprised that he didn't ask for a new title to reflect current government concerns. He'd be an ideal minister for driverless cars, delayed runways and signal failures outside London Bridge.

12 JANUARY
MAY COMMUNES WITH NATURE

Theresa May had come to a wildlife reserve to talk about the environment, so naturally her speech was held indoors, well away from any fowl play that the photographers had planned for her.

Tarquin and Iolanthe, her advisers, had been sent ahead to scoop up any limping mallards that might hobble past, providing an awkward metaphor, and the news on the wetland's website that the redpolls had been doing well was played down. The feather report also spoke of snipe, pintails and a peregrine, although that might have been another press officer.

Everything had to be controlled, which meant that while we could hear all about the Great Outdoors, we weren't actually allowed to see it. 'It's wonderful to be here at a true oasis,' Mrs May began. And if you wiped the condensation off the windows and looked into the distance you might glimpse it. The only tweeting came from our phones.

There was, however, a nice backdrop of the countryside behind the Prime Minister to put us in the mood. It was like the time she took the press all the way to Florence to see her speak about Europe in front of a piece of office chipboard painted in the shade they call Think Tank Guff.

In fact, the speech was rather good and deserved our full attention, undistracted by all that pesky nature. In the front row, noisily lowing whenever his boss made a good point, sat Michael Gove, wearing a mint-green tie to go with his new reusable coffee cup. When Mr Gove has a new cause, he goes in with gusto.

Names of great champions of nature – Gilbert White, Stanley Spencer, Beatrix Potter, Shakespeare, Wordsworth, Constable – were drizzled throughout the text, rather than the customary lines of tedious Mayese, such as 'let me be very clear'. It made me wonder if a good chunk of it had been written by Mr Gove himself. It had a columnist's flourish.

The Prime Minister clearly shared its vision. She appeared to believe in what she was saying more than usual. Her eyes shone at the thought of the new Northern Forest that she wants to plant and the wildlife that Mr Gove will reintroduce. Otters and beavers and bears! Oh my!

A main sprig of her cause seems to have come straight from *The Graduate*. One imagined Mr Gove sitting her down. 'I want to say one word to you. Just one word.' Mrs May nodded. 'Are you listening?' Another nod. 'Plastics.' Unlike for Benjamin Braddock, however, there is not a great future in plastics. Mr Gove knows because he has been watching *Blue Planet*.

Eight million tonnes of plastic pour into the oceans each year. In Britain alone we waste enough single-use plastic each year to fill the Royal Albert Hall 1,000 times. 'In years to come, people will be shocked at how today we allow so much plastic to be produced needlessly,' Mrs May said. 'It is one of the great environmental scourges of our time.' And she is determined to tackle it. The power of Attenborough is mighty.

As Mrs May wound up in Barnes, Labour was staging its own wildlife stunt at London Zoo. Emily Thornberry leapt into the penguin enclosure for a photo. From afar, her motivation was unclear – perhaps Labour intends to rename emperors as the people's penguins – but it did at least provide an answer to the old question about what's black and white and red all over.

19 JANUARY
BRITAIN WELCOMES THE YOUNG NAPOLEON

Theresa May looked across at the fresh-faced Frenchman and reflected on what a difference a year makes. She had decades more experience than her guest – heck, she was old enough to be Emmanuel Macron's sister-in-law – but the balance of power had tipped.

Twelve months ago, Mrs May was heralded as a new Iron Lady for talking tough to Brussels while Mr Macron was a fringe candidate for the French presidency, just a young man with an Instagram following. Who can predict anything in politics these days? Mr Macron won. France went for that hopey-changey thing.

One month later, Mrs May blew an invincible poll position in her election and so here they were for a summit at Sandhurst looking like a rematch of Waterloo: the new Napoleon versus an old boot.

'*Je swee trez orreurs de vooz aquee*,' the Prime Minister told Mr Macron as they came out for their press conference at the end of an afternoon of talks. She didn't look all that '*heureuse*'. In the joint photograph of ministers outside the barracks beforehand, Mrs May had one of those slightly fake smiles on, the sort you see in wedding photos when someone has been placed next to a disastrous ex.

Perhaps Mr Macron had made a disobliging comment about the duck served at the Prime Minister's favourite pub that lunchtime, or maybe it was just the chilly weather, which was *comme singes en cuivre* (brass monkeys), as they say in the less refined parts of Paris.

Some had come prepared. Jean-Yves Le Drian, the French Foreign Minister, wore a puffer jacket without shame. Boris Johnson, his opposite number, appeared much broader above the waistline than below, as if he had strapped a few hot water bottles around his chest under the jacket. Philip Hammond, the Chancellor, had apparently borrowed a coat from a general who was two sizes bigger than him.

Gavin Williamson, the Defence Secretary, hoped to impress the military on their home turf by wearing neither a coat nor a jumper and leaving his jacket unbuttoned. Matt Hancock, the Culture Secretary, looked absurdly pleased just to be there, beaming in the back row like a fourth-former invited to play for the first XI during an injury crisis.

Once they were inside, Mrs May tried to speak with warmth about her guest and his country. *Ententes cordiales* were flung around. 'We have a uniquely close relationship,' she said. 'Lots of Britons live in France.' Lord Lawson of Blaby and Peter Lilley for two, who love the land of their second home so much that they campaigned for Brexit.

She welcomed, of course, Mr Macron's generous loan of the Bayeux Tapestry and said this would be 'only the start of a cultural exchange'. They're giving us an embroidery of the Battle of Hastings; we'll offer a box set of *'Allo 'Allo* and a subscription to *Viz*. '*Magnifique*,' Mr Macron replied.

He wants to use the tapestry as a symbol of our future ventures rather than a relic of the past. 'It is an invitation for us to be humble,' he said. 'See how much creativity the tapestry represents. We are making a new tapestry together.' Hopefully this one won't end with the British leader getting one in the eye from the French and the slogan '*hic Theresa interfecta est*'.

And so, yet again, another UKIP leader leaves the stage.

23 JANUARY
SO BAD, EVEN FARAGE CRINGES

Henry Bolton hung a 'Do not disturb' sign on the outside handle of his hotel door, removed his trousers and put them in the Corby for a quick pressing, then helped himself to a complimentary finger of shortbread before facing his radio interview with Nigel Farage. Grimly, Mr Bolton began to dial the number, then suddenly put the receiver down. He kept forgetting to press nine for an outside line.

Earlier, Mr Bolton had emerged from the seaside hotel where he now lives since leaving his wife for a 25-year-old racist and told the press that he would not be standing down as UKIP leader. The party's executive committee had told him to go and half of his spokesmen had resigned. All he had left was his defiance. 'It is time to put an end to infighting,' he declared, and so he would be removing anyone in a position of power who wants him to resign. The committee had lost his confidence, not the other way round, and thus they must be replaced. There's only fourteen of them, he later told Mr Farage. 'But 4,000 voted for me.' It doesn't sound like many.

'It is time to drain the swamp,' this Folkestone Poundland version of Donald Trump concluded. Not that UKIP has enough members to form a swamp. 'Wring out the bar towel' might have been better.

The resignations had come in steadily throughout the day. Four MEPs and a few former and present deputy leaders took turns to stick daggers into Mr Bolton. *Et tu*, the tenth Earl of Dartmouth? David Kurten, the little-known education spokesman, also resigned and was immediately installed as the bookies' favourite 'Kurten's for UKIP' had a certain ring to it.

Others may not even have existed. Hands up who had heard of David Meacock, the now former culture spokesman? Someone called Star Anderton, who had been the equalities spokeswoman, claimed to have resigned two weeks ago but no one noticed so she was doing it again. At least Stuart Agnew was loyal. The agriculture spokesman said he would not follow the herd.

After refusing questions from the press, Mr Bolton went back into the hotel, checked the evening specials in the restaurant and returned to his room to call Mr Farage's radio show, where he was told by the former UKIP leader that he had turned the party 'into a soap opera'.

'It's getting to the level of being a liiiiitle bit cringeworthy,' Mr Farage said, which is like being told by a professional darts player that you're putting on weight. 'How are you getting through it?' Mr Bolton explained that 'the occasional whisky does help'. A sad image formed of a selection of miniature bottles lined up on the desk in front of him, ready for an evening reshuffle. Who needs David Meacock and the tenth Earl of Dartmouth when you have Jack Daniel and Johnnie Walker?

31 JANUARY
HOPE AND PANNICK CREATE PEER PRESSURE

When Britain really ruled the waves, as W. S. Gilbert wrote, 'the House of Peers made no pretence to intellectual eminence'. Britain set the world ablaze, he went on, while the same 'did nothing in particular – and did it very well'. How timely that a new production of *Iolanthe* opens at the Coliseum next month.

To the red end of Parliament, then, where 191 peers, a record number, had signed up to debate the EU (Withdrawal) Bill. 'This is not about revisiting the arguments of the referendum,' Baroness Evans of Bowes Park, the Leader of the House, pleaded. Fat chance.

There they all were: Lord Has-Been, Lord Claimform, Baroness Toady and dozens of Lib Dems, all desperate to have their six minutes' worth on the withdrawal from the EU. 'We are experts at being boring,' Lord Hill of Oareford said, knowing his comrades well.

This is the cut and paste bill, the means by which European law becomes British law after Brexit. It was originally called the Great Repeal Bill, as big a misnomer as Lord Adonis, who wants a second referendum. Quoting George Orwell, he said 'political language is designed to make lies sound truthful and to give an appearance of solidity to pure wind'. There was certainly a lot of the latter. After almost three hours, the peers 'adjourned during pleasure', which sounds filthy but is just Lords slang for 'strapped on the nosebag'. Only twenty-four had spoken by this point.

The Lord Bishop of Leeds was concerned by how the referendum had torn 'the veneer of civilised discourse in this country and unleashed an undisguised language of suspicion, denigration, hatred and vilification'. Leavers are stupid and narrow-minded, Remainers are traitors (or so he characterised the arguments); he prayed for moderation.

At least you get restrained debate in the Lords. None of that ugly cat-calling and jeering that we see at the plebeian end of Parliament, although there were a few subtle digs. Lord Patten of Barnes, who lamented the way the EU has torn his tribe, said that 'loyalty is the secret weapon of the Conservative Party – sometimes so secret it can barely be discerned by the human eye'.

In a typically boisterous speech Lord Pearson of Rannoch, the former UKIP leader, railed against the 'silly mirage' that the EU ensures peace in Europe, to which Lord Foulkes of Cumnock sniffed, 'That was the comedy interlude.'

Lord Pearson was one of two Ukippers in action; there was also Lord Willoughby de Broke, whose name reflects his party's finances. I started to look for other apt names on the speakers' list but the Earl of Sandwich, Lord Crisp and Baroness Young of Old Scone just made me feel peckish. Baroness Northover then noted that three of the lords putting pressure on the government over the bill are called Hope, Judge and Pannick.

On they went, round and round. It was ninety-six down by the close of play, ninety-five to come today. Lots of words, little progress. As Lord Bridges sighed with feeling, 'The years of Brexit are like dog years – each one feels like seven.'

1 FEBRUARY
TRAPPED ROBIN PLEADS FOR MAY TO BE RELEASED HUMANELY

The Commons was far from full as we neared Prime Minister's Questions – surprisingly empty, in fact, considering the absence of Theresa May and Jeremy Corbyn, those no-score-draws in human form – when MPs were roused from their lethargy by a sudden invasion.

A robin! Flitting back and forth across the chamber, dancing from perch to perch, this red-breasted visitor had somehow sneaked past the serjeant at arms. Like children who spy snow out of the classroom window, MPs stopped pretending to listen to the Welsh Secretary and started pointing in excitement. All tweeting was briefly suspended, except, perhaps, by the robin.

This made a change from the usual birds of ill omen that we see in the press gallery, such as that albatross that Mrs May has been forced to carry since the referendum. Robins are said to be lucky, symbolising life and new starts. Sod's law the Prime Minister was in China when it appeared.

Emily Thornberry was not flustered by the sideshow. The shadow Foreign Secretary, taking Mr Corbyn's place at PMQs while David Lidington stood in for Mrs May, gave herself a preen and hopped up to the dispatch box. When Lidders had last deputised for Mrs May thirteen months ago, she said, the Tories held a seventeen-point lead in the polls and, as Leader of the House, he had joked about Labour being in chaos.

'Well, woddadiffrensayearmakes,' Ms Thornberry crowed in that wonderfully sassy way of hers, part Miss Piggy, part Pink Lady in *Grease*.

The robin, now watching from a light fitting, did not seem all that impressed. Nor was Mr Lidington. 'What a delight to see her still there,' he said, hamming it up a bit, when no fewer than ninety-seven members of Labour's front bench have been sacked or resigned under Mr Corbyn. 'I pay credit to her sticking power.'

Ms Thornberry wanted to know when the government will allow sixteen-year-olds the vote, something the Tories aren't keen on because young people will only go and waste their cross on the other lot. It is an easy win for Labour on social media, a promise that will win support without carrying any awkward cost implications. Before question time had finished, a party video about extending the franchise to those doing their GCSEs was circulating online.

Mr Lidington observed that the last Labour government had raised the legal age for buying cigarettes and fireworks and for using a sunbed to eighteen – without acknowledging that using a stubby pencil is perhaps less likely to cause injury – and said that the voting age is eighteen in twenty-six of the other EU members as well as the United States, Canada and Australia. Pah, facts!

When he tried to point out that Labour were just playing a rather cynical game, Ms Thornberry made it sound as if the Tories want to deprive young people of their mobile phones, a breach of their human rights. 'They are the coalition of cavemen,' she scoffed with glee. Love her or loathe her, but she is so much better at this than her boss. 'Oh, grow up,' Mr Lidington huffed, losing the high ground with his final reply. God knows what the robin made of it all.

In the briefing room at the back of the chamber, where hacks go to be told what MPs had meant to say after questions, an official spokesman said that the Prime Minister hoped this unexpected visitor would be 'rescued in a humane fashion and released outside'. Funnily enough, a spokesman for the robin later said exactly the same about Mrs May.

2 FEBRUARY
MR DOGSBODY TAKES LEADING ROLE IN FARCE

You may not be all that familiar with Steve Baker, the Brexit minister. He's a tall chap with badgery hair who resembles one of those cruise-ship singers who croon about wanting a 'deep and special partnership' while looking into the eyes of women of a certain age. In his own mind he is rather more A-list. Apparently he told fellow MPs recently that he would like to be played by Ben Affleck, Batman himself, in a Hollywood film of the Brexit saga. In reality, he's more a batman with a lowercase B, employed to clean up after David Davis.

It must be a frustrating life for Mr Dogsbody, sent to the dispatch box whenever the Brexit Secretary has put his foot in his mouth. You can understand why he craved to perform his own dontopedalogy. Yesterday, he got his chance. Jacob Rees-Mogg, who will surely be played by a resurrected Charles Hawtrey, is upset that the civil service are not playing cricket.

He asked Mr Baker to confirm a rumour that the Treasury 'have deliberately developed a model [of analysis] to show that all options other than staying in the customs union are bad'. In other words, will he confirm that his officials are up to no good? Mr Baker rose slowly and laid his hands on the dispatch box. 'I am sorry to say,' he said, 'that my honourable friend's account is essentially correct.' Sitting beside him, Mr Davis gave a sudden, uncontrolled wince, looked up at the ceiling and then shot his junior a Captain Mainwaring sort of glare. You stupid boy.

The backtracking began almost immediately. 'At the time, I considered it implausible,' Mr Baker insisted. 'Civil servants are careful to uphold impartiality. We must proceed with caution. It would be quite extraordinary if it turned out that such a thing had happened.'

'You said it was correct!' protested Labour's Paul Blomfield (Sheffield Central). 'I said it was correct that the allegation was put to me,' Mr Baker clarified. 'I did not seek to confirm the truth of it.' But if anyone wants to think that it may be true then that's, of course, up to them.

Next to Mr Baker, Robin Walker appeared rather relieved that it had not been him at the dispatch box juggling with this hot potato. Mr Walker, who is crying out to be played in the film by a young Tim Brooke-Taylor, is often asked to clean up the department's mess whenever Mr Baker's bucket is full. His method is to say everything very quickly in the hope that no one ever notices what he says.

In fact, should Hollywood not show an interest in making *Article 50: Brexageddon*, this whole saga could be recreated as a Gilbert and Sullivan sort of comic opera, with Mr Walker employed to sing the patter song.

'Here's a first-rate opportunity to reject Europe's community,' he would sing, 'and indulge in the felicity of a break from synchronicity. We shall quickly all be brexified, monetary gains unspecified. Though it looks like asininity, we'll defend it to infinity.'

Then he would do a little dance, Mr Baker would sing a madrigal, Mr Davis would announce that by an implausible twist Britain had never actually joined the EU in the first place and everyone would get married. I think we have a hit.

8 FEBRUARY
ELLIS THE LICKSPITTLE DIGS IN

Politics finally went through the looking glass yesterday and everything was turned on its head. Jeremy Corbyn asked a series of pithy questions at PMQs and praised the words of a Tory right-winger, who himself then called for help for vulnerable people, before Dennis Skinner described the Tony Blair years as a 'golden period'. It could not have been more weird if Jacob Rees-Mogg had sung the 'Ode to Joy'.

Mr Corbyn avoided asking about Brexit for the sixth successive week, since it's all going so well, and went instead on what was supposedly Theresa May's specialist subject. 'With crime rising, does the Prime Minister regret cutting 21,000 police officers?' he asked. A decent opener. Mrs May disputed his assertion.

'Actually crime is at record low levels,' she said. Surely one of them was wrong. It all depends on which figures you read. Philip Davies (Con, Shipley) must have been reading the same reports as Mr Corbyn, for a comment he made last month about the lack of police resources was then deployed by the Labour leader. Mr Davies gave Mr Corbyn a thumbs-up.

'I never thought I would see the day when where I lead, the Leader of the Opposition follows,' the Tory said a few minutes later. 'There is hope for him yet.' This scourge of political correctness, melter of snowflakes, a man who makes the *Daily Mail* look like a wishy-washy liberal rag, then called on the PM to revive the abolished post of disability commissioner. Jaws dropped.

It was followed by Mr Skinner singing a hymn to the Third Way. The Blair years, this veteran Trot said, were 'the best period anyone in the NHS had ever experienced'. He called on the Chancellor to be more like Gordon Brown. Curiouser and curiouser.

At least amid all this topsy-turvy there was one politician on whom we could rely. Michael Ellis is the champion toady in the Commons, beating stiff competition from the likes of Chris Philp, who gave the PM another good slurping, and Rebecca Pow (Con, Taunton Deane), who is always telling us how government initiatives will be 'a real fillip for the people of Taunton Deane'.

Mr Ellis, wearing a grey check suit that made him look like a 1950s bingo-caller, has a talent for gasping and pointing that recently earned him promotion to the most junior role in the culture team: minister for first nights and openings. His dream job.

He was lounging lazily on the backbenches yesterday when something that the PM said made him spring to life. Mrs May told the House that Andy Burnham, the former shadow Home Secretary, had once said that police budgets could be cut by 10 per cent. There came a loyal bellowing from over her shoulder. 'Aha! Yes!' Mr Ellis roared. 'Ten per cent!' And he stabbed his finger at Labour.

He then turned his attention to another of his talents, excavating his nostrils like Schliemann at Troy, and waited for the next opportunity. It came from the response to Mr Philp's sycophancy on Brexit. Mr Ellis wrenched his finger from his nose, sending flecks of dried snot over his neighbours, and did the 'aha!' routine again.

A third turn came when Mrs May said she would take no lessons from Labour on the abuse of MPs. 'Exactly!' brayed Mr Ellis. 'Disgraceful! Apologise!' The finger jabbed and jabbed. It was a performance we in the gallery have seen many times, but on a day when Mr Davies became the champion of the weak and Mr Skinner outed himself as a Blairite, such trademark lickspittling was rather reassuring.

While Jeremy Corbyn's sympathies for Mother Russia were hardly hidden, it was claimed in February 2018 that he had been an informant for the Czech communists during the 1980s. Mr Corbyn, who according to a file in the Czech archives was given the codename Agent Cob, admitted meeting a Czech agent but said he thought he was just a diplomat.

22 FEBRUARY
THE SPY WHO CAME IN FROM THE COLD FRAME

Agent Corn-on-the-Cob shook off the virtual snow from his boots, handed his ushanka to an aide and went up to the doorkeeper. 'In Moscow, April is a cold month,' he whispered. 'Yer wot?' the custodian replied. 'My lighter needs more fuel,' the arrival tried. 'Eh?' came the response. The agent sighed. 'I'm here for PMQs.'

'Oh, go right in, Mr Corbyn,' the Commons official said. Then, as the Leader of the Opposition headed to the chamber, the doorkeeper muttered, 'Every bloody week…'

The idea that Jeremy Corbyn was the Kim Philby of the 1980s is slightly absurd. If he belongs in a John le Carré novel it would be *The Constant Gardener*, though he doesn't spend as much time on the allotment as he would like. Spectre – the Special Executive for Courgettes, Tomatoes, Radishes and Endives – is having to manage without him. He is the spy who came in from the cold frame.

Still, there he is, firing shots at M across the dispatch box every Wednesday. Most go into his own foot but yesterday he hit the target by asking about Brexit. David Davis had tried to reassure people that life outside the EU would not be a '*Mad Max*-style world borrowed from dystopian fiction'. Mr Corbyn asked if the Brexit Secretary could not set the bar 'just a little bit higher'. Theresa May did her usual trick of ignoring the question and saying, 'I've been very clear.'

As usual, Mr Corbyn didn't bother with a question on his sixth and final rising. He prefers to shout something that can be clipped for social media. The Speaker should tell him off for not asking something. Mrs May could have ignored him, but she had a spy joke prepared. 'Normally he asks me to sign a blank cheque,' she said. 'I know he likes Czechs, but really…' This 'cheques-it means Czechs-it' twist on her usual mantra was not all that good but the troops loved it.

Agent Cob had no chance to reply. As James Bond was fond of saying, 'That's a Smith & Wesson [Cockney rhyming slang for "PMQs session"]. And you've had your six.'

23 FEBRUARY
WALKER GOES FOR A QUICK RUN

While the Cabinet headed to Chequers for Brexit boot camp, where they played 'pin the fail on the Boris' and a game of 'I went to the single market' in which no one could even think of anything they wanted beginning with A, it was left to Robin Walker to face the inquisition of Sir Bill Cash.

Sitting under an enormous portrait of the first Duke of Wellington, regarded by Sir Bill as very sound on European domination, the chairman of the European Scrutiny Committee grilled Mr Walker, a junior Brexit minister, about how much longer we must toil under the Brussels yoke.

Sir Bill is concerned about this implementation period after Brexit. 'It could be as long as a piece of string!' Sir Bill exclaimed. German string at that.

Mr Walker shook his head and spoke quickly. I think he disagreed, though it is hard to tell with him. Words flow from the Walker mouth like the Severn through his Worcester constituency during a spring tide. Take this reply to Darren Jones (Lab, Bristol North West), who asked him to confirm that Britain will still have to abide by EU law and contribute to its budget during implementation. I give the minister's response with little punctuation and no spacing since he didn't use any. 'Wellit'sa time-limitedextensionoftheexistingrulesandregulationsasthe PrimeMinistersetoutinherFlorencespeech,' he said, 'andofcourse we'vealreadyreachedthatagreementintermsofcovering theUK'scommitmentsunderthemulti-annualfinancialframe-work.'

'So … yes?' an unsure Mr Jones replied. The minister let fly again. 'The committee likes clear answers, Minister,' Mr Jones said. Again the Walker lips whirred. 'Yeeees. You've just said that,' Mr Jones scolded.

The minister may speak in fast-forward mode but the committee was concerned that the Brexit team is dragging its feet. 'Why not get on with it?' Kate Hoey said. 'I don't think the public will think there is much momentum.'

'Show some backbone!' urged Sir Bill. 'We give the EU too much respect,' added Ms Hoey. 'The British government always gives in.' Poor Mr Walker could only blink and burble.

In late February 2018, Britain shivered under a cold snap that brought heavy snows and was labelled The Beast from the East.

1 MARCH
NO BUSINESS LIKE SNOW BUSINESS

The Beast from the East whipped across Westminster, striking the crumbling old building with such force that snow even fell inside one of the corridors, but nothing will have made them shiver in Downing Street like the Flurry from Surrey as Sir John Major threw snowballs at the Prime Minister. Snowballs with pebbles at their heart.

It was a very polite mugging, laced with those archaic expressions that Sir John has always been fond of, such as 'we are now the laggard at the bottom' and 'I'll have no truck with that', but the blows were meant to sting. Sir John is not altogether unperturbed, as he would say, by the way Theresa May is handling things.

'I don't say this to be critical,' the former Prime Minister insisted, but you don't write lines like 'this is not only grand folly, it is bad politics' without wanting to draw blood. You don't call Britain's negotiating strategy 'not credible' or suggest that any half-decent opposition would be fifteen points ahead in the polls without seeking to be a little censorious.

What happened to the Prime Minister who once told his party not to bind his hands when negotiating with Europe? Sir John used to hate back-seat drivers. He once called Margaret Thatcher's criticism of his decisions in office 'intolerable'. Yesterday, however, he reached across Mrs May's shoulder, grabbed the steering wheel and tried to spin the car around. A risky manoeuvre in these icy conditions.

He flung snowballs not just at Mrs May but at her whole Brexit team. Michael Gove took a glancer to his ear – 'I'm rather in favour of experts,' Sir John said – while the grand claims made a few months ago by Boris Johnson and David Davis were shown to be as slippery as my driveway yesterday morning.

The Foreign Secretary also got a withering rebuke for his suggestion that sorting out the border in Northern Ireland would be no harder than arranging a congestion charge zone that covered Camden and Westminster. 'I will not comment on that,' Sir John said. 'I would still like to be a serious politician.' Ouch.

In the Commons earlier, MPs shivered as they waited for Prime Minister's Questions, which usually resembles Narnia, whether there is snow on the ground or not, as Mr Tumnus begs the White Witch to ensure that it will be always Christmas and never winter.

Clive Lewis (Lab, Norwich South) was wearing a padded gilet under his jacket and glorious knitwear abounded. Jeremy Corbyn was wearing hiking boots, having trekked in from the frozen tundra of Islington. He asked six questions about Brexit, but it didn't cause the avalanche he was hoping for. As Sir John later showed, a few gentle but barbed comments can do much more damage than shouting.

14 MARCH

CHANCELLOR HAMMOND HAS A SPRING IN HIS STEP

It was half past twelve; time for a little smackerel of something, as Pooh would say, and the Chancellor bounced in full of enthusiasm. 'I am at my most positively Tigger-like today,' Philip Hammond told MPs. 'If there are any Eeyores in the chamber, they are on the opposition benches.'

The wonderful thing about Chancellors, he explained, is that Chancellors are wonderful things! Their growth forecasts are made out of rubber! Their deficit reduction plans are made out of springs! They're bouncy trouncy flouncy pouncy fun fun fu... Well, you get the message.

Under the Conservatives, Mr Hammond said, the sun will always shine on the Hundred Acre Wood (or Seventy-Five Acre Wood after Brexit). If Labour took control, he warned, heffalumps and woozles would come for your hunny. Jeremy Corbyn gave a stage yawn. He prefers his Milnes to be of the Seumas variety.

There were not many jokes in Fiscal Phil's statement but it was mercifully short. He seemed to include one section on innovation just so that he could make fun of Matt Hancock, who is now an app as well as a Culture Secretary, and there was the obligatory Red Book gag, now rather tired, about John McDonnell liking Chairman Mao.

The funniest line, or at least the one that drew the most laughter from Labour MPs, was when he said that 'we have made substantial progress in our negotiations with the EU'. There were lots of aspirations, though. Plenty of 'looking at' this and 'consulting on' that. 'Get on with it,' one Labour backbencher shouted, while another suggested that his big infrastructure idea was to 'build more long grass' to kick things into.

In reply, Mr McDonnell justified his Eeyore image. 'Good afternoon,' his expression seemed to say. 'If it is a good afternoon. Which I doubt.' He called the speech astoundingly complacent. 'We face in every public service a crisis on a scale we have never seen before. Has he not listened to the doctors, nurses, teachers, police officers, carers and even his own councillors?'

Attacking Tory hecklers as 'bully boys' (Mr Pot, meet Mr Kettle), he said it was 'indefensible' for the Chancellor to congratulate himself on improved forecasts while councils went bust, school budgets were cut and homelessness had doubled.

Mr Hammond's rebuttal seemed to have been written in advance. Rather than busking from a few scribbled notes, as usual, he read from a typed script, attacking Mr McDonnell for presenting the 'smooth reassuring mien of a bank manager', masking 'the sinister ideology beneath'. As he went on and on, Mr McDonnell mimed a typing gesture. 'He's making a second speech,' he protested to Mr Speaker.

Mr Hammond did not care. His second speech, rather better crafted than his first, set out the ideological differences. 'No one watching our exchanges can be in any doubt that Britain faces a choice,' he said.

What a choice, though. Tigger or Eeyore? An overexcitable fantasist or a moaning pessimist? Give me a humble, decent, kind-hearted bear of very little brain any day. In difficult times, the nation needs a Winnie. In the absence of Churchill, I'd take Pooh. Tiddely pom.

16 MARCH
PRIVATE PIKE FIRES HIS PEASHOOTER AT THE KREMLIN

Is this what they mean by a 'robust dialogue'? Making his first appearance of this crisis, the Defence Secretary was asked how bad things might get. Now was the moment to prove his mettle. 'Frankly,' Gavin Williamson declared, 'Russia should go away and shut up.' He resisted the urge to add, 'And yah boo sucks to you, Putin.'

Moments of national emergency call for great oratory. Edward Murrow wrote that Winston Churchill 'mobilised the English language and sent it into battle'. Mr Williamson clipped it round the ear and told it to meet him behind the bike sheds at break.

Perhaps he thought that such words would sound tough. Maybe they would have been if delivered in something other than a squeaky Yorkshire accent. He sounded like a young Alan Bennett after taking a cricket ball in the box. They will not be tremblin' in the Kremlin.

If his attack seemed puerile, it was also ungenerous given that the wife of one of Mr Putin's former cronies had bid £30,000 for dinner with Mr Williamson at a recent Tory auction. Maybe he thinks he is worth more. The same woman once paid £160,000 to play tennis with Boris Johnson. 'Sigh… OK, I'll do it,' a fuming Mr Williamson will have told Tory HQ. 'But just two courses. And no coffee.'

Still, his playground taunt got Mr Williamson, the Private Pike of the government platoon, a place on the news. Not since he won Regional Salesman of the Year in his former career after flogging a shop-soiled Vulcan 2000 fireplace for more than list price has he earned such attention for a really weak burn.

20 MARCH
BREXITEERS BEWARE BARNIER'S BONHOMIE

Michel Barnier was in a jolly mood. Positively perky. He looked like a Frenchman who had arrived late for lunch and discovered that the chef had just received a large and particularly ripe Livarot denied to earlier diners. All was *en fête chez Michel*. This did not bode well.

'*Bonjour*, allo, good to be back here for this – ah – little press event,' the EU's lead negotiator told journalists in Brussels. '*Je suis très heureux*.' This was a bit of a vowel shift for Mr Barnier. The last time he did a little press event his emotion had been more *horreur*.

Mr Barnier began by praising David Davis. 'I applaud the whole of the UK negotiating team for their commitment and competence,' he said. Their efforts had resulted in what he called 'a decisive step'.

Ta-dah! A document suddenly appeared on the screen behind him, colour-coded to show the progress that had been made. 'The writing is symbolically on the wall,' he said, which made me think of the bad omen that appeared at Belshazzar's feast, but was presumably a reference to the streaks of green across the pages, indicating areas in which they agree.

Mr Davis's expression was more one of 'oo-er' then *heureux* as he began to contemplate the difficult discussions that would follow with his backbenchers. Negotiations involve give and take but had he given away too much? There was already a nasty whiff coming from the British fishing ports.

He looked like a man who had been told to be happy but wasn't quite sure why. 'It's an *entente cordiale*, sir,' an aide might have explained after the agreement was concluded and Mr Davis will have nodded earnestly, assuming that this was something to do with drinking squash under canvas.

'It is a powerful vision,' he said. 'Ambitious. This will allow us to sign and ratify new deals with old friends and new allies for the first time in more than forty years. We are seizing one of Brexit's greatest opportunities.'

It will be, he said, 'a trade deal like no other in the world … the biggest, most comprehensive trade deal ever' but we will not have much time in which to sort it out. Theresa May had wanted twenty-four months after Brexit Day to get our affairs in order, the EU offered twenty-one and so we settled on twenty-one. A green line was drawn through the PM's red one.

When it was suggested that this did not seem a very long time – with Mr Barnier helpfully observing that Britain will have to renegotiate 750 international agreements that the EU has with third parties – Mr Davis bizarrely said that we should 'just look at some of the things Chile has done' in the world of speedy trade deals. Perhaps they get a boost in performance from negotiating at altitude, or maybe their economy, ranked No. 43 by the IMF, is a little less complicated. Just to be safe, let's send Liam Fox up a mountain for the next two years.

21 MARCH
GOVE GETS A GRILLING AND BATTERING

Michael Gove looked a bit green around the gills. The Environment Secretary had been sent into the Commons to defend the latest position on Brexit, even though he tended to agree with those who carp about it being bad for the fishing industry. 'The EU's intransigence was disappointing,' he said. 'I make no bones about it.' Deboned and gutted, Mr Gove lay there on the slab, waiting to be battered.

An urgent question had been granted to Alistair Carmichael (LD, Orkney and Shetland), who said that 'the mood in fishing communities today is one of palpable anger'. The government had promised them that they would be free from EU quotas come the end of March 2019, but now they will be stuck in the system for a further year on worse terms than they have at the moment.

Mr Gove acknowledged their anger. He reminded MPs that brine was in his blood. His father was a fishmonger, his grandparents went to sea to fish. He spends every waking hour watching *Blue Planet II*. He wants to be the champion of the fisherfolk – one day the world will hear his great 'I have a bream' speech – but sometimes you have to accept a short-term stitch-up, even if you're a Kipper.

The SNP members, minnows compared with Sturgeon and Salmond, created a lot of noise. 'What a load of codswallop,' said Pete Wishart. 'They're throwing our fishing industry over the side,' wailed Drew Hendry (Inverness, Nairn, Badenoch and Strathspey).

This charge really got up Mr Gove's nose. He said that the SNP 'have a damn cheek' to moan when they want Britain to stay in the EU. He added that their party 'has raised grievance to an art form', which reminded me of P. G. Wodehouse's famous line about rays of sunshine and Scotsmen. It clearly inspired John Bercow, too, for the Speaker soon piped up to tell the House that Jeeves always said that eating fish was good for the brain.

Labour MPs were also cross. They can often smell when there is blood in the water. 'Who was negotiating this?' demanded Kate Hoey, who can be a bit of a red snapper. 'Did they care about fishing?' Chi Onwurah (Newcastle upon Tyne Central) said that no one should have believed that the Tories would prioritise a deal on fishing over one on finance.

Mr Gove's biggest problem, though, was the shoal of angry Scotsmen sitting to his right. Douglas Ross (Con, Moray) repeated that there was no way he could sell this as a good deal to his voters. John Lamont (Con, Berwickshire, Roxburgh and Selkirk) said, 'Like many fishermen, I feel badly let down by this deal.' John Redwood, who isn't Scottish but likes a good moan, told the government to 'just get on with it'.

Mr Gove tried to reel them all in with a reminder that Britain will be fully out of the common fisheries policy by the end of 2020, which is more than other parties have offered. 'The opportunities available to us after the transition deal are critical,' he told them. 'We must keep our eyes on the prize.' Never mind the pollocks, hear the Brex pistol.

30 MARCH
BLAIR URGES PEOPLE TO THINK AGAIN

The will of the people is fickle. Stars rise and fall and so do political causes. When Tony Blair talks about people growing disillusioned with politicians who fail to deliver a bright tomorrow, he speaks from experience. Ironically, the thing that could be most likely to shore up national opinion in favour of Brexit is Mr Blair saying that we should reject it.

That will not stop him trying. Yesterday, with a year to go until B-Day, when supporters of Brexit claim that the stain of Brussels' rule will be washed away by the douche of democracy, the former Prime Minister kicked off a conference on Britain's place in a changing Europe by demanding a second referendum.

His call went down well inside the hall but most of these seemed to be believers already. A woman sitting next to me wore blue mittens with gold stars across the knuckles. Mr Blair would have needed only to sing '*Freude, schöner*' to this crowd and a cry of '*Götterfunken*' would have come in reply as sure as armagnac follows cheese at lunch with Jean-Claude Juncker.

The problem for Mr Blair is winning over those who sent him to Downing Street three times with a huge majority but now consider him to be as trustworthy as an Australian cricketer with a sheet of sandpaper.

Like Cassandra standing beside the Trojan Horse and asking if anyone could hear bouzouki music, Mr Blair predicted disaster – but how many will believe him? His voice now rather gravelly, his grey hair receding so he has begun to resemble Alec Douglas-Home, Mr Blair said that Britain was too small to prosper on its own in the twenty-first century. 'To give up a huge alliance on our doorstep is an extraordinarily self-defeating act,' he said. The EU had been created by his father's generation to ensure peace in Europe; now it was needed to preserve the old world's power.

'We shouldn't kid ourselves. The rest of the world do not see

[Brexit] as globally ambitious. They really don't. They think: "Brits, you guys were always commonsense people."' The idea that Britain can get the benefits of the single market without following its rules is for the birds.

'It's known as cakeism,' he explained. 'And the EU is not going to agree to that. At some point, it will become clear that cakeism is not on the menu.'

So Parliament should reject whatever deal the Prime Minister could get, he advised, because it wouldn't be all that good, and then Mrs May, far from resigning after a defeat, should use this rejection as an excuse to give the final decision back to the public on the question of 'take the deal or stay in the EU'.

It would be the Conservatives' best chance of winning the next general election, he added. If Brexit is to happen, let the public own it, knowing exactly what it means.

'I've got a feeling that the 17 million who voted to leave are going to be short on gratitude [come the election in 2022],' Mr Blair said, 'and the 16 million who voted to remain are going to be long on memory.' If the Tories pushed Brexit through without a referendum on the final deal, it would create bitterness against them and be the 'gateway to a Corbyn government'. This, he implied, would be almost as ghastly as Brexit.

That Mr Blair is giving strategic advice on winning elections to the Tories may be one reason that he never gets invited to karaoke night at the Labour Party conference these days, but there was some logic to his argument. He believes that everyone can have second thoughts. After all, when he first stood to be an MP in 1983 his own manifesto said he wanted to leave the European Economic Community.

The war against Islamic State trundled on. Theresa May was forced to seek Parliament's approval for missile strikes on chemical weapons sites in Syria.

18 APRIL
BERCOW GOES ON A BOMBING MISSION

This must be what they mean by the fog of war. At the end of an emergency debate on whether Parliament should be consulted before military action, Jeremy Corbyn moved a motion that the matter had been 'considered', then whipped his MPs to vote against it and show that it hadn't.

To confuse things further, he had ended his speech by calling on MPs to approve his motion, even though he didn't want them to, making this possibly the first time that the Tories had ever done what he asked.

Syria has not been under-debated, even if it was shutting the hangar door after the PM had bombed. Over two days MPs spent ten hours on it; an hour and a quarter for each bomb. Mr Corbyn made one of his better speeches. Holes could be picked in his argument, but it was not the usual string of petulant tribal whines.

Jacob Rees-Mogg said this had all been sorted out in the Glorious Revolution. He's become a modernist since he joined Twitter. The Tory argued that it would have been better procedurally for Mr Corbyn to call a vote of no confidence if he felt the PM lacked support. 'I think democracy can go forward even from 1688,' Mr Corbyn replied. The Mogg seemed sceptical.

Mr Corbyn's speech was punctuated by repeated blasts from the chair. The Speaker's finger is always on the trigger when it comes to noisy Tories. Mark Francois had been on his radar for decades. 'He used to misbehave thirty years ago when he stood against me in Conservative student politics,' John Bercow announced as he fired a missile at Rayleigh and Wickford.

North Dorset got it next, again with a student anecdote. Simon Hoare had been at Oxford with Mrs Speaker. 'She says he was a well-behaved young man,' Mr Bercow grumbled. 'He seems to have regressed since then.' Boom!

More bombs fell on the Forest of Dean – 'Resume your seat, Mr Harper, you do not stand when I am standing and that is the end of it.' – and Elmet and Rothwell when the Speaker leapt from his chair to tell Alec Shelbrooke to shut up or get out. 'I am not having you shouting out,' he said. 'You are over-excitable and need to contain yourself.'

Mr Shelbrooke could have replied that the same was true of Mr Speaker, but he might have gone nuclear. Boom! Boom! Boom! Bomber Bercow was in his element.

25 APRIL
HANDEL WITH CARE: THE MOGG IS MAKING THREATS

Jake 'The Filibuster' Rees-Mogg looked at the Pugin wallpaper and busts of dead legislators and whistled softly. 'Nice little upper chamber you've got here,' the whistle seemed to suggest. 'Verrrry nice. I would hate for anything to happen to it. Amazing how delicate some of these neo-gothic edifices can be.'

He wasn't wrong there. Only last week a large piece of masonry had fallen 200 feet from a stone angel on the Victoria Tower at the Lords end of Parliament, almost causing a by-election in the hereditary peerage. An accident they say, but was that a chisel-shaped bulge under The Filibuster's double-breasted suit or a rolled-up Hansard? Perhaps it had been a warning. Amend the Brexit legislation at your peril.

Mr Rees-Mogg was speaking in Parliament to a think tank and it was clear that recent votes in the Lords had got his dander up. The impertinence of these popinjay peers, many of them with EU pensions, to think that they could defy the Will of the British People! The Tory backbencher made it clear where this defiance would lead. 'Their lordships are playing with fire,' he warned. 'And it would be a shame to burn down an historic home. They have to decide whether they love ermine or the

EU more.' You think that Parliament's moth problem is bad for your robes, just see what a disgruntled Somerset Tory can do with a Tommy gun.

He spoke extremely politely but with determined menace, like a gangster who will perform dentistry on you whether you want it or not but will place his blood-soaked pliers on a coaster afterwards so that it doesn't stain the mahogany. Do not mess with The Mogg.

There was also a warning for his colleagues in the Commons who want Britain to stay in some form of customs union and remain under the Brussels yoke. 'It's completely cretinous,' he said. 'A betrayal of good sense. I cannot understand why the government is faffing around with this.'

He warned that the electorate would punish the Tories if they botched it on Brexit. 'It would be put right through the ballot box,' he said. 'Remainers would think we were useless because we had got out and Leavers would think we were useless because we hadn't.'

In fact, he went on, the Tories would risk not getting a single vote at the next election. 'Well, one,' he conceded, 'but I am such a die-hard Tory I always would.' An idea suddenly formed of Bruce Willis playing The Mogg in a pin-striped vest in a movie that fuses guns and parliamentary procedure. *Die Hard with a Closure Motion.*

Mr Rees-Mogg said that he would grudgingly accept the proposed 21-month transition period, but only if it led to a full Brexit, not a fudge. 'What is twenty-one months in our Great Island Story?' he said. 'It is a price worth paying. It means twenty-one months of purgatory but the good thing about purgatory is that it leads to heaven.'

But will Theresa May take us all the way to the throne of grace? He thought so. 'She is a very enigmatic figure,' he said. 'She is carrying out the Will of the British People and it is hard to tell with what enthusiasm she is doing it. She doesn't express her emotion. That is A Good Thing. I rather like a Prime Minister who exercises self-control.'

In fact, he thinks that Mrs May will go on and on in the job, so long as she sticks to her last. 'May the Prime Minister live for ever, amen, amen, alleluia, alleluia, amen,' Zadok the Mogg said. He really does talk like this. Handel with care.

27 APRIL
RUDD BECOMES CHIEF TARGET FOR REMOVAL STRATEGY

Amber Rudd looked up at the green annunciator screen that hangs above the chamber. 'Urgent question: removals targets in the Home Office,' it said. 'Oh, that sounds interesting,' Ms Rudd thought. 'I wonder which poor sap is going to have to answer that.'

'The Home Secretary,' announced Mr Speaker. Ms Rudd didn't move. 'That's you,' he hissed. 'Golly,' Ms Rudd replied. 'Why did none of my officials brief me on this?' It turned out that she was, indeed, the Home Secretary, not that bossy woman with expensive shoes who keeps popping into the office to tell her what she thinks. But Ms Rudd has only been in the job for two years. You can't really expect her to have picked up trivia like who runs the department in such a short time. She has only just learnt how to use her swipe card in the canteen.

Ms Rudd had been hauled to the Commons to account for a mistake. She had told the Home Affairs Committee that her department didn't have regional targets for removing people from Britain, but it turns out it does. Someone googled it very quickly. It's just that no one had told Ms Rudd. Or the senior adviser who had sat beside her.

These were, she now knew, 'local targets for internal performance management' but nothing to do with HQ. The Home Secretary has no more say over regional removals targets than she does over deciding where the Wolverhampton branch should hold its Christmas party.

She had not misled Parliament, as some claimed. John Woodcock (Lab, Barrow and Furness) pointed out that her statement had been too easily disproved for anyone to think she had deliberately lied. What she was guilty of was cluelessness. Though how many Home Secretaries have ever known what goes on in that jambalaya of a department? Diane Abbott, her shadow, had declared earlier that Ms Rudd 'can't get basic facts right'. That is the same Ms Abbott who, announcing a new policy last year, said in the space of five minutes that Labour would create between 2,000 and 250,000 extra police officers a year at a cost of either £30,000 or £80 million. Both women would struggle to find a haystack in a field of needles.

Ms Abbot had asked for this urgent question in the hope of drawing blood. Ruddigore, you might call it. She said that Lord Carrington had resigned over the Falklands as 'a matter of honour' and called on Ms Rudd to do the same. In fact, while Lord Carrington was an honourable man, he also took note of the angry reception he received when he briefed 200 Tory backbenchers on Argentina's invasion. Sir John Nott, the Defence Secretary at the time, later wrote that Lord Carrington's problem was that, being a peer, he didn't know the character of some MPs and took them all seriously.

He did not know, Sir John wrote, that 'A is an idiot, B always talks nonsense, C is a pompous twit and only D and E carry some respect'. There are plenty of As, Bs and Cs in the modern Tory Party, if not quite enough Ds and Es, but they all rowed in behind Ms Rudd yesterday.

Sir Nicholas Soames began the defence. 'Be assured that she has the total support of Conservative members,' he said. Michelle Donelan (Con, Chippenham) said that Labour was being 'morally wrong' and 'playing politics with people's lives'.

Anna Soubry blamed the last Labour government for leaving a 'dreadful obsession with targets' as a legacy.

A healthy number of Cabinet ministers bayed support. Labour would not get their Ruddigore. The Home Secretary is going nowhere. Which is not quite the same as saying that she is going somewhere.

After several days of refusing to resign over the Windrush scandal, Amber Rudd stood down when she was found to have inadvertently misled MPs over removals targets.

3 MAY
RUDD BACK IN THE SADDLE AND CORBYN HAS BIT BETWEEN HIS TEETH

When you fall off a horse, get straight back in the saddle. Amber Rudd endured a difficult ride last week on Unfitfor-purpose, that troublesome nag, eventually being thrown after two refusals at a fence called 'Deportation Targets', but she was back in the paddock yesterday for the 12.05 PMQs Stakes, hoping to be given a new ride before too long. Preferably a horse with four legs.

Ms Rudd was right behind the Prime Minister for question time, literally as well as emotionally. We wondered if she would sit in Soubry Corner with the Tory rebels but she chose a seat mid-chamber, in what we might call Paintbox Row. A ruddy splash in the middle of a canvas that also featured Damian Green, James Gray and Bob Blackman.

There, looking more relieved than disappointed after her liberation from the Home Office, Ms Rudd bobbed up and down for half an hour before being called by Mr Speaker. Her question was phrased a little clumsily – in effect, 'Last year we had five terrorist attacks in which thirty-six people were killed, aren't the security services doing well?' – but it's been a while since she was asking rather than answering.

Since it was the eve of the local elections, Jeremy Corbyn ditched his usual strategy of failing to hit a cow's backside with six swings of his banjo and instead swung wildly at a whole herd of cows in the hope that he might clip one of them.

His first question was succinct. Did Mrs May feel 'the slightest pang of guilt' that Ms Rudd had carried the can for her boss's failures? After Mrs May gave what she assumed would be only the first slice of Windrush waffle, he changed tack and asked about growth figures. Then, like a child dipping into a bag of pick-and-mix, he plucked out A&E waiting times, followed by a question on school funding and then one on police budgets.

It was not a bad tactic since it did not allow Mrs May time to settle. She flicked back and forth through her folder, reading out stock prepared answers, but was unable to deploy killer lines. It didn't allow Mr Corbyn to build momentum, though. His argument may have been that the Tories are hopeless at everything but it got a bit lost.

Naturally, he didn't ask about Brexit. There was a hollow laugh when Helen Grant (Maidstone and The Weald), a Tory toady, asked Mrs May if she agreed with her that 'it is only under the Conservatives that you get decision and vision'. (Spoiler: Mrs May did.) This was then followed by one from Labour's Karen Buck (Westminster North) about the customs union and the Irish border that showed they have neither.

Never mind, Peter Bone was happy. The Tory has an app on his phone that counts down the time to Brexit by the second. We could see it whizzing from the gallery. 'In 331 days, eleven hours, forty minutes and twenty-two seconds,' he said, 'the Prime Minister will lead us out of the EU.'

He invited her to visit his seat on B-Day, 'where she will be carried through the cheering crowds' and shown the site where a statue will be erected to her. Mrs May said she was tempted. She seemed delighted to have had a question from a Brexiteer that didn't contain a trap. Mr Bone was also delighted. By the time she had finished her answer, B-Day was eighty-five seconds closer.

10 MAY

ED THE EVANGELIST PRESSES HOME HIS PRIGGISH POINT

How kind of Ed Miliband to come in to work. We don't see much of the former Labour leader in the Commons these days. You might think the party would welcome his experience in the trenches, but he seems loath to dirty his hands in combat. He has made only fourteen speeches in the past year and shown up for barely three quarters of the votes. Lucky it isn't a hung Parliament.

Yet there he was yesterday, clutching the sword of sanctimony and shield of priggishness, out from his tent and prepared to fight with all his might against the evil forces of a free press. That photo of him struggling to eat a bacon sandwich daintily still stings.

Let us be fair to Mr Miliband, though, for it was a magnificent piece of theatrics. Four stars, rising five, with a good chance of a transfer to Broadway. We see so many dreary politicians these days, reading a tepid script from pages held in front of their face and fluffing every third word, that it is a treat to get someone who can orate, even if it was pious claptrap.

His eyes shone with the fervour of an evangelist; he flung his arms around like an auctioneer at a cattle market. 'No, I will not give way,' he bellowed at Tories who tried to interrupt. 'How dare they?' he said of the government for being anti-Leveson. 'This is about honour.' And he clutched a fist to his chest and breathed in the air of self-righteousness.

Jacob Rees-Mogg eventually got a word in after Mr Milib- and said that Parliament should act because David Cameron and Nick Clegg had told the victims of phonehacking that they would. The Mogg was so exercised by this that a few of his hairs had fallen out of place and flapped about as he observed that Mr Cameron and Sir Nick are no longer in Parliament. It is unconstitutional, he said, to say that their actions can bind their successors.

Mr Miliband looked as if he had got a whiff of something foul. 'I give way to his constitutional knowledge,' he said. 'But I do not give way to him on morality.'

The Mogg got more of a turn later. Freedom of the press is a matter of ancestral interest to him, of course. His mother used to be a secretary on the *Sunday Times*'s City desk. Having licked his errant forelock into place, The Mogg spoke with el- oquence and no less passion, though he didn't wave his arms about. Leave that to the Italians and the Milibands.

'Freedom of the press,' he said, 'is so overwhelmingly pre- cious that we should preserve it even if sometimes the press upsets us. It is amazing how many people who have had run- ins with the press suddenly find that they think it should be more tightly regulated.' Embarrassment, he said, should not be followed by shackling. 'We must not be pressurised by those who have sometimes had the sharp lash of the press's tongue.'

Speaking of shackles and lashes, The Mogg wondered why Labour are so keen to press the agenda of Max Mosley, the dungeon-loving son of a fascist demagogue who had given heavily to their deputy leader. 'It reeks of self-interest,' he said. 'In bed with a man who gave them £540,000 to pursue his cause.' Oddly, when Mr Miliband spoke of honour and morality, he didn't mention this. Perhaps he'll bring it up next time he pops in.

23 MAY
PRIVATE WILLIAMSON GOES OUT ON PARADE

Gavin Williamson has now completed six months of his work experience at the Ministry of Defence and he is loving it. The uniforms! The boats – ships (sorry, still learning the lingo)! The things that go bang! The things that go whoosh! All those people who salute when you walk into a room! This is better than working in a restaurant.

Like anyone doing a YTS (Young Tory Statesman) placement, Mr Williamson has had to learn on the job. After a few fruitless trips to the quartermaster to request elbow grease and half-inch holes, he has learnt not to trust the pranksters in his private office. And after the press conference in which he told Russia to 'go away and shut up' they realised that he could play jokes too.

Now he was being let loose on the Defence Select Committee, a group with more experts than amateurs. Chaired by Julian Lewis (PhD in post-war military planning), it has the likes of Captain Johnny Mercer (three tours of Afghanistan with the Royal Artillery), Captain Leo Docherty (Scots Guards and author of a memoir called *Desert of Death*), Mark Francois (Territorial Army and an MA in war studies) and John Spellar (ex-armed forces minister). God knows what they think of Private Pike running the MoD.

He lacks military bearing. Partly this is his youthful appearance (perhaps a moustache might help?) but mainly it's because he says things like 'haitch em ess', 'foreign secutary' or, as he did at the start of yesterday's session, 'the core things what we are aiming to deliver'. He even, rather sweetly, said 'righty-ho', when asked to describe our military relationship with the US.

Nonetheless, the committee members were polite enough to him despite the wetness behind his ears. For two hours they watched him do a gentle stint on the parade ground – an 'about turn' here, a 'shoulder arms' there, an awful lot of 'stand at ease' – without giving him the full Windsor Davies treatment.

Mr Francois, for instance, got very little out of Private Williamson about exactly what he plans to do with the 400 extra troops who, it has been reported, are being sent out to Afghanistan. 'You're assuming a decision has been made,' Private Williamson, the man in charge of making decisions, said.

Later, though, when the minister shed a moderate wattage on a different issue, Mr Francois went out of his way to encourage him. 'You answered that much better,' he said, and it sounded less patronising than it might read. Perhaps this is what they mean by civil defence.

The only act of aggression came at the end when Captain Mercer grew annoyed with the lack of answers on protecting troops who had served in Northern Ireland from vexatious litigation. As Mr Williamson said, 'We need to do more' for the third time, Captain Mercer blew up. 'I know that,' he snapped. 'The question is why we haven't. This is literally wasting time.' The work experience minister nodded. True, but it beats stacking shelves.

5 JUNE
GRAYLING GOES OFF THE RAILS

Well, at least the Transport Secretary turned up early for his kicking. Some expected his statement to be cancelled altogether but the 5.30 p.m. Failing Grayling service from Shambles

Magna to Much-Chaos-on-the-Mainline rolled into the Commons twenty-eight minutes ahead of schedule.

It caused a frantic rush of MPs, swarming through Central Lobby like commuters at Manchester Piccadilly after a late platform alteration. No one wants to miss a whipping. 'I'm pleased to come back at the earliest opportunity to update the House about the recent difficulties,' Mr Grayling began. He did not look especially chuffed.

He had come to address the problems experienced on Northern Rail and Govia Thameslink Railway during last week's Whitsun recess, but MPs from other parts of the country were keen to use the occasion to tell him how dreadful the trains are where they live, too. Clackety-clack went the Labour backbenchers as they rode up and down what remains of Mr Grayling's spine.

He was also attacked by MPs on his own side. From Letchworth, Sevenoaks and East Grinstead, a trio of Tory knights laid into their colleague. Sir Oliver Heald said children were in tears at his station yesterday because they couldn't get to school. He ordered Mr Grayling to tell the train operator to 'get on with it'.

Sir Michael Fallon said that two villages in his seat have been completely cut off by timetabling changes, while Sir Nicholas Soames called the whole mess 'an absolute disaster' that was destroying lives. Crispin Blunt said his constituents in Redhill, next door to Mr Grayling's seat, were promised an improved service in 2014 but 'even when it works properly it is worse'.

The pressure seems to be taking its toll. A muscle in Mr Grayling's left cheek twitched uncontrollably for most of the ordeal. He began to resemble the tortured Dreyfus in the *Pink Panther* films. If Mr Grayling were a railway station there would have been an announcement for Inspector Sands to report to the operations room immediately, the railway code for a crisis.

'We need to find out who is responsible for this,' Mr Grayling pleaded at one point as he announced an inquiry into what had caused the chaos. 'YOU ARE!' came the shout from all sides.

He thought this was a bit unfair. What was the good of privatisation if ministers still get the blame for the rail network being a disaster? 'I share people's frustration,' Mr Grayling pleaded, a duffer hitting the buffers. 'What exactly are you for?' heckled Labour's Jess Phillips (Birmingham Yardley).

Tim Loughton, a Sussex Tory, asked for an assurance that the Transport Secretary would take back rail franchises within six months of his inquiry making its report. This seemed optimistic. He may not last another six days. The lolloping Mr Grayling, 6ft 5in. in his socks, resembles a rather dim Great Dane and plenty of MPs wanted him to get the Rinka treatment.

Chuka Umunna witheringly called him an 'utterly pointless Transport Secretary'. It would be unfortunate if he is. Without points, he cannot be moved into the siding where he belongs.

6 JUNE
TRANSPORT SECRETARY HAS ANOTHER BUMPY FLIGHT

———

It's all go, go, go in Chris Grayling's world these days. The Transport Secretary knows this because every time he rises at the dispatch box MPs shout 'go' at him. Sometimes it is 'in the name of God, go,' but he knows what they mean. They see in him a man of dynamism and versatility.

One day he's gone off the rails, the next he's got his head in the clouds. Having told the Commons on Monday that he can handle Govia (it's like Michael Gove only more so), he appeared again yesterday to say that he has received clearance from the Cabinet's air traffic control to taxi down a third runway at Heathrow.

'I come to this House to mark a historic moment,' Mr Grayling announced grandly. Perhaps he dreams of one day getting a statue on Parliament Square for aircraft to make their descent over and pigeons to defile. Churchill, Mandela, Grayling: the 'New York, Paris, Peckham' of political figures.

'The time for action is now,' he added. Or nowish. It has been, after all, nine years since Labour won a vote on Heathrow expansion, only for the Tories to ground the idea.

On that occasion, John McDonnell, then just a rebellious Labour backbencher with a local grievance rather than the shadow Chancellor, had marched down to the table and grabbed the ceremonial mace, shouting that his party's decision was 'a disgrace to the democracy of this country'. Mr McDonnell is trying to pass himself off as a statesman these days, so he just sat there in silence, glowering.

Andy McDonald led Labour's response and spoilt his shadow's moment of history by saying that on the evidence of how well he has handled the rail crisis 'his assurances are not worth the Hansard they are printed on'. The twitch in Mr Grayling's left cheek, which had put in a long shift on Monday, began to spasm again. It went off, I noted, whenever an MP mentioned rail links to the runway. Some sort of Pavlovian response.

"The only reason he is at the dispatch box is that the Prime Minister is too weak to sack him,' Mr McDonald added. 'He simply does not enjoy the confidence of the House.' Twitch-twitch. A few Tories gave a loyal honk of support but it did not threaten to breach noise-pollution standards.

With fifty MPs circling in the Speaker's stacking system, Mr Grayling was looking most nervously at those coming in over his left shoulder. Zac Goldsmith and Justine Greening, MPs for west London constituencies, were side by side in Soubry Corner, where the Awkward Squad fly.

They gave the minister a threatening buzz, asking him about what the project is likely to cost and raising concerns about pollution, but did not drop any bombs on his runway. That will come when the issue returns next month for a vote.

Other Tories, ones further from London, were supportive. Robert Goodwill (Con, Scarborough and Whitby) said he had read about potential barriers to construction. 'May I offer my services as someone with some experience of driving bulldozers?' the farmer said. Mr Grayling welcomed this Goodwill gesture, a reference to Boris Johnson, who has promised to lie in front of the Heathrow bulldozers. Mr Johnson is fond of lying.

The Foreign Secretary had stayed away from the statement, but he remained the (flying) elephant in the room and Mr Grayling hinted at his enduring opposition when he said that the decision had 'almost entirely universal Cabinet support'. The Uxbridge Dumbo may yet have a role to play in grounding his colleague's historic plan.

7 JUNE
CURSES! MUTTLEY CREW PUT PM IN A FLAP

At last a straight answer from Theresa May. It came near the end of PMQs in response to a question on next week's big showdown between the Commons and the Lords. Not the Brexit Bill but the parliamentary pigeon race.

'Would she like to sponsor a pigeon?' asked Chris Davies (Brecon and Radnorshire), a newish Welsh Tory who didn't want to ruffle any feathers. Mrs May beamed. This was one coo she was happy to encourage.

Jeremy Corbyn is also a pigeon-fancier. In 2004 he was one of three Labour MPs to sign a motion condemning a plan to use pigeons as flying bombs in the Second World War. The motion said that mankind deserved to be wiped out by an asteroid as punishment, even though it had only been an idea and Speckled Jim never got his payload. A touch

OTT, perhaps. The peapod burgundy must have been strong that year.

The Labour leader asked something even more ridiculous yesterday. He wondered whether the government would publish a long-awaited White Paper on its Brexit negotiating position before next week's debate.

Mrs May grimaced. This is a particularly elusive bird and her Brexit team's efforts to catch it have resembled Dick Dastardly pursuing the pigeon in the Hanna-Barbera cartoon. The plot is always the same: the General (Mrs May) demands results, DD and his chaotic team come up with some outlandish scheme that fails dismally and it ends with Boris, I mean Muttley, that 'snickering floppy-haired hound', begging for an undeserved medal.

This week, however, DD had gone AWOL and the General had to tackle the mission herself. 'Muttley, do something!' she howled, borrowing DD's catchphrase. 'Rashin' fashin' Rayvid Rayvis,' growled Boris, which wasn't much help. Mrs May waffled.

It did not get her out of trouble. Mr Corbyn tried again. If the White Paper won't be ready for the debate, will we have it by the EU summit on 28 June? His MPs waved the clear back of their order papers at the PM, either to show what white paper looks like or to suggest the extent of its contents.

'Curses! Foiled again!' Mrs May growled, while Muttley just gave a wheezing laugh beside her. She flannelled some more, wishing that Mr Corbyn would get bored and ask about something else, though preferably not the railways.

Mr Corbyn has, however, finally realised that Brexit is a problem for the government. It does not matter that he lacks a coherent position of his own on this subject or that there is as much disunity about it on the Labour benches as the government ones. He just has to keep on punching the bruise and watch the Prime Minister wince. He did this with glee. When she tried to attack his lack of policy, he pointed out simply that 'the opposition are not conducting the negotiations'. When some Tories shouted 'hallelujah' at this, he gave a stinging reply: 'Sadly, the government aren't either.'

Mr Corbyn was enjoying himself now. After praising Mrs May for uniting Ireland in thinking that her ideas are 'bonkers', he pivoted to the other chaotic issue of our time and asked, 'Which will last longer: Northern Rail or her premiership?' The General crash-landed. All that she had left to say was one of DD's other catchphrases: 'Drat, double drat and triple drat!' Meanwhile, the Brexit pigeon flies on unmolested.

The government faced another defeat on Brexit when rebels sought a vote on giving Parliament the final say on any deal. It was seen off with a concession that MPs would be consulted, but one minister resigned in order to abstain.

13 JUNE
MR DARCY TACKLES PRIDE AND PREJUDICE

Chief Whips should be felt and not seen. Omnipotent, omniscient, omnipresent, they shimmer into the chamber when a difficult vote is in prospect, appearing at the shoulders of the weak and the wavering, cajoling them to do the right thing and lay down their principles for the party. Some are charmers, some are thugs, few have a face that is recognised outside.

You may never have seen Julian Smith (Con, Skipton and Ripon), the current Chief, but you know his type from BBC period dramas. Tall and brooding, with keen eyes and cheekbones you could slice cheddar on. A man who knows how to wield a riding crop. He is Westminster's Mr Darcy.

The Chief glided in and out of the chamber for four hours

yesterday, dripping honey into the ears of those who needed encouragement ('The Prime Minister is a big fan of yours') or reminding the naughty to stay in line ('I saw some verrry interesting photos the other day'). And all the time he was counting, ever counting.

When George Freeman (Con, Mid Norfolk) tweeted that he was still mulling over what to do, the eternal footman was soon at his side, reminding him of the value of loyalty. Before that he had been up in Rebels Corner, showing MPs his thumbscrews catalogue.

He knew he could count on a few Labour votes, such as Frank Field, a rebel on the other side who arrived with his arm in a sling. 'Whips' office?' enquired David Davis cheerily. 'I hope ours is kinder than the government's will be in getting this through,' Mr Field told the Brexit Secretary.

For every Field, though, there were Tory boulders he could not budge. Ken Clarke, of course, and Anna Soubry, whose speech was like Mark Antony at a funeral, praising Robert Buckland (Con, Swindon South), the Solicitor General trying to find a fudge, as an honourable man.

And then there was Phillip Lee (Con, Bracknell), who had just resigned as a minister to oppose the government. His turn came later than he had hoped – Mr Speaker appeared to give him the nod before calling Sir Bill Cash, whose views on the EU have not been underexposed – but it was the most anticipated.

Hesitating at the start, through nerves or perhaps because, as a GP, he couldn't quite read his handwriting, Dr Lee said that he was 'devastated' to have had to make his decision. 'This is a matter of deep principle,' he said. 'We need to leave our children a legacy of which we can all be proud.'

As he spoke, Mr Smith stood silently beside the Speaker, looking along the rows, counting and then counting again. Twenty minutes before the close, he summoned four potential rebels out for a chat. A few minutes later, another three were sent to Room 101. Some explained on their return how they had won the victory over themselves. They loved Big Brexit.

Before the vote, Mr Smith walked in and sat on the front bench. A minister raised an eyebrow and received a broad Robert De Niro sort of smile. Job done. It all added up.

As MPs filed out at the end, Mr Davis found himself next to the newest rebel and suddenly put a friendly arm around his shoulders. 'Cheer up, Phillip,' he seemed to be saying. 'I used to make grand futile gestures myself once.'

14 JUNE
BABY SHOWS THE BUTCHER'S BAND HOW TO BEHAVE

The Commons had not heard such a sound for a long time. Whole benches of Conservative MPs were cheering John Bercow. The Speaker has seldom felt such love from his old party and all because a stroppy Scotsman disrupted Prime Minister's Questions.

The shoulders of the Scottish Nationalists in Westminster are not unburdened by chips even on their cheeriest days, but their grievance settings were turned up to maximum yesterday because of the progress of the Brexit Bill against their wishes. 'A democratic outrage,' bellowed Ian Blackford, their leader. 'We will not be disrespected.' He looks and acts like a butcher: renowned for his beef.

Then he pushed a little-known parliamentary button in the knowledge that it would cause an explosion. 'I have no option', he said, 'but to ask that this House now sit in private.' Clear the galleries! Everybody out! Cancel your lunch plans! The SNP is having a huff! This device is little more than an attention-seeking filibuster, a means of wasting time on a vote that will be defeated. It is the parliamentary equivalent of a schoolboy trying to get out of detention by holding a cigarette lighter to the smoke alarm.

Mr Bercow saw through this stunt. We'll deal with this later, he told Mr Blackford. Let's finish PMQs first. No, Mrs Soubry, he added to the Tory MP chirruping to his right, I don't need any of your help on this. The Chair has spoken.

But Mr Blackford was not willing to listen. He got to his feet and demanded an immediate vote. 'Resume your seat, young man,' Mr Bercow said to the SNP leader, who is two years his senior. The butcher refused. How could he, with his own MPs now egging him on and the Tories barking their contempt? 'Order! Order!' barked Mr Bercow until his voice began to crack. The Hansard scorers credited him with saying it fourteen times but I counted at least twenty-eight when watching it back. Yet still Mr Blackford maintained the perpendicular.

'You'll have to chuck him out,' the clerk muttered to Mr Bercow. This, of course, is what the SNP wanted. Martyrdom. The Speaker read out the *Nunc dimittis* and Mr Blackford strutted out, accompanied by the rest of his party.

Some went quietly, others brandishing their dirks and flashing their kilts. Mhairi Black, the petulant MP for Paisley and Renfrewshire South, stabbed her finger at the Speaker and spat out words that may not have been allowed by Erskine May, Parliament's rulebook, if they had been caught. She would not be missed: her speaking and voting record are rated as 'well below average' by the number-crunchers. It fell to Luke Hall (Con, Thornbury and Yate) to break the ice. Called as the massed pipes and drums headed out into Central Lobby, he drew a laugh. 'Given the number of people who are leaving the chamber, I feel as though I am making one of my after-dinner speeches,' he said.

Watching in the gallery was the Speaker of the Ukrainian Parliament, who John Whittingdale (Con, Maldon) remarked would have been 'utterly mystified by what just took place'.

Only by how tame it was, I suspect. Debates in that legislature frequently develop into an all-in brawl in which MPs remove their jackets and punch their opponents in the groin.

Mr Blackford's stand was also overseen by Zana, the eleven-week-old daughter of Clive Lewis. Suddenly spotting the child above, Mr Bercow remarked that 'for all the turbulence and discord of the proceedings, the little baby … has been a model of impeccable behaviour from start to finish'. The SNP should follow her example. Ms Black may hold the title Baby of the House on account of her age, but she lacks the maturity to wear it.

21 JUNE
PINCHER NIPS REBELLION IN THE BUD

Vote Grieve, Take Control. That was supposed to be the mantra for those who wanted to secure the right of Parliament to have the final say on the Brexit deal. It did not work out that way. In the end, not even Grieve voted Grieve.

Twenty minutes before the debate finished, Theresa May walked quietly into the chamber and stood for a while behind the Speaker's chair, almost unnoticed, a smile playing on her lips. At the same stage in last week's debate on this bill she had been hauling rebels out of the chamber to beg for their support. Now, she was confident of victory.

That had been secured when Dominic Grieve (Con, Beacons-field), whose amendment had caused sweats in Downing Street, rose to say that he had tasted the government's latest fudge recipe and it worked for him. This fudge involves a vote on a 'neutral motion' about the final deal, probably as bland as the one MPs passed last night after a debate on defence: 'This House has considered NATO.' Mr Grieve perhaps hopes that MPs will consider the Brexit deal and, if necessary, consider it a duffer.

The Tory whips' office had put in another hard shift for this win. In the original *House of Cards*, Francis Urquhart, the Machiavellian Chief Whip, leaves the dirty work to a lackey called Stamper. Julian Smith has a deputy called Pincher, which may reflect gentler times in the whips' office. They'll appoint a Nudger and a Tickler next.

Pincher, a weaselly little fellow with a nasty twitch (better a twitching Pincher than a pinching twitcher...), wandered along the benches during PMQs, whispering encouragements or threats into wavering ears. Justine Greening got much of his attention and duly stayed loyal; her rebellion may come on Heathrow expansion next Monday.

After the collapse of Mr Grieve, described by George Howarth (Lab, Knowsley) as 'the Grand Old Duke of York' for marching his troops towards a rebellion and back down again, I saw another Tory whip flick an imaginary speck off the shoulder of Phillip Lee, who had resigned as a minister to rebel, and grind it under his foot. Reminiscent of Donald Trump's gesture to Emmanuel Macron the other week, it sent a clear message: remember who is the big dog here.

Dr Lee still rebelled, though, along with five other Tories. One of them was Anna Soubry, who was very hoarse and expressed a fear that the editor of the *Daily Mail* owned a voodoo doll of her and was sticking pins in its throat. I doubt that would silence her.

26 JUNE
DUTY-FREE JOHNSON FLIES FROM DIFFICULTY

Kabul is an awfully long way to go for a sicknote. There was not even much on the agenda, to judge by the flimsiness of the folder that Boris Johnson was seen clutching as he arrived for a hastily arranged chinwag with the Afghan Deputy Foreign

Minister. A 9,000-mile round trip and he didn't even get to see the top chap! As they might say at Boris's alma mater, this really puts the rot into aegrotat.

One imagines that his briefing went something like this: 1) Ask how the Taliban situation is going. 2) Talk a bit about cricket. 3) Make a joke about coming to Kabul to escape the heatwave in London. 4) Explain joke. 5) Apologise for joke. 6) Ask the Afghans to sign a chitty explaining to the British press that this was a very important meeting that couldn't be held over Skype or on another day and not a desperate attempt to get out of honouring a promise to his constituents.

This was just a flying visit, in and out in a day, which is ironic given the subject of the debate that he was bunking off from. The Foreign Office planners had needed to find a destination that was both too far away for him to get back in time for the Heathrow vote and close enough that he could still attend departmental questions in the Commons this morning.

Plan A had been to send him to Luxembourg for an EU council meeting (see, Boris, they do have some uses) but the vote was at 10 p.m. and no one would believe that it was impossible to get back in time from there. Plan B should have been to send him to Manchester and blame Northern Rail for the cancellation of his scheduled arrival in London, which would have been credible, but might have upset Chris Grayling, who sees the Heathrow decision as his great legacy and gets a nasty spasm in his cheek when anyone mentions the railways.

'This is a really important moment in the history of this country,' beamed the Transport Secretary as he began his statement. 'It will set a clear path to our future as a global nation in the post-Brexit world.' Mr Grayling is no poet.

Acknowledging the Uxbridge Dumbo, that flying elephant in the room, he admitted this had been a 'divisive issue' for his party, with Greg Hands (Con, Chelsea and Fulham) resigning as a trade minister to oppose it. Andy Slaughter (Lab,

Hammersmith), who had resigned himself for the same reason when this was voted on in 2009, reminded Mr Grayling that he, and for that matter Theresa May, were also once opponents of a third runway.

Mr Hands told the Commons that he had not resigned willingly but that as a former Deputy Chief Whip he knew the form. Sitting beside Phillip Lee, who had resigned as a justice minister this month to oppose Brexit, he told MPs that this debate was about more than just laying some tarmac west of London. 'It is also a debate about being true to your word,' he said. 'This is a vote about integrity.'

Something for Mr Johnson to look up in the dictionary during his return flight from Kabul.

This sketch, looking ahead to what turned out to be a fractious Cabinet meeting at Chequers, was written not for The Times *but for Radio 4's* Broadcasting House.

1 JULY
SQUABBLING SPOILS MAY'S QUIET GAME OF CHEQUERS

Theresa May looked around the wood-panelled room at the members of her Cabinet. 'Well,' the Prime Minister said. 'I suppose you are all wondering why I have called you here.'

The guests all nodded and murmured expectantly, all except Gavin Williamson, who was looking in the mirror trying to decide whether they would respect him more with a moustache, and Liz Truss (Con, South West Norfolk), who was taking photographs for Instagram. It was the most extraordinary collection of egos and strong opinions to be gathered together in one room since the last time that Piers Morgan had dined alone.

'No, seriously,' May said. 'Why have I called you here? What was I thinking? We are only 266 days away from leaving the European Union and we still cannot agree on what we want from Brexit.'

At this David Davis gave one of his irritating chuckles. 'Two hundred and sixty-six days, as little as that?' he laughed. 'Oh dearie-me, how time flies. No wonder Michel Barnier's been trying to call me. I thought he just wanted Wimbledon tickets.'

The Brexit Secretary stabbed at his phone. '*Michel, mon bonnet de douche,*' he said. 'Ha ha! Long time, no speak…'

The Prime Minister looked at the others with desperation. It had been a frustrating day that began badly when Boris Johnson tried to explain his Max Fac idea again. 'Look, think of it as a cross between a Big Mac and a fax machine,' he told them. 'Both were popular in the 1980s. And so were we! Ipso facto bingo bongo.'

After lunch, Matt Hancock tried to break the tension with a football match but it fell apart when Sajid Javid kept swapping sides. In the afternoon, Philip Hammond delighted in turning down any idea that would cost money with a tart comment of 'sorry, Jeremy Hunt's taken it all', while Greg Clark had brought lots of interesting ideas but couldn't stop sending his colleagues to sleep. Poor Damian Hinds (East Hampshire) kept being asked who he was.

Now they had gathered for one last attempt to find a solution. Suddenly, Michael Gove leapt up. 'I want to say one word,' he said. 'Just one word. Are you listening?' May nodded. 'Plastics,' Gove said and sat down. He says nothing else these days.

'If only Brexit was black or white,' May mused, reflecting on the irony of saying this at a place called Chequers. 'More like fifty shades of Grayling,' quipped Boris. The Transport Secretary wasn't there, of course, having decided to come by train.

'Look, shall we just have a vote on it,' May said. 'I know it will be difficult and possibly unpopular but to lead is to choose and...' There was a sudden yelp from Boris. 'Difficult vote?' he said. 'Unpopular? Sorry, just realised I'm meant to be elsewhere.' As he dashed out, they heard him on his phone. 'Can you get me on a flight to Kabul urgent?' he said. 'Yes, yes, again.'

As the Cabinet continued to squabble, May looked up at the stained-glass window in the long gallery, installed by the last private owners of Chequers, that describes the sixteenth-century mansion as a 'house of peace and ancient memories, given to England as a place of rest and recreation for her Prime Ministers'.

'Fat chance of that,' she sighed. 'Oh well, they'll be gone soon and I'll have my peace back.' And then her eyes fell on the calendar and the entry for the following week: 'Donald Trump visits Chequers.'

Her scream could be heard as far away as Beaconsfield.

4 JULY
A SIRI-OUS ERROR AS WILLIAMSON IS HECKLED BY HIS OWN PHONE

An irritating tinny sound came from Gavin Williamson as he delivered a statement on the latest situation in Syria. Those who have heard the Defence Secretary speak before found nothing unusual in this, except that it came from his breast pocket rather than his lips. Had he taken up ventriloquism?

'I have found something on the web for Syrian democratic forces supported by...' his pocket said, before Mr Williamson reached in and pulled out his iPhone. The interruption, it turned out, was caused by Siri, the voice-activated mobile assistant that had evidently misheard Syria as a call to arms. Or at least a call to Google.

As Speaker Bercow huffed about how 'rum' this all was, Mr

Williamson apologised. 'It's very rare that you're heckled by your own mobile phone,' he said. Almost as rare, perhaps, as a Cabinet minister with top-level security clearance not disabling the voice-recognition software on his phone.

There was something different, though, about Mr Williamson's delivery. For a couple of weeks there has been gossip in the Commons about him having voice coaching to make him sound less like Alan Bennett on a lungful of helium. A Yorkshire squeak may be authentic – and we mustn't be snobbish – but Mr Williamson's voice has tended more towards gravy than gravitas. Pretty thin gravy at that.

Yesterday, he seemed to speak much more slowly and deeply. Perhaps his voice has broken at last. The Private Pike jibes have probably stung. What worked at the Scarborough fireplace salesmen's guild needs to be taken down an octave when dealing with military top brass.

Dropping one's voice is often the sign of a leadership bid. Margaret Thatcher lowered her pitch on the path to power and Liz Truss, another Tory who fancies herself rotten, demonstrated in Treasury Questions yesterday a timbre that is both deep and slightly camp, making her sound a bit like Bernard Bresslaw.

It matters more what a minister says than how he says it, of course, and Mr Williamson didn't do a bad job of his statement on Daesh, though he kept stumbling over the word 'counter' as if he could never work out whether it was being used as a verb or an adjective.

He neatly sidestepped the bear traps, such as one from Khalid Mahmood (Lab, Birmingham Perry Barr) on what efforts we are taking to monitor the terrorists we have no knowledge of – 'well, obviously it is difficult to monitor people we have no knowledge of' – and one from Ged Killen (Lab, Rutherglen and Hamilton West) on office gossip.

'He will be aware of reports of a number of private

conversations and correspondence between himself and the Prime Minister that have been leaked to the press,' Mr Killen said. 'Can he shed light on how these came into the public domain? Has he instituted a leak inquiry?' Mr Williamson gave him a hard stare. 'I was waiting for a question about Daesh and our operations in Iraq and Syria,' he said, before moving quickly on. Cynics might wonder if he had been briefing the press himself. My money is on Siri doing a spot of moonlighting.

6 JULY
BETTER TO BE THOUGHT STUPID THAN A LIAR

Esther McVey would have made a brilliant theatre promoter in the days when it was sharp practice, until banned by an EU directive, to mislead audiences by selectively quoting from reviews. Indeed, if she wanted to use this sketch to promote her one-star performance yesterday she would probably go for, 'Brilliant ... star performance — *The Times*.'

The Work and Pensions Secretary had been hauled to the Commons to answer an urgent question from Labour's Frank Field after she had received a remarkable rebuke from the National Audit Office. The spending watchdog, in a report on universal credit, had said that the government did not have any better ideas. Ms McVey, with her eye on the box office, had interpreted this to MPs as 'brilliant, let's have more of it right now'. The NAO said that wasn't quite what it had meant.

Mr Field, who has been an MP for almost forty years and knows what he can get away with, accused the minister right from the start of 'dissembling'. This would normally have got a stern ticking-off from the Speaker – it is unparliamentary to accuse an MP of lying – but John Bercow contented himself by saying that he was being 'rather naughty' (oops, said Mr Field) and let it pass.

Ms McVey did not own up to lying, for that would mean that she had deliberately misled the Commons. Damian Green and Amber Rudd had resigned for less. Instead she explained that she had just 'used the wrong words', misinterpreting what the NAO meant. I'm not a liar, just a bit dim.

It was admirable sophistry but poor oratory. Since Mr Field had given a day's notice that he would be asking this question, you might have expected her to draft a statement. Instead she had a few scribbled notes on a piece of paper from which she tried to busk. It came out sounding like John Prescott on one of his less lucid days.

Here is the first sentence: 'I had information that the question was on the letter that I received yesterday, so that is obvious-ly where we will be going; the letter that I received yesterday. Opening the letter...' It was like Anne Elk, John Cleese's ram-bling dinosaur expert. 'That is the theory that I have and which is mine and what it is, too.'

She also disagreed with the NAO's assessment that the roll-out of universal credit was not going smoothly. The government has made changes to the system, she said, and they may turn out to be good changes and so it would be wrong to claim that it is all a mess now because it may get better.

This long view was reminiscent of Zhou Enlai, the former Chinese Premier, who when asked in 1972 about the impact of the French revolution replied that it was 'too early to say'. Some have since claimed that Zhou thought his questioner meant the uprising in Paris in 1968, not 1789, but that's what Ms McVey might file under 'nit-picking'.

'There I'd like to leave it,' she said, optimistically, at the end of her brief meander but, curiously, MPs wanted to question her a bit more. Some forty of them tried to catch the Speaker's eye, though only eighteen got a go. Some were very angry.

To all of these, Ms McVey just acted as if she had been unlucky to be caught. 'Sometimes I think we are blessed in this House that the opposition never get anything wrong,' she tut-tutted. 'I have never asked Labour to apologise for its misleading figures.'

It was a performance, in short, that was so lacking in sparkle, so incoherent, so eager to dodge the blame and move on that it made Chris Grayling look like Pericles.

13 JULY
STABLE GENIUS GETS BIGGER AND BIGGER

If men were dominoes, P. G. Wodehouse wrote of one of his trademark duffers, Sigsbee H. Waddington would have been the double-blank. Yet in politics, the double-blankers have their merits. Superficially pointless, they can be deployed to get you out of a tricky hole and if they're with you to the end they are worth more than the multi-spotted.

Donald J. Trump is not a double-blank. If he were a domino, he'd claim to be the double-seven: far bigger than anything you've got but unable to make a connection with anyone else. Ultimately not something you want in your hand, whatever Theresa May first thought.

The American President bulldozed into Brussels for the NATO summit, told the other delegates how great and generous he is, beat some more money out of them for the communal defence coffers and then called an unscheduled press conference to tell the world.

'We are doing numbers that have never been done before,' he boasted of the new deal. Presidents from Reagan to Obama had been too soft, he said, but The Donald had shouted at them for a bit and they had coughed up. And they were grateful that he had asked. Why hadn't anyone done so before?

'The Secretary-General thanked me,' he said. 'Everyone in that room thanked me. They said it was a great thing that we were doing.' What a remarkable man he is. And as if we were in any doubt he then added, 'I am a very stable genius.' Course you are, Donald. And I have a 28-inch waist.

The American President is not a man given to huge self doubt. He is the Ethel Merman of diplomacy. Anything you can do, I can do bigger. He told the press that he had explained to the other leaders that 'our equipment is so much better than everyone else's equipment' and they had been won over.

He had a point, to be fair, about America bearing an over-heavy burden when other nations could contribute more, but he hinted that he could be even more generous since his own economy was booming. 'Our GDP has increased since this thing called an election,' he explained. 'It's, like, gone way up.'

Speaking of the election, he then told the room, for no reason other than insecure bragging, that he had won Wisconsin in 2016. 'Reagan didn't,' he preened. 'That was the one state he didn't win when he swept the board. And we did.' Well done, Donald, although you probably meant Minnesota. Reagan actually won Wisconsin twice. Fake news, as someone once said.

Still, at least he speaks to the press and takes their questions. He hogged the stage for half an hour after his speech, which is about twenty-seven minutes longer than Mrs May usually gives. He spoke glowingly of President Xi of China ('I spent two days with him, they were among the most magical two days I have ever lived.') and President Putin of Russia ('He's a competitor, hopefully he'll become a friend.').

And what about us? (Sorry to be needy, Donald, but you'll understand.) Not much other than to say that talk of protests for his visit to Britain was overplayed. 'They like me a lot in the UK,' he insisted. That's why he's being kept outside the M25: to share his luminescence around. Got a view on Brexit? 'It's not for me to say what they should be doing.' Blimey, that was uncharacteristically coy. 'Brexit is Brexit,' he finally added. Maybe Mrs May has greater influence than we thought.

14 JULY
FAKE NEWS! THIS IS THE SPECIALEST RELATIONSHIP

Only a week ago Theresa May thought that she had united her party over cream tea at Chequers by threatening to call a cab for any Cabinet cabal. That dream soon crumbled like a stale scone. Then yesterday the peace of the Chilterns was broken again when Marine One landed on her garden, dispensing the Great American Man-Toddler and a collection of unflattering headlines.

If their morning meeting had been a testy one, Mrs May did not show it as they walked out for a joint press conference. In fact, she seemed almost jolly. Donald Trump, bronzed and brazen, grabbed her wrist as they walked down the garden stairs and she didn't flinch. It probably just felt nice to be needed.

Mr Trump said that it was a 'true honour' to be at Chequers ('truly magnificent'), which he had learnt all about in history lessons at school. He said that Mrs May and the 'Dook of Marlboro' had given him 'very gracious hospitality' the night before at Blenheim Palace. 'A memorable evening that I will not soon forget,' he said. Nor will Mrs May after she had been informed over the petits fours of his interview in *The Sun*, the diplomatic equivalent of a guest relieving himself on his host's fireplace. An electric fireplace at that.

'Fake news!' insisted Mr Trump. 'I said tremendous things about the Prime Minister! She's doing a terrific job!' In fact, as the man from *The Sun* was keen to point out, they had printed what the President had said about her on page two. 'But you didn't put it in the headline,' whined Mr Trump. Perhaps that was because he had just called her 'a nice person'. A rather subdued adjective as tremendousnesses go, but perhaps more sincere and flattering than the exaggerated superlatives he normally sprays around.

Boris Johnson, on the other hand, had been described to *The Sun* as 'a very talented guy ... who's got what it takes' to be Prime Minister. What made him say that? Ego. 'He thinks I am doing a great job,' Mr Trump explained. 'And I am doing a great job, in case you hadn't noticed.'

Mr Trump has more of a beef with his own media than ours. 'We have a lot of false reporting,' he told Mrs May. He then refused to engage with the CNN reporter – 'I don't take questions from fake news' – and was rude to the man from NBC. 'Such dishonest reporting. Possibly worse than CNN.' A reporter from Reuters got off lightly: Trump only mocked his lack of hair. What a guy.

So how special is the special relationship these days? So special, that's how special. 'I'd give it, like, the highest level of special,' Mr Trump said. 'Am I allowed to go higher than that? I don't know.' It truly is the specialest.

He wouldn't reveal the advice he had given to Mrs May over how to play Brexit. 'It was a suggestion, not advice, and I think she found it was too brutal,' he said. Bomb Brussels? Yet he was eager to be a better guest in person than he had been in print. 'I've been watching her and she is a tough negotiator,' he insisted. 'Very smart and determined. I'd much rather have her as my friend than my enemy.'

At this, a little too needily, Mrs May leant across from her lectern. 'And we are friends,' she insisted. It was hard to tell who was playing who. Like all toddlers, Mr Trump just craves attention and to get whatever he demands. They walked off together, him clutching her elbow as they climbed the stairs, the most specialest of friends. For now.

17 JULY
STORM ANNA FINALLY BREAKS OVER THE COMMONS

Westminster has needed a good storm. There has been too much hot air, rancorous and unstable, rising above Parliament.

Rumbles have been heard for weeks. Finally, at the start of a debate on cross-border trade, the wind picked up and lightning flashed. Storm Anna had broken.

Anna Soubry has been fighting Brexit since the referendum but yesterday she lost patience with her Tory colleagues who want to leave the EU with no deal. Speaking of the damage this would do to manufacturing, she wondered how many Brexiteers had bothered to speak to businesses.

'Shame on you,' she thundered at Ben Bradley (Con, Mansfield), who resigned as a party vice-chairman last week. 'Codswallop,' she said to Sir Bernard Jenkin, who had told Radio 4 in the morning that businesses were opposing Brexit only to protect their bottom line. 'The stuff of madness,' she said to Charlie Elphicke (Con, Dover) as he explained how easy trade would be once we left the EU.

Some colleagues, she claimed, admitted privately that hundreds of thousands of jobs would go as a result of Brexit but thought it worth it to regain sovereignty. 'Tell that to the people of my constituency,' she demanded. 'Tell that to the people who voted to leave. Nobody voted to be poorer.'

'And nobody,' she roared, firing an almighty lightning bolt, 'voted Leave so that someone with a gold-plated pension and inherited wealth would take their job away from them.' The bolt could have struck any number of colleagues, but I suspect it was aimed at North East Somerset.

Like the storm in *King Lear*, this scene also featured a fool. Sir Edward Leigh felt that Ms Soubry's grandstanding was too much. He sees her as more rust than iron. 'I knew Margaret Thatcher,' he told her. 'I worked for her. And my honourable friend ain't no Margaret Thatcher.'

This was a bit petty and deserved the heckles it received. 'Is that the best you can do?' a Labour woman shouted. Nicky Morgan (Con, Loughborough) remarked that the only trade Sir Edward seems keen on is trading insults. Still, as Mrs

Thatcher once said: if they attack one personally it means they have not a single political argument left.

Bravely, Dame Eleanor Laing, the Deputy Speaker, suggested that Ms Soubry might be nearing a conclusion. 'More! More!' several MPs shouted. 'This isn't music hall,' Dame Eleanor said. 'Oh yes, it is,' came the inevitable reply.

Ms Soubry had plenty more to get off her chest. She said that three people had been jailed for making death threats against her and she was 'a bit tired of being called a traitor'. Next she attacked her own front bench. 'They should be shaking their heads with shame,' she said, In reference to them accepting Jacob Rees-Mogg's amendments to the Trade Bill. 'It's madness. They are scared of forty members. Hardline Brexiteers who should have been seen off a long time ago.' Is Theresa May in charge, she wondered, or Mr Rees-Mogg? 'The time has come for the nonsense to be stopped.'

It was the sort of barnstorming speech that used to be delivered by a member of the opposition. Alas, the Labour benches were largely empty. Their MPs were having a meeting to discuss how much antisemitism is too much. Again.

Another tough night for the Tory whips as pro-EU rebels tried to pass a law obliging Britain to join a customs union if it can't agree a free-trade deal with the EU. The government defeated the motion by six votes.

18 JULY
GOVERNMENT SCRAPE LATE WIN IN STOPPAGE TIME

It was, as Sir Alex Ferguson used to say, squeaky bum time in Westminster. Deep into stoppage time, the government were defending for their lives to preserve a slender lead. Players were collapsing everywhere you looked and many of Theresa May's fans had already given up. A late goal for the Reds, condemning the Tories to another season in Europe, would surely be it for the gaffer.

'I wonder if the Prime Minister will be going to the palace this evening,' mused a colleague in the gallery as MPs scurried like ants. There was a whiff of panic and urgency. Tory whips looked miserable; Tory rebels looked worse. Regicide is never easy. Stephen Hammond, the Wimbledon MP who had tabled an amendment to keep Britain in a customs union, almost choked on his words as he moved it. 'With a heavy heart,' he sighed. He knew the likely consequences.

Throughout the debate the whips had been at work, trying to separate the weaker rebels from the herd. Paul Masterton (Con, East Renfrewshire), one of the new intake, had a long chat with his whip and stayed loyal. Mr Hammond kept being called out and each time he returned his face seemed sadder. George Hollingbery (Con, Meon Valley), the trade minister who looks as if he has been dipped into a barrel of creosote, then made an oily offer: drop the rebellion now and it can be amended in the Lords. 'Oh no,' the rebels replied. 'We're not falling for that trick again.'

Tick, tick, tick. Chris Pincher, the Deputy Chief Whip, was now up in Rebel Corner but no one wanted to talk to him. Then Julian Smith, the Chief, shimmered into the room. 'Would you like to come and inspect my new thumbscrews?' he invited the rebels. Nicky Morgan and Sarah Wollaston told him to bugger off. Mr Smith shimmered out.

As this went on, David Davis was sitting merrily on the backbenches, chatting to old friends, not looking remotely like a man who had just resigned. Of Boris Johnson, who, like Mr Davis, had stood down from the Cabinet in protest at the position agreed at the Chequers summit, there was no sign. The former Foreign Secretary was described by one MP as wandering the corridors like an ex-girlfriend at a wedding.

Mrs May couldn't watch. She voted without entering the chamber, a sure sign that it was too close to call. A narrow defeat on an amendment to do with the regulation of medicines did not bode well. Up the MPs got and voted once more. This was the biggie. A whisper went round that the Chief Whip was threatening a confidence vote if the government lost. Do you really want to bring us down?

Jeremy Lefroy (Con, Stafford), a rebel on the medicines amendment, returned to the fold; yet Guto Bebb (Con, Aberconwy), a minister twenty-four hours earlier, went into the rebels' lobby. Ten rebels, eleven, twelve. Was the Chief Whip squeaking? Suddenly I spied Jeremy Corbyn, wandering round tieless. The Labour leader stopped in front of the mace and looked rather forlorn, as if he had just realised he might actually have to be Prime Minister after all.

In came the tellers. From the gallery we watched as they whispered to a clerk, who wrote the numbers down in pencil. Was that last digit a one or a seven? Was that a grin from Mr Smith or a grimace? 'The ayes to the right…' There was a late winner all right, but it was scored by five Labour MPs in their own net. Afterwards, you could hear the Brexiteers singing, 'It's coming home, it's coming, sovereignty's coming home…'

19 JULY
SHOWMAN SHUFFLES OFF STAGE WITH A MUTED PARP

Boris Johnson surely knew what he was doing when he entered the chamber for Prime Minister's Questions – at precisely the same time as Theresa May, though from opposite doors – and headed for a seat below the gangway, three rows back.

It was from there, or a buttock or two to the right, that Geoffrey Howe had battered Margaret Thatcher with his broken cricket bat.

What we got from Mr Johnson in his statement, however, was more Reggie Perrin than regicide. A futile gesture by a disillusioned man in search of a new start. If an attack from Howe was famously like being savaged by a dead sheep, Mrs May was gummed by a toothless lion.

That was still two hours away. Boris's arrival for PMQs at least caused a stir. He had come to mark his territory. Sitting with him were other members of the recently unemployed: David Davis and Steve Baker, once the Del Boy and Rodney of DExEU, and Scott Mann (Con, North Cornwall), a former postman who resigned as a bag-carrier because he couldn't deliver Mrs May's Brexit catalogue.

First blood went to Andrea Jenkyns (Con, Morley and Outwood), another departed aide whose greatest achievement in three years as an MP has been winning Westminster Dog of the Year (or, to be precise, her two Schnauzers did). She asked the PM 'at what point it was decided that Brexit means Remain?' Mr Johnson beamed. 'Brexit means Brexit,' Mrs May replied, as she always does. She survived PMQs easily.

Unlike Mrs Thatcher in 1990, the Prime Minister did not have to stay and listen to the resignation statement. Labour had done her a favour by tabling three urgent questions and the government had a statement on space policy. Some MPs would like to blast Boris into orbit, although he thinks the world revolves around him, not vice versa.

All the big names had left by the time the Speaker finally called him. Michael Ellis, the tourism minister, was as heavyweight as it got on the front bench and Julian Smith, the Chief Whip, was the only Cabinet-level minister. It felt rather low-key.

And what followed was a curiously low-wattage speech. For

such a natural showman, it was flaccid and underwhelming. It was Harry Kane in the second half of England's World Cup semi-final or a Paul McCartney concert featuring only songs from his new album. Whether you love or hate Boris, this was way below his potential.

There were none of the verbal flourishes and twiddly bits. No Latin or pentasyllabic archaisms. No vivid claims about how Brexit will be a success because they love *Harry Potter* in the Punjab. I think he was trying to be a statesman. He had even brushed his hair.

He began by thanking the Foreign Office staff for putting up with him for two years and praised Mrs May for her 'courage and resilience' (subtext: is she still here?). Then we got straight to the nub. Mrs May's Lancaster House speech on Brexit in January 2017 had been brilliant, he said. Everyone loved it. He glossed over her losing her majority in an election five months later. And now that bold vision had gone.

'A fog of self-doubt descended,' he said. 'It's called "reality",' heckled Labour's Chris Leslie. 'We allowed the Northern Ireland border to dominate,' Mr Johnson went on. The Chequers plan would mean 'economic vassalage ... a miserable permanent limbo'. He ended by saying that it was 'not too late to save Brexit' but it was a muted parp rather than a fanfare.

His supporters in the chamber liked it, though they were not many, and his online fans lapped it up, but the mood in the room was flat. The buzz had gone. As he walked out, you could hear them all thinking, 'Aaaanyway, moving on...'

24 JULY

MAYDAY! MAYDAY! PM FACES HUMANITY PROBLEM

Should the air get too thin on the Matterhorn, or wherever Theresa May plans to spend her holidays, and an idea form in her oxygen-deprived mind about calling a snap general election, the Prime Minister should watch the tape of her appearance at a factory near Newcastle yesterday and remind herself what happens when she meets the people.

They terrify her. And she, in return, cannot connect with them. Her question-and-answer session had all the energy and excitement of a nervous librarian reading the phone book to a conference of narcoleptics. They sat there like wet fish on a slab, all open mouths and unblinking eyes, as she explained her vision for Brexit and desperately hoped that no one would ask something tricky.

This must have been the only place in the country without any sunshine yesterday. For thirty dreary minutes, Mrs May said nothing on a variety of topics, using trademark phrases such as 'a future partnership that works for everyone' that just left her audience looking bewildered.

They asked questions more out of politeness than interest and the answers were rather low-wattage. Boris Johnson would have bounded in and enthused about how the future for trade is bright because they love *Inspector Morse* in Tonga.

This was the beginning of a tour in which Mrs May will sell her Brexit proposal to the nation. She is not a natural saleswoman. Diazepam in speech form. After she addressed the staff of an engineering factory yesterday, half of them would have been banned from operating heavy machinery for the rest of the day.

Still, if they were bored by her, she was petrified by them. Especially the person, a budding Andrew Neil, who asked how she likes to unwind. Mayday! Mayday! Humanity alert!

Here is her verbatim response to this stinker of a question. 'Hahahaha,' she said. 'Hahahaha. Well. It's, er, um, there's lots, several, er, things I like to do. I like walking. So we, er, we, er, my husband and I, er, enjoy going walking when we can, er, taking holidays, er, walking.' Let no one be in any doubt that walking is something she enjoys. Discovering that this answer had not gone down badly – Gateshead may not be the Lake District but some people enjoy walking there too – she developed her list of interests.

'I enjoy cooking,' she said, followed by a long pause as she considered what to add to this. 'It, er, has a benefit because you get to, er, eat it as well as, er, make it.'

(Then a long pause as her internal voice screamed 'what are you going on about?' at her.) 'I have over 150 cookbooks,' she added, 'so I, er, spend a lot of time looking at cookbooks.' Painful though this sounds, it was more interesting than her answers on Brexit.

Sensing that this was still not enough, Mrs May thought she had better throw in a TV show. But which? She tried to remember the box sets David Cameron had left in the Downing Street flat. 'Does anyone know *NCIS?*' she asked. 'I like watching that when I can.'

And suddenly she looked scared that someone would ask for her favourite character. The only thing worse for her than explaining Brexit is trying to appear normal.

25 JULY
OLD BOY RAAB HAS END-OF-TERM BLUES

It was almost the holidays and the Brexit select committee had welcomed back one of its former pupils to give a talk. 'It's really good to have you in your new role,' said Hilary Benn, beaming like a proud headmaster. 'It shows there is hope for us all.'

Dominic Raab sat with his hands clasped as if in prayer. He knew from his time on the committee that this would be testing. David Davis had been Brexit Secretary for two years without giving much sign of knowing what was going on. How could Mr Raab get it in two weeks? The first fifteen minutes were full of honesty, if not information. 'I don't know, I'll write to you,' he said. 'I'll have to look into that and get back to you … I would need to check … I'm sure we must have done some work on that … Just write to me.'

Sitting beside him was a man who would have known the answers but Olly Robbins, the Prime Minister's Europe adviser, let him flounder. You don't rise in the civil service by speaking unless forced to. Gradually, he was eased into the discussion, inasmuch as a man built like a back-row forward can ever be eased, but he said as little as he could.

'Shouldn't you swap places?' John Whittingdale suggested. Mr Robbins just smiled at Mr Raab, like a clever wife does to her stupid husband. 'Oh no, honey, you can do all this politics stuff by yourself.' Mr Robbins, some say, has been quietly trying to clean up the mess created by the Brexiteers' mad ideas. He is Gromit to Mr Davis's Wallace.

After one question about tariff arrangements, Mr Benn suggested that the answer could be provided in a diagram. 'A DI-a-gram?' Mr Raab gasped, sounding like Lady Bracknell. 'I'll see if I can find someone with the artistic talent.'

He then got confused over red lines and Northern Ireland and spoke about 'a border down the Red Sea'. Maybe he sees himself as a second Moses, leading his people from their European bondage to a land of milk and honey. Read all about it in the Book of Brexodus.

From Moses to Jacob. Since it was the last day of term, Mr Rees-Mogg had come in mufti, picking a daring navy tie to go with his double-breasted suit. Called near the end, he suggested that Mr Robbins had drawn up the Chequers compromise in secret without telling Mr Davis.

Mr Robbins gave a wary look as The Mogg asked when he had first sat down 'with pen in hand' to write it. 'Or probably more with a computer,' he conceded, realising which century he was in. 'Forgive the assumption of accusing you of being modern.' Mr Robbins said that he had been working on it for about two weeks, that it was an extension of work already done, and that he had only been doing what the Prime Minister had asked.

'That is worrying,' hummed The Mogg. It did not seem so to Mr Benn. 'For those of us who have been Cabinet ministers,' he said, pointedly at The Mogg, 'that sounds fairly normal. You are the Prime Minister's Europe adviser and you are accountable to her.'

Mr Robbins nodded, relieved that someone got it. The Mogg did not look convinced. He clearly felt that something was up, something so rum you could make it into a daiquiri. As for Mr Raab, he just looked like any drink would do.

1 SEPTEMBER
RAAB OF THE YARD LOOKING FOR RESULTS

The Brexit negotiations are getting closer and closer to a deal. We can tell that by the way that the lecterns from which the lead negotiators brief the press after each Brussels summit and the national flags that stand behind them have slowly moved towards convergence.

In the early days of these talks, David Davis and Michel Barnier stood so far apart from each other on the stage in the press room at the Berlaymont that their earpieces were needed for amplification as much as translation.

'Can you repeat that, Michel?' '*J'ai dit "non", David.*'

By the start of this year it was being reported that the two men were barely meeting at all.

With Dominic Raab replacing Mr Davis two months ago, the negotiators' lecterns have shifted inwards and the flags yesterday were placed so close together that a gentle draught might have made them touch. Concord, this image seemed to suggest, is in sight. And perhaps this time the French will allow it to be spelt the English way after Tony Benn conceded in 1969 that the supersonic aircraft should have a terminal 'e'.

Mr Barnier spoke of the 'ambitious and unprecedented partnership' that is being created and said that Theresa May's latest White Paper had a lot in it that was positive. Mr Raab flinched a little at this. 'Steady with the praise, Michel,' his gesture suggested, 'we still have to get it past our backbenchers.'

Much of the remaining dispute, Mr Barnier added, was now of a technical nature. Northern Ireland? It has come down to 'minutiae'. His main beef now is over Britain's refusal to recognise the EU's protection for where certain foods can be produced. Perhaps beef is the wrong word. The British suggestion that we might sell beaufort produced in Bristol and raclette from Rochdale has left this proud Savoyard a bit cheesed off.

At least they are making an effort to find consensus. After six hours together yesterday, the pair will meet again next week and Mr Raab said that he was 'stubbornly optimistic' of resolving a deal by the EU council meeting next month. Asked to offer odds against that happening, he replied, 'I'm a negotiator, not a gambling man.'

Mr Barnier also seemed reasonably relaxed about the work that needed to be done. While he conceded that a 'measure of flexibility' might be needed in the timetable, he said it would delay things by no more than a 'few days or weeks'. He repeated a quotation by one of the EU's founding fathers, Jean Monnet, that he had used on the opening day of these negotiations in June 2017. 'You ask me if I am an optimist or a pessimist; I am neither,' he said. 'I am determined.'

Yet Mr Raab also looks like a man on a mission. The jokey *joie de vivre* style of Mr Davis has been set aside. This Brexit Secretary seems to have a bit of steel about him. He is certainly growing into the job.

I wrote in July that he resembled a slightly too ambitious inspector in the Metropolitan Police. At the end of what has been a good week he looks set for promotion to superintendent.

8 SEPTEMBER
BEACH BOY CABLE TRIES TO AVOID LOOKING WASHED-UP

The Liberal Democrats need a better theme song. Sir Vince Cable walked out for the relaunch of his party yesterday morning to the sound of the Beach Boys. 'Wouldn't it be nice if we were older?' sang Brian Wilson. Sir Vince is seventy-five. Maturity is not their problem.

We were gathered in the National Liberal Club, hearth of liberalism, under the bronze gaze of a bust of David Lloyd George, though it was the busts and bronzed bodies heading upstairs that caught the attention of some Lib Dems. Chilean expatriates were also using the club facilities. 'They're much better looking than us,' one leading Lib Dem grumbled.

Sir Vince had come to explain how he will revive his party's flatlining fortunes by encouraging people to become Lib Dems without paying a subscription. They will be able to vote for the next leader, too, who won't even have to be an MP. Parliamentary politics is so nineteenth century, said Sir Vince, whose Commons colleagues could fit into a minibus.

It remains a mystery that the only national party opposed to Brexit, a position apparently supported by half the country, is mired in single figures in the polls. Sir Vince has failed, in his first year in charge, to shift the dial. He just lacks stardust.

You can tell how exciting a speech is by the sound of the photographers' shutters. The snappers crouch in the gangway, waiting for a dynamic movement or exaggerated expression that will make The Picture. Then rattatattatatta. During Sir Vince's speech, their trigger-fingers were not over-employed.

He began by saying that Brexit is stifling progress in other important policy areas, such as how we face the challenge of new technology. No one outside the room could hear him, though, as the live stream on the party website had failed.

Liberal democracy, he said, is facing its biggest threat since the 1930s, in Britain and around the world. The two main parties are being taken over by their extreme wings but there is a gap in the centre to be filled. He hopes that the Lib Dems can emulate Justin Trudeau's Liberals in Canada and go from third place to government. That would be some leap.

Sir Vince acknowledges that he is too old to take them into Downing Street. 'I do not wish to emulate Gladstone, who kept going into his mid-eighties,' he said. And when Gladstone was the age that Sir Vince is now, he had already spent more than ten years as Prime Minister.

The challenge is to find their Trudeau. While Sir Vince was anxious to say that any of his party could be a leader, his plan to throw the job open to outsiders suggests a party desperate for a messiah, a deus ex machina with a yellow tie and a sparkling smile. As the Beach Boys' song continues, 'Maybe if we think and wish and hope and pray it might come true. Baby, then there wouldn't be a single thing we couldn't do.'

21 SEPTEMBER
SO LONG, FAREWELL, AUF WIEDERSEHEN...

High on a hill was a lonely PM.
Lay-ee yodelay-ee yodelay hee hoo!
Sat by her own at a lonely banquet.
Lay-ee yodelay-ee yodel-oo!

Theresa May had hoped to flee Salzburg last night, like the von Trapps so many years earlier, to a land of peace and freedom. The hills were alive with the sound of Brexit. She had even prepared a little tune to impress the leaders of the twenty-seven other EU countries.

> Stopping migration; a fair deal for Britain;
> Choosing the laws we'd prefer are rewritten;
> Frictionless trading without any strings:
> These are a few of my favourite things.

Alas, they were deaf to her song. Not for the first time, the Prime Minister left a European summit with steam coming out of her ears. Ten days before her party conference, Mrs May's endeavours had received a loud raspberry.

It had been, she said in a press conference, a 'frank bilateral meeting'. The word 'frank' seldom expresses something positive when reporting back on a summit. It normally means Frank as in Spencer: a disaster. Mrs May wore an expression that suggested that the EU had done a whoopsie on her Chequers proposal. Some PMs do 'ave 'em.

Earlier, Donald Tusk, the president of the European Council, had bluntly told the press that Chequers would not work. It would undermine the single market, he said. Not since Michael Gove declared war on the ivory trade has Downing Street held such a dim view of tusks.

Thirty years to the day after Margaret Thatcher's Bruges speech, in which the former Prime Minister had sung of shared prosperity and security but rejected the proposal to make the European Community 'a narrow-minded, inward-looking club … an institutional device to be constantly modified according to the dictates of some abstract intellectual concept', Mrs May again tried to talk tough.

'Ours is the only serious and credible proposition on the table,' she insisted, saying that while Britain would bring forward a revised proposal shortly, it would be nice if the EU27 could offer some thoughts of their own, too. 'A lot of hard work is to be done,' she said, 'but, if the political will is there on the other side, I am confident that we WILL reach a deal.' She said 'will' with added firmness, but they were not the eyes of a confident woman.

Mrs May was wearing a striking red jacket with a white top as if to present herself as a living, breathing flag of St George, but what caught the eye was the chunky chain-link necklace, the sort of thing you see used to deny Staffordshire Bull Terriers their liberty. For all the good intentions that she expressed about improving Britain when she became Prime Minister – all that talk of helping the just-about-managings Mrs May's premiership has been as firmly shackled to Brexit as a Staffie to a railing. She cannot escape it.

'There will be no second referendum,' she insisted. 'We gave people their choice, they made their choice. It's the duty of the government to deliver on that vote.' Climb ev'ry mountain, ford ev'ry stream… If only David Cameron had kept his von trapp shut.

And so, as Mrs May followed Maria out of Salzburg, it was to a different tune from The Sound of Brexit:

> No to deal, the Chequers deal.
> May, she hopes they change their mind.
> ('Me' says Boris, yet again.)
> Far, far off from being signed.
> So the situation's rough.
> Argh, there's six months left to go!
> Tea? No more, I've drunk enough!
> And that brings us back to No.

22 SEPTEMBER
FURIOUS MAY DEMANDS R-E-S-P-E-C-T

Theresa May had come dressed for a funeral, but not her own. Not yet, anyway. Her mood was as black as her jacket, her anger bubbling close to the surface. Hell hath no fury like a Prime Minister scorned.

The headlines will have been painful, with their variations on a theme of 'humiliation', but the mockery that came from Donald Tusk's Instagram account really rubbed Salzburg into the wound. She had an expression that suggested she had told the president of the European Council where he could stick his cake, cherries and all.

The theme of her statement, delivered in what seemed to be a Downing Street broom cupboard in front of two Union Flags, was 'respect' and it came in two forms. Her determination to respect the result of the referendum, whether it is good for the country or not – summed up, with apologies to Jim Hacker, as 'I am their leader, I must follow them' – and the lack of respect she feels from her fellow European leaders. 'I have treated the EU with nothing but respect,' Mrs May said. 'The UK expects the same. A good relationship at the end of this process depends on it.'

'R-E-S-P-E-C-T,' she sang. 'Find out what it means to me. Sock it to me, sock it to me, sock it to me, sock it to me.' At Salzburg, the EU had listened to her and then gently slipped lead into the end of the sock.

Mrs May gave them a warning, therefore, that unless Mr Tusk and the others started showing her more respect – just a little bit – 'you might walk in and find out I'm gone'. The Aretha Franklin of Maidenhead wanted her protest song to be a threat; given the EU's attitude to threats, 'I Say A Little Prayer' might have been useful.

In fact, the Brexit negotiations have been like a Motown

greatest hits album. First we got 'I Want You Back' and 'It Takes Two' but that was quickly followed by 'Money (That's What I Want)', 'Ain't No Sunshine' and then 'Don't Leave Me This Way'. Meanwhile, on the sidelines we find the record stuck on 'What's Going On?' It looks as if we will never make it to 'Signed, Sealed, Delivered'.

25 SEPTEMBER
LEFT-WINGER SHOOTS AND SCORES

There are few easier ways to get a standing ovation in Liverpool than to invoke the blessed memory of St Bill of Anfield. Jeremy Corbyn had a Shankly moment here in 2016 and John McDonnell began his shadow Chancellor's speech yesterday with a video about the man he calls 'my hero'.

He did not mention the former Liverpool manager's adage that 'if you are first you are first; if you are second you are nothing', for it might have reminded people that, despite 'winning' last year's election (as many a delegate here insists), Labour still have fifty-eight fewer MPs than the Tories. Instead, he sang of a shared belief in socialism as the foundation for success. Though even Shankly needed people who could play on the right wing.

In the past, Mr McDonnell has softened his words with a ladle or two of honey, canny enough to realise that if you scare voters you are less likely to win power. The Tories find him far more dangerous than Mr Corbyn as a result. As Shankly defended one of his players by saying, 'Yes Roger Hunt misses a few, but he gets in the right place to miss them,' so the shadow Chancellor recognised that you can change nothing, for better or worse, if you are not in Downing Street.

Yesterday, however, Mr McDonnell let rip. Perhaps he now sees the route to power as an inevitability. He was shankled but certainly not shackled. It was the most openly, proudly left-wing speech by an aspiring Chancellor since the 1980s. From the overture, in which he merrily bashed the bankers, via a hymn of praise to Clause IV, that Labour shibboleth that Tony Blair tried to bury, to a rousing finale – 'And we'll be proud to call that future "Socialism". Solidarity!' – this performance was one of the deepest red.

27 SEPTEMBER
CORBYN TAKES LABOUR ON A WHISTLE-STOP TOUR TO POWER

In the Labour Philharmonia, sounding more philharmonious than it has for years, even the triangle player has his moment. As the conference drew to its close with the traditional sing-along, Barry Gardiner (Brent North) finally got the role his talents deserved.

The shadow Trade Secretary, who a recent poll found to be the most anonymous member of the shadow Cabinet (an accolade up there with being the tallest citizen on Lilliput), stepped forward, recalling what Lauren Bacall had taught him years ago, put his lips together and blew. The first verse of 'The Red Flag' whistled around the hall. And back came the chorus from 13,000 comrades: 'So raise the scarlet standard high...'

Mr Gardiner's skill at whistling is well known in Westminster. You can find a video of him on YouTube whistling the 'Queen of the Night aria' from *The Magic Flute*. Researchers in the neighbouring offices have been known to leave early whenever Baz is in an *Oklahoma!* mood. When Jeremy Corbyn speaks of wanting to harness the hidden talent of everyone, no matter how insignificant they seem, he means people like his purse-lipped pal.

Mr Corbyn certainly gave the members a reason to be in good voice yesterday. To praise the Labour leader's oratory is like remarking on Emily Thornberry's modesty or Boris

Johnson's celibacy. Not the first attribute that comes to mind. Yet when the moment came, he nailed it. He had the hall in the palm of his hand from the moment that he walked out to 'You'll Never Walk Alone'. 'Please welcome the next Prime Minister, Jeremy Corbyn.' You know, I think he really believes it now. And they believed it in the hall as well.

He looks confident and chipper, not tetchy and sanctimonious. 'This is the conference of a Labour Party that's ready to take charge,' he said.

The speech was riddled with applause lines. He gave the media a bashing early on and then crowed about the local election results on Merseyside. And in the audience they waved their red scarves and sang 'Oh Jeremy Corbyn'.

This conference has had two clouds overhead and he confronted antisemitism early on. The row, he said, had caused immense hurt. Some might correct him on that: it's the antisemitism that really upsets them, not the row. Nonetheless, this felt like a stronger rebuke than he has issued so far — one that should have come months ago — though it was delivered in a whisper as if he feared who might hear it.

The other cloud, the one called Brexit, was left dangling for fifty minutes. When he finally reached it, all we got was more fudge. 'We respect the result of the referendum but we don't respect the way the government have handled the negotiations. Move over, Theresa.' This section did, though, have the best joke of the speech. 'Brexiteers dream about a Britannia that rules the waves and waives the rules.'

The audience didn't mind. He had given them enough show tunes by then. A catalogue of Tory failures — prisons, trains, Carillion, bankrupt councils — and then some new policies on childcare and taxing second homes. The Palestinians, Yemen and Burma, favourite causes, all got more attention and appreciation than Brexit.

By the end, when he told them with a subtle nod to the

city's most famous sons that 'when we meet next year, let it be as a Labour government', they adored him. This was, however, also a good speech for the Tories. For too long they have relied on the fact that Mr Corbyn is rubbish. It has made them lazy.

This speech, and the general professionalism of the whole conference, might shake them out of their complacency. If they don't start to demonstrate why they can make people's lives better, they can go whistle for another term. And they will be doing it without the talented Mr Gardiner.

2 OCTOBER
MOGGMENTUM

In 1997, when campaigning for election in Fife, Jacob Rees-Mogg arrived at a hall for a public meeting to find only one woman and a small child there. Undaunted, he addressed them as if he were Gladstone for half an hour until the lady raised a hand. 'Excuse me,' she asked. 'Is the mother and toddler group cancelled?'

How times have changed. The honourable member for Fusty-upon-Tweed is now the star attraction on the conference fringe. Forty-five minutes before his event yesterday, there were forty people in a queue. Come kick-off there were getting on for 300 in a room with 100 seats. And this at the same time as the Chancellor's conference speech in the main hall. Moggmentum is real.

Jacob beamed as they cheered his arrival. '*Et cum spiritu tuo*,' he may have murmured in benediction. He was there to explain how the Tories can win in places like Middlesbrough and said he had brought a 'modern message'.

The Mogg is not noted for such things. One can imagine his speech-writing session: quill in hand, little Sixtus upon his lap, the other Mogglets – Anselm, Genuflect, Chasuble and sweet

Panis Angelicus – cross-legged at his feet as he declares that he intends to give them a bit of Augustine of Hippo down at the conference. 'Lord, make me Prime Minister but not yet.'

At this, Nanny, who has become a radical since Jacob bought her a wireless, suggests he goes for something more modern. 'Hmm, possibly,' he muses. 'Aquinas, perhaps? Or William of Ockam?' And Nanny sighs and says, 'I was thinking more Alan Titchmarsh.'

Which I imagine is how, as a sop to Nanny and her modern ways, The Mogg told a packed room that the party needs to find the spirit of that up-and-coming thruster Benjamin Disraeli. 'He built a coalition of interests,' The Mogg said, 'and was interested in "the condition of the people".' Modern Tories need to grasp that nettle once more.

'We have to be saying that "we are going to improve your lives",' he said. 'And frankly we are not saying that at the moment.' For all his otherworldliness, there is a sensible, sellable philosophy lurking in the Mogg cranium. And just to mess with our sense of the way things are a little bit more, The Mogg then announced that 'a sepia-tinted vision has never been my thing'. Much more of this and he will be wearing double(-breasted) denim.

Fortunately, just before the fringe dispersed, he then revealed his big planning vision: a new bypass for Bath that is designed as 'a beautiful Georgian pastiche bridge with little pavilions'. With a sigh of relief, the world shifted back on to its axis.

The Mogg was also, albeit in absentia, the darling of the Bruges Group's fringe where the members endured a half-hour lecture on 'Johnny Continental and his Perfidious Allies' by Sir Bill Cash – sample line: 'Margaret Thatcher was assassinated by the pro-Europeans' – and were asked to vote for who they want as Prime Minister. The Mogg got 49 per cent, the most by a long way. Boris Johnson is yesterday's eccentric.

If the fringe is busy, with the likes of Dominic Raab and

Liz Truss also speaking to crowded rooms, the main hall has been uncluttered with members, even when Ruth Davidson was speaking. It was at its emptiest when Jeremy Wright (Con, Kenilworth and Southam), the Culture Secretary, had his turn. He was originally meant to give his speech remotely as a hologram (a Matt Hancock idea) but this was ditched when organisers realised that being there in person would push the attendance into double figures.

3 OCTOBER
BORISMANIA IS BACK

There was plenty of room to stretch out in the stalls as Sajid Javid made his big speech. Another half-empty conference hall. He gave those who had shown up a riff on an old John Major poster. 'What does the Conservative Party offer a working-class son-of-an-immigrant kid from Rochdale?' he asked. 'You made him Home Secretary.' It got a polite ripple. Cricket applause, you might say, the sort you hear at Taunton when a batsman nurdles a boundary early in his innings.

What, on the other hand, do the Conservatives offer an Old Etonian son-of-an-eccentric Bullingdon boy from Balliol who made a hash of being Foreign Secretary? Adulation, ululation and a fringe event packed to the gunwales of its 1,500-capacity. Borismania is back.

The queue had started to form three hours earlier and snaked around the conference centre, past the party treasurer's office where Theresa May was due to arrive to thank staff. Awkward. As members took their seats for Boris Johnson, a Queen song was played over the speakers, sending a message about the coming attraction: It's 'A Kind of Magic' – 'one prize, one goal, one golden glance of what should be' – not 'Good Old-Fashioned Lover Boy'.

In the front row we saw a glimpse of a future Johnson Cabinet as friendly MPs took their seats: Priti Patel, Owen Paterson, IDS, Peter Bone, Zac Goldsmith, John Redwood. There were about twenty-five in all, a claque but not an army.

Mr Johnson walked out with purpose, almost rolling up his sleeves as he went, like Churchill in the famous 'we're all behind you' cartoon by Low. They were certainly behind him metaphorically in the hall, lapping up what he had to say.

He opened with a joke about how so many thoroughfares in Birmingham are now named after the Tory mayor (Andy Street) and then thanked the Chancellor for saying that he will never be PM. 'The first Treasury forecast to have a ring of truth!' The Tories do love self-deprecation, especially when it is insincere.

Then straight into his main theme: bashing the hapless leader. Not Mrs May but Jeremy Corbyn. It was the standard Boris fare of hyperbole and colourful phrases: 'Weaselly cabal'... 'Kremlin apologists'... a bit on beards and allotments. After a drizzle of crowd-pleasing policy on how people will vote Tory if they own a house, why cutting taxes is good and a call to revive stop and search, he finally came, via an odd detour about Toblerone, to Brexit.

The key message, of course, was 'chuck Chequers', a phrase that drew the biggest cheer, but he did not attack Mrs May directly. Brussels was to blame, he said, for forcing her down that path. They want to make Britain 'parade in manacles like Caractacus'. He failed to mention that the old Catuvellauni chieftain managed to talk himself out of execution, was pardoned by Claudius and ended up having a nice retirement in Rome. Chequers is a 'cheat' to his eyes. And he knows a cheat when he sees one.

If Mr Johnson said one thing that everyone can agree with, Leaver and Remainer, it was that squabbling over Brexit is a 'toxic, tedious business' that puts off many normal people. So he ended not with a military fanfare but emollience. He called on members to back Mrs May by asking her to change her plan 'softly, quietly and sensibly'. Not adverbs you associate with him. It was a muted challenge but perhaps a more effective one. He had not parked his tank on her lawn but on a nearby street so that she can see it whenever she goes to the shops.

4 OCTOBER
METHINKS I SEE A MARVELLOUS OLD HAM ACTOR

What magnificent oratory! Exactly the pick-me-up we all needed at the end of a rather drab party conference. Whoever cast Geoffrey Cox (Con, Torridge and West Devon), QC, as Theresa May's warm-up man deserves a pay rise.

Mr Cox, the new Attorney General, given his big chance at the tender age of fifty-eight, seemed to have wandered in from rehearsals for *Iolanthe*. In a rich baritone that was part Rumpole, part RSC ham, with a hint of Terry Wogan, he addressed the hall as if they were jurors at the Old Bailey and he was pleading for Mrs May's life.

He leant casually on the lectern, puffing his cheeks in regret at his client's predicament, before pulling the lapels of his jacket together as if it were a gown and stiffening his back to show the nobility of the law. Then he raised a hand to heaven and bellowed, jowls a-quiver, 'We need not fear self-government.'

He even quoted from Milton. 'Methinks I see in my mind a noble and puissant nation...' How rarely we get puissance in speeches. And after that, with a gentle wave, he strolled off for lunch at El Vino's and to submit his bill. It was glorious.

The Prime Minister also gave a speech. So forcefully had her defence counsel put his case that I wondered if Mrs May would not be risked in the witness box, but out she trotted, doing a little shimmy to ABBA's 'Dancing Queen', before starting with a joke, in reference to last year's disaster, that if her voice failed she could borrow Mr Cox's.

This was not a normal May speech. Like Jeremy Corbyn last week, she had raised her game. It was thin on policy but hefty on purpose and delivered with greater confidence and competence than usual. There were light moments – 'I've seen the trailers for *Bodyguard*: it wasn't like that in my day' – and sombre ones, such as when she spoke of the selfless sacrifice in the First World War and the death of her goddaughter.

In a powerful section, she attacked the polarisation of politics, the bitterness and the bile that turn people away. She called on her party to 'set a standard of decency that will be an example for others'.

She heaped praise on colleagues as a head does to her pupils on Speech Day, then contrasted them with the shadow Cabinet. Labour has good people, she said, the heirs of Gaitskell, Castle and Healey, but not on the front bench. Another party squats there – the Corbynists – who do not deserve to lead the party of Attlee. 'What has befallen Labour is a national tragedy.'

On Brexit she stuck to her guns. No mention of Chequers by name but she defended her policy. 'If we pursue our own visions of the perfect Brexit we risk ending up with no Brexit at all,' she said, 'If we stick together and hold our nerve, we can get a deal that delivers for Britain.' It was a fudge, but one presented with enough confidence and optimism that it kept the hall.

By now it was starting to drag – it was fifteen minutes longer than Mr Corbyn's speech – and her sections on ending austerity and improving people's lives felt cobbled together. But it was delivered with vim and vigour and a sense of humanity and purpose. It was not her usual robotic performance. We need to see more of this. She left the stage to 'Mr Blue Sky' by ELO, a song whose chorus asks, 'Please tell us why you had to hide away for so long.' Many of us were saying exactly the same thing.

16 OCTOBER
MAY PLAYS A LONELY GAME OF CHEQUERS

On the day that the government launched its loneliness strategy, a 62-year-old woman sat forlornly by a table in Westminster and tried, as she has done for the past three months, to encourage someone, anyone, to join her in a game of chequers.

The board is rather battered and some of the pieces are missing. Theresa May is not even sure that she can remember the rules – is a huff a special move, she wonders, or just something that David Davis does? – but still the Eleanor Rigby of Maidenhead sits and hopes that someone will play with her. She was there for almost two hours yesterday and had not a single taker.

More than eighty people engaged her in conversation but they wanted to talk to her, not with her. They had no interest in her silly game. They wanted to tell her what games she should be playing instead: Patience, Risk, Scrabble or just Go. Some wanted to warn her, others to advise her. Sir Vince Cable cut to the chase and asked why she was even there. No one understands an existential crisis like the Lib Dems.

Jeremy Corbyn knows all about talking without anyone listening. The Labour leader did it for the first thirty years of his parliamentary career. Yesterday, he tut-tutted at Mrs May. 'This really is beginning to feel like *Groundhog Day*,' he sighed. Ironically, Sir Keir Starmer, his Brexit spokesman, had said exactly the same thing in reply to last week's Commons statement.

Brexit does indeed now resemble the 1993 film in which Bill Murray is unable to escape the ghastly Andie MacDowell no matter how often he kills himself. No matter how many statements we get, the same things always happen. Remainers want a new referendum, hardline Brexiters want to leave right now, John Bercow tells a few MPs to calm down and no one wants to play chequers. Never in the history of human conflict has so much been owed by so many to déjà vu.

Mrs May did have something slightly new to say, though, on the subject of the backstop. Now backstop, like Groundhog Day, is a term that never should have entered the Brexit lexicon. It's the sort of expression used by people who follow sports teams with the word 'Sox' in the title. A bit Ed Miliband. No wonder no Brit understands it.

If the Prime Minister had spoken instead, using her mother tongue, of the need for a longstop, a fielding position that was all the rage when cricket pitches resembled potato fields, it would have been much clearer. A sensible precaution until the pitch has flattened out and the keeper's got his eye in. No one, Brexiteer or Remainer, could have objected to that. And to think that Mrs May is a member of Marylebone Cricket Club.

The EU, she told the Commons, has now asked for a 'backstop to the backstop', in case her first one fails. She should have offered Monsieur Barnier instead a deep fine leg and a third man right on the rope. Throw in a backward point, two short legs, one of them silly, and a man out at cow corner and suddenly it would all make sense. Or at least confuse the hell out of them in Brussels.

Instead, she explained, which I don't think I've heard her do before, that the backstop is really just an insurance policy that she hopes never to have to call on. And what the EU wants, she clarified, is 'effectively an insurance policy for the insurance policy'. I fear this all just ends with us getting cold calls in ten years' time from people asking if we've ever been mis-sold a Brexit.

23 OCTOBER
THE LADY IS FOR TURNING, ROUND AND ROUND...

Round about and round about and round about they go. Like
the child in the A. A. Milne poem, Parliament went for another
circular trot – 'all round the table, the table in the nursery' –
yesterday, seeking an answer to the Great Brexit Question. 'I'm
feeling rather funny and I don't know what I am BUT round
about and round about and...'

Theresa May assured MPs in her latest Commons statement
that we are almost there with the Brexit negotiations. Almost
– 95 per cent done. Yet as anyone who has installed updates
on a computer knows, the first 95 per cent is easy. It's the final
bit, as the circle spins or the hourglass keeps flipping over, that
drives you mad.

The Prime Minister began, as she usually does when reporting back on a summit, by stating the obvious. The EU leaders
had discussed chemical weapons last week and they agree that
they are still bad. Ditto cyber attacks. And slavery, that's a big
no-no. Anything else? Oh. Yes. Brexit.

'The shape of the deal is now clear,' Mrs May said. 'We have
agreed the broad scope of provisions.' The typeface for the withdrawal agreement, for instance, is now settled and we are almost
there in terms of which shade of green to use on the back cover.

The Maynframe churned through the updates. 'Installing
protocol on aircraft bases in Cyprus... DONE. Installing under-
lying memoranda over Gibraltar... DONE. Installing citizens'
rights... DONE. Installing Northern Ireland arrangements...
WAITING... WAITING...' The counter had whizzed to 95
per cent but now it seemed to have stalled.

'There is one sticking point left, but a considerable one,' Mrs
May conceded, wondering if the hourglass might stop rotating
if she gave the table a kick.

Labour backbenchers, and a few of her own, went for the

traditional solution whenever computers or diplomacy get stuck. 'Have you tried turning it off and back on again?' The so-called People's Vote, or Referendum 2.0, is the control-alt-delete of modern politics, the last resort of the desperate.

'Just give it more time,' Mrs May pleaded. But how long? Another three months? Six months? 'I do not want to extend the implementation period,' Mrs May insisted. Come on, computer, come on... Some of her backbenchers look as if they would rather whack the machine with a sledgehammer. John Redwood suggested she should just chuck it out of the window and buy another one.

Yet the violent impulses have gone too far. Some Tory MPs had got carried away when briefing the Sunday newspapers and thought they were running with the Krays. One said he wanted to plunge a hot knife into Mrs May's chest, another said she should bring her own noose to the 1922 Committee. Charming.

This was too much even for her critics. 'They have thoroughly disgraced themselves,' Steve Baker, the former Brexit minister, said. 'I hope they're discovered and that she'll withdraw the whip from them.' Jacob Rees-Mogg said that for all their political differences he held Mrs May as a role model for the way to speak to colleagues.

The mood in the chamber was one of sympathy rather than anger. It may be enough to buy the PM the time she needs to load her Brexit. Until then, round about and round about and round about we go...

25 OCTOBER
DANTE METAPHOR SIGNALS ONE HELL OF A MESS

Geoffrey Cox is not short of literary allusions. A long career at the Bar does that to you. The Attorney General, who deployed Milton to talk up the opportunities of Brexit at the party conference, followed that in Tuesday's Cabinet meeting by comparing a backstop in Northern Ireland to being stuck in Dante's first circle of hell.

Actually, as the underworld goes, the first circle isn't all that bad. It's where virtuous pagans – Homer, Cicero, Aristotle and that gang – spend their days conversing in green meadows. Estate agents might spin it as 'paradise borders', though the neighbours can be diabolical.

The Dante metaphor works better for Prime Minister's Questions. There we sit in the limbo of the press gallery, surrounded by the wailing souls of the uncommitted, as we look down upon the lustful, the wrathful and the gluttons as they suffer eternal torment by watching Jeremy Corbyn take on Theresa May. Abandon all hope, ye who enter.

The latest outing felt even more awful than usual. Mr Corbyn challenged the Prime Minister on whether austerity was over, a claim she made at her party conference, albeit with the sort of optimism you hear from a British holidaymaker who has spotted an inch of blue sky in a week of rain showers and declares that 'summer is here'.

. They don't think it's over in Tory-controlled Walsall, Mr Corbyn crowed as he read out a comment from the council leader, nor Derby. 'Will the Prime Minister try to cheer them up?' What an odd question. Effectively an invitation for Mrs May to launch into some spin about the employment figures.

She then produced a book of economic essays, edited by the shadow Chancellor, in which one of Mr Corbyn's advisers had written that the Institute for Fiscal Studies thought the sums in the last Labour manifesto didn't add up. It was a cynical piece of selective quoting to get her off the hook. It worked.

Mr Corbyn moved on instead to complain about cuts to the police force. 'There are 21,000 less police officers than eight years ago,' he said. 'FEWER!' bayed the Tory backbenchers, missing the point.

Barely pausing for breath, the Labour leader changed tack and threw in attacks on universal credit and nurse bursaries. They were so clumsily delivered and unfocused that they failed to trouble the Prime Minister. After more than two years in the job, Mrs May is still playing PMQs on the easy setting.

'You're completely out of touch,' Mr Corbyn sniffed as she refused to engage with his questions. Suddenly I spotted Boris Johnson standing in the doorway by the exit to the voting lobby. The former Foreign Secretary chose that moment to let loose an almighty yawn, almost revealing his tonsils. For once, Mr Johnson spoke for everyone in the House.

This had been billed as 'hell week' for Mrs May. Or was that last week? Or even the one before? Amid all the talk about letters of no confidence being submitted, still she trudges on stoically like Dante through the damned.

At the end of the day, she had to confront that great three-faced beast, the 1922 Committee. Yet again she passed the trial unscathed. The whips had gone to work and she was greeted with desk-thumping and yodelled loyalty. Far from being thrown to the lions, one MP later said it was like a petting zoo. The Tory Party was keen to show that it stands firmly behind its leader. There's no better place to be if you want to stab them in the back.

26 OCTOBER
SUGAR BITTER ABOUT BREXIT FAILURE

Bored by Brexit? Blame Lord Sugar for not stopping it. The businessman told the House of Lords yesterday that he could have single-handedly kept Britain in the European Union two years ago. 'Alan, you muppet,' he chides himself every morning. 'This is all your fault. Why did you have to be so bloody modest and self-effacing?'

History pivoted, this reticent software mogul explained, on his decision not to appear in a BBC television debate on the eve of the referendum. 'I was invited by David Cameron to take the lead,' Lord Sugar told peers. 'And to this day I kick myself for turning it down. I felt I wasn't qualified.'

Sadiq Khan, the Mayor of London, went in his place. 'Sadiq did the best he possibly could,' Lord Sugar said, with as much condescension as he could muster. Then, realising that he could patronise the mayor just a little more, added, 'Look, I'm being polite.' The inference was clear: he thought Mr Khan was as much use as a chocolate teapot.

What, though, would Lord Sugar have done differently? Simple. 'I would have made Boris Johnson admit he was lying. And maybe that could have swung the vote.'

It may seem surprising that no one had tried to make Mr Johnson tell the truth before but few have the persuasive talents of the Chigwellian Cicero. Why, Lord Sugar even managed to talk himself into a U-turn during his six-minute speech yesterday. He began by saying that a second referendum would be a 'complete farce' and concluded by saying that the public were entitled to be given a vote on the terms of the deal. Lord Sugar is a man who deals in certainties, even if they are contradictory.

Perhaps he changed his mind in the belief that, even if it were a complete farce, a second vote for Brexit would tie the public into taking responsibility for the lies. As the old saying goes, 'Fool me once, shame on you; fool me twice, we've got a viable business model.'

There is no pussyfooting around with Lord Sugar. He even called during yesterday's speech for Mr Johnson and Michael Gove to be sent to prison – 'or at least prosecuted' – because they had made a debatable claim on the side of a bus. That sort of thing would not be tolerated in business, he said. What a pure and innocent world he must inhabit.

30 OCTOBER
BUFFET BUDGET COULD HAVE DONE WITH MORE MEAT

The TV listings for BBC One said that from 3.45 p.m. onwards there would be *Money for Nothing*, followed by *Flog It!* and then *Pointless*, which seemed like a rather brutal prediction of Philip Hammond's big fiscal event until I realised that the Budget was being shown on BBC Two.

A flood of emails from public relations departments giving their verdict began to arrive as soon as Mr Hammond sat down – 'The National Gruntfuttock Federation welcomes the Chancellor's extra money for gruntfuttocking...' – with his statement appearing to offer something for everyone, if not all that much of it.

It was a buffet Budget, with lots of small spoonfuls piled upon the plate that might seem temporarily filling but doesn't make a square meal. The Tory backbenches were satisfied enough at the end but not all that enthused. Some of his biggest announcements, such as a cut to business rates, barely registered on the clapometer.

This was, Mr Hammond said, a Budget for everyday people. 'The strivers, the grafters and the carers, people we are proud to represent.' It was especially aimed, the Chancellor added, at 'those who care little for the twists and turns of Westminster politics'. And they will have loved the joke he soon threw in about the 1922 Committee.

Another line about 'fiscal rules OK', playing on a graffiti trend from forty years ago, may also have passed over many heads. It made me wonder, with the threat of blockades at Calais after Brexit, whether we will end up with graffiti saying 'French customs officials rule *au quai*'.

While the NHS got the biggest dollop, schools were given a one-off serving of £400 million to spend on 'an extra bit of kit', which sounded patronising when many of them are asking parents to supply paper and pens, while £420 million was provided to mend potholes in the hope of a less bumpy road ahead. There was also £90 million for research into providing 'on-demand buses', when people would just be happy with ones that come on timetable, and a few million for something called the Medicines Discovery Catapult. Perhaps that is how we are going to get drugs into the country after Brexit.

Northern Ireland also got its cream with a £350 million city deal for Belfast, which was greeted with a rally of cross-chamber nodding between David Lidington, the PM's second in command, and Nigel Dodds, Leader of the DUP at Westminster, who may now be less keen to make threats about voting down the Budget.

Mr Hammond even found some money to allow himself a series of jokes based around rates relief for public lavatories — 'for the convenience of the House ... without wanting to get bogged down ... at least this hasn't leaked' – though disappointingly he failed to shoehorn in anything about being flush with cash or always keen to spend a penny.

Speaking of shoehorning things in, Liz Truss, Mr Hammond's deputy, had come wearing an eyecatching scarlet dress but was almost denied her plum seat next to the boss when Sajid Javid refused to move. Sharp-buttocked Ms Truss eventually squeezed herself in, shunting the Home Secretary out of camera shot. Yet again Mr Javid had backed Remain only to become a reluctant Leaver.

This was the first Budget held on a Monday since 1962. Selwyn Lloyd's statement was apparently a formative event in the life of the infant Hammond. He told MPs that he remembered watching it and that his parents had told him, 'Philip, that could be you one day.' He failed to mention that Mr Lloyd was sacked three months later.

31 OCTOBER

MCDONNELL'S MISERY TURN PLEASES THE WEEPING CHORUS

John McDonnell is not a man with levity in his soul. There is no sunny side to his street. I suspect that the shadow Chancellor is someone who likes to watch *It's A Wonderful Life* and stop at the point when George Bailey leaps into the river in case it spoils the ending. He has all the jollity of the leading man in one of Ibsen's less frivolous works.

That is his Commons persona, anyway. In private, he may cuddle kittens and sing 'Zip-a-Dee-Doo-Dah' as he dances into the office, but his game face is grim with a capital G. This is someone who can look at the word 'splendour' and see only the 'dour' bit.

Not that the Budget was all sunshine and sparkles. A shadow Chancellor never praises his opposite number, but Mr McDonnell presented it as something that made *Oliver Twist* look like a sitcom. When George Freeman asked if there was anything he could welcome – the increased funding for mental health, say – Mr McDonnell gave him a blank stare and said it was still not enough.

Those watching on TV may have thought that the Labour benches were packed for his speech but apart from the shadow Cabinet there were two rows of six loyalists squashed together behind Mr McDonnell with barely fifteen other MPs dotted around the chamber. He knows how to dress the stage. These dozen companions played the same role as the chorus in a Greek tragedy: to reinforce the protagonist's tales of woe with the odd 'aiai'.

'Four weeks ago, the Prime Minister promised to end austerity,' Mr McDonnell began. 'She raised people's hopes.'

'For shame!' sang the chorus.

With a quiver in his voice, he spoke of those whose hopes

had been dashed. Teachers who have to write begging letters to parents, police officers who cannot tackle violent crime and councils who cannot support families when – and here he bit his lower lip – 'a record number of children are being taken into care. Taken. In. To. Care.'

'Disgrace!' sang the chorus.

Was he overplaying it a bit? There were times when he almost pulled the old onion-in-a-hanky trick. If it was just an act, it was one that deserved an award.

'Austerity is not ending,' he said. 'But it is the beginning of the end of the dominance of an economic theory. People no longer believe the myth that austerity was necessary.'

'Yes! Yes! That's right!' sang the chorus with a ripple of nods.

The Tories, he went on, were so 'ideologically crushed', so 'bereft of ideas', that the Chancellor had been reduced to making toilet gags. This was a fair point. Philip Hammond's speech at that point had felt like a crude vaudeville act.

Tory backbenchers tried to intervene and read out the lines that the whips had given them. 'Desperate! Desperate!' sang the Labour chorus. 'Sit down!' To Marcus Jones (Con, Nuneaton), who pointed out the state of the economy left by Labour in 1979, Mr McDonnell gave a withering response. 'A former local government minister gets to his feet in this House and he does not express a word of apology for what the government have done to local government,' he preached.

'No wonder you lost your job,' one of the chorus shouted. Mr Jones, now a party vice-chairman, might argue that he was promoted, but it was not the time to quibble.

Mr McDonnell smothered another heckler, Chris Philp, with sarcasm. 'He gets excited,' he said. 'I've been excited myself in the past. George Osborne used to tell me to calm down. I said: "I'll calm down when you resign." And he did.'

Sitting next to Mr McDonnell, Jeremy Corbyn kept wincing.

Was this in sympathy with those affected by the awful tale that was being laid out or in the rueful realisation that the shadow Chancellor is just much better at this sort of performance than he is?

Finally, Britain and the EU agreed a draft text of a withdrawal agreement and immediately, perhaps without even reading all 585 pages, there were complaints from Brexiteers, particularly over the so-called Irish backstop, a means to prevent a hard border being established on the island of Ireland if no trade deal had been agreed before the end of a post-Brexit transition period. This dispute would drag on for months.

14 NOVEMBER
PLENTY OF ASSES BUT FEW WISE MEN

The Archbishop of Canterbury switched on the Christmas lights at Lambeth Palace last night, indecently early, some might say, with almost three weeks to go before Advent, while across the river at the Palace of Westminster auditions were being held in Central Lobby for the Brexmas nativity.

Wise men seemed to be in short supply and there were not as many loyal sheep as Theresa May had wanted. Instead, we saw several men from Northern Ireland who were anxious to play the role of Herod to the newborn withdrawal agreement, while a string of asses and donkeys lined up to say 'neigh' to the deal and bray that this wasn't the saviour that they had been promised.

The news had come out in the traditional way, with a tweet from an Irish broadcaster. Gallantly, as she had with her Chequers proposal in July, Mrs May decided not to seize the news agenda and talk up what had been decided, but to allow her political enemies a free evening to complain noisily about something that they had not yet seen.

Boris Johnson bounced into Central Lobby to wail and gnash his teeth for the evening news bulletins. This new arrangement would mean eternal servitude, he complained, even though he hadn't read it. Perhaps, like Ken Clarke and the Maastricht Treaty, he never will. What would be the point? Empty vassals make the loudest noise.

Boris begat Jacob; and Jacob begat Steve; and Steve begat Iain; and Iain would have begat Priti but no one seemed to notice the former International Development Secretary, who was hanging around on the fringes of the room hoping that someone would ask her for a quote. Alas, her vox did not pop.

Suddenly, from the heart of a rolling maul that had formed around Jacob Rees-Mogg, came the booming voice of Mark Francois, deputy chairman of the European Research Group, cutting through the hubbub. 'What members of the Cabinet do over the next twenty-four hours is the most important thing that they do in their lives,' Mr Francois said. 'They have an opportunity to stand up for their country and defend its destiny.'

Iain Duncan Smith was sceptical, however, that there would be Cabinet resignations over this. 'I never expect anything,' the former Tory leader sighed. He recalled the harsh criticism that Margaret Thatcher had once given to John Whittingdale, a backbench colleague, during the Maastricht debates: 'The trouble with you, John, is that your spine does not reach your brain.'

Brexiteers and Remainers were in agreement about one thing: that the Prime Minister's deal must be rubbish, even if none of them had read it. They just could not agree upon the next course of action.

16 NOVEMBER
MAY STAYS AT THE CREASE ON A STICKY WICKET

The first departure came over breakfast. 'Shailesh Vara's gone,' Philip May remarked. 'Oh good,' his wife replied. 'Who took his wicket?' By the time he had explained that this wasn't an update from the Test match but the resignation of an obscure minister, more bad news had arrived.

'Dear Prime Minister,' the note from Dominic Raab began. 'You'll recall how surprised I was recently to discover that Dover is an important trading port. Imagine my shock when I found out that I was Brexit Secretary and responsible for that load of rubbish you made us read in Cabinet.'

One down became two and there were now nasty rumblings coming from Esther McVey and Penny Mordaunt. Late-night pizza can have that effect. In the car to the House, Mrs May asked for news. 'Dickwella's out,' an aide told her. 'Dick Weller?' she replied. 'What was his job?' 'He's a cricketer not a minister,' the aide clarified. 'Sri Lanka are collapsing.' Mrs May sighed. 'I know the feeling,' she said.

She walked into the chamber as defiantly as can a woman who knows that she has just had a 'kick me' sign slapped on her back by a colleague. 'My draft treaty means we will leave the EU in a smooth and orderly way,' she insisted to hollow laughter.

They had come to bury Theresa, not to praise her. Most questions from her side came with a 'but' in the first sentence. Mark Francois: 'She has done her best but it is mathematically impossible to…' Justine Greening: 'I respect her efforts but this is not a good deal…' Anna Soubry: 'Nobody can doubt her dedication to doing her duty but the harsh, cruel truth is…'

Mrs May gave her best 'but me no buts' response. The troops were unconvinced. A note was passed to her by David

Lidington. 'There's been a rally,' it said. 'In the pound?' she asked. 'No, in Sri Lanka,' her deputy replied. 'We can't get rid of the one at No. 10.' Mrs May smiled. She would take every omen going.

Then rose Jacob Rees-Mogg, the double-breasted assassin. After praising Mrs May for being honourable, he ran through the promises she had made that were now broken. Since she could not deliver, he said, why should he not submit a letter of no confidence to the chairman of the 1922 Committee? It was a rallying call that others would follow, though it was disappointing that The Mogg had not ended his oration by declaring '*nunc est scribendum*', adapting the poet Horace's take on the fall of Cleopatra. If ever a time called for a Latin gerundive it was now.

The day passed and so did people of whom no one had previously heard: Perera (cricketer) fell, then Jayawardena (ministerial bag-carrier), Dananjaya (cricketer) and Chishti (Tory vice-chairman) but no more big hitters. Despite a rumour, or just wishful thinking, the Chris Grayling express service to Backbenches and Obscurity was eventually cancelled, held up by Leavers on the line.

At 5.20 p.m. Mrs May emerged to make a statement. Not a resignation, but defiance. I fight on, I fight to win, as another Prime Minister said on a previous November evening. The final question summed up her day, asking how many more wickets must fall before the captain stands down.

Mrs May reflected on all the dismissals in the past two years and reasoned that most of them had been self-inflicted: hit wicket, stumped, caught by silly point. And of course there had been the loss of Damian Green in that ball-tampering incident. None of this was her fault.

Instead, she told the press that she would grind it out like her childhood hero, Geoffrey Boycott. 'He stuck at it,' she said – and she will protect her deal with the same determination and lack of flair as he had guarded his wicket. If her team want to remove her, they will just have to run her out.

21 NOVEMBER
CAPTAIN MOGGERING COMES UNDER FIRE

Who do you think you are kidding, Mr Chief Whip, if you think we're on the run? The plot to overthrow the Prime Minister may have run out of puff faster than a chubby boy on a cross-country run but its architect did not mind his hapless gang being compared to *Dad's Army* yesterday. 'I've always admired Captain Mainwaring,' Jacob Rees-Mogg said.

This was a surprise. Surely he is more of a Sergeant Wilson, the upper-class deputy who likes to mutter 'Do you think that's wise?' at the leader. Perhaps he simply appreciates Mainwaring's patriotic refusal to give in. Not enough letters for a vote of no confidence? Why, as his hero would say, that's a typical, shabby whips' office trick.

Captain Moggering was at a meeting of Procrastinators Anonymous, the pro-Brexit group he chairs, which sometimes goes by the name of the European Research Group. For once, they had lived up to their billing and produced a pamphlet of analysis that 'exploded the myths of leaving the customs union', but all people wanted to ask him about was the attempted removal of Theresa May.

He rejected the claim that this is a failed coup. 'Stupid boy,' Captain Moggering seemed to grumble at the hack who suggested it. 'That is a silly word,' he said. 'It isn't an illegitimate act but something completely proper.' He spoke as if he had merely tried in vain to get the Prime Minister to use the correct cutlery at dinner. The Night of the Wrong Fish Knives.

Asked whether the moment for toppling Mrs May had passed, he insisted that 'patience is a virtue and virtue is a grace'. And Grace is Nanny's whist partner, who would do a better job of playing the Brexit cards than the PM.

With Steve 'Pike' Baker a non-combatant (his mother had sent an excuse note as he is suffering from a bout of footin-mouthitis), Captain Moggering was joined by the spivvery of David 'Walker' Davis and that remembrancer of old campaigns, Peter 'Corporal Jones' Lilley.

'Don't panic!' said Lord Lilley, in response to the idea that a no-deal Brexit would cause congestion on the M20. That already happens every time French customs officials feel bolshie, he said. We can see those Frenchies off with our pluck. After all, they don't like it up 'em.

Then Mr Davis tried to flog us some tat. All that fuss about a new customs deal, he scoffed. He's got a nice used one up his sleeve that we can have, no questions asked. 'We start with no tariffs and we want to end up with none, so that should only take ten minutes to arrange,' he said. It's amazing he didn't try it when he was Brexit Secretary.

Would the ERG back down if Mrs May took their advice? Here, The Mogg wavered. It has gone too far for him. But Lord Lilley was more forgiving. Noting the religious centre in which they were sitting, he quoted from St Luke.

'We are in a place of God and there is more joy in heaven over one sinner that repenteth than in ninety-nine righteous people,' he preached. Which is all well and good, but so far the ERG are finding it tough to find more than two dozen of the righteous to join their mission.

23 NOVEMBER
PINGS CAN ONLY GET BETTER FOR CAN-KICKING MAY

Theresa May took aim at a point on the far horizon, clasped her hands together like Jonny Wilkinson, and stepped forward, swinging her right foot. Ping! The can sailed high into the air, bounced on the road and took a skip forward, coming to rest beside half a dozen other deferments. No one kicks cans like the Prime Minister. It's either that or kicking the bucket.

The Travolta–Micawber strategy, a combination of stayin' alive and hoping something will turn up, was identified when Gordon Brown was PM. Mrs May is an adherent. As long as she is still kicking, even if screaming in private, her time is not up. Ping!s can only get better.

She wore her best kicking boots to the Commons to present her new, expanded declaration on our future relationship with the EU. Unfortunately, so did many other MPs and Mrs May was the target.

'It's twenty-six pages of waffle,' Jeremy Corbyn complained. 'What have the government been doing for the past two years?' He drew out one section that blandly said 'the parties should consider appropriate arrangements for co-operation on space' and scoffed, 'Well, what a remarkable negotiating achievement that is.'

Ian Blackford, of the SNP, said the PM was 'spluttering forward in a haphazard, chaotic way', while Sir Vince Cable, the Lib Dem leader, called it 'pathetically weak' and 'an agreement to have an agreement'.

Mrs May tried to kick back, claiming that her deal met Labour's heralded tests for Brexit. 'Does it do X?' she read. 'Does it do Y?' And the Tories and Labour shouted 'yes' or 'no' as if they were at the panto, though a clapometer would not have awarded her side the win.

It was the kicking from her own side that hurt more. Iain Duncan Smith, whom she had thanked for his advice, even if it was not taken, called the Northern Irish backstop 'toxic'; Owen Paterson spoke of 'the horror' of being stuck in a customs union; and Sir Bill Cash said he was damn well going to hold an inquiry into how these negotiations have been handled.

'Oooooh!' squealed MPs, not taking Sir Bill as seriously as he may have hoped.

Boris Johnson 'regretfully' pointed out some of the flaws and 'respectfully' suggested a tweak, though the polite tone was spoilt by him concluding that the deal was 'complete nonsense'. Dominic Raab, until recently the Brexit Secretary, said it gave away more control over our laws. 'Resign,' heckled Labour's Chris Ruane (Vale of Clwyd).

Throughout the statement, Mr Raab's successor, Steve Barclay (Con, North East Cambridgeshire), just sat there beside Mrs May, stony faced and impassive. With a granite forehead and solid jaw, he looked like one of the Easter Island sculptures. He must have wondered what on earth he'd got himself into.

5 DECEMBER
GERIATRIC HAMSTER KEEPS TRYING TO TURN THE WHEEL

With exquisite timing a story appeared on the wires at 5 p.m. saying that Theresa May, according to *Forbes* magazine, was the world's second most powerful woman. This came between her second and third defeats in the voting lobbies and before she opened a debate on a Brexit deal that more than 100 of her side have said they will oppose. You would get more power out of a geriatric hamster on a rusty wheel.

Yet still she keeps going, running on fumes, the slave of duty. Even if Parliament itself were to collapse into rubble – and there are times when it seems to be one sneeze away from doing so – she would stand firm in the dust, insisting that she has been very clear about whatever it is she is clear about. (It's not clear.)

It would be admirable if only some of the damage were not self-inflicted. Take the row over publishing the legal advice on Brexit. The government had hoped that by refusing to engage with an opposition motion on this they could ignore the result.

'Sorry, doesn't count if we don't play.' Some might call that naive; yesterday Parliament voted that it was also contemptuous. Geoffrey Cox, the mahogany-voiced Attorney General, had been unable to convince MPs with his statement. Two and a half hours of this venerable QC's time wasted, and he couldn't even bill the government for it.

In the distant past, an MP found in contempt could be imprisoned in the clock tower by the serjeant at arms. There would be something magnificently Iolanthine about Mr Cox being marched out by a man in tights carrying a sword, but that was never going to happen. Not least as the clock tower is a building site.

Labour's beef was not with Mr Cox but with the Chief Whip who had pulled the troops from the field to avoid what Sir Keir Starmer called 'a short-term humiliation'. Well, that plan worked marvellously.

Mr Cox arrived seven minutes late for the debate, wiping the lunchtime *ris de veau aux truffes* from his jowls, but he was there to hear Sir Keir urge the government to 'pull back from the brink' and release the advice rather than be found in contempt. The government hoped instead that MPs might vote to kick the decision down the road. Andrea Leadsom, Leader of the House, said that releasing the advice would not be in the national interest. (For which read 'Tory interest'.) But this is what happens when you lack a parliamentary majority.

Poor Mr Cox looked devastated when the vote came. He threw his head back and gave a long sigh. 'It is a far, far better thing that I do than I have ever done,' he muttered.

After another defeat on the terms of the Brexit debate, Mrs May rose and gave one of the best speeches of her tenure. With MPs sharpening their stilettos, she warned against falling for sound and fury. 'Don't let anyone think there is a better deal to be won by shouting louder,' she said. 'I do not say that this deal is perfect. It was never going to be. We should not let the search for the perfect Brexit prevent a good Brexit.'

It was passionate, heartfelt, even persuasive. It also had the whiff of a valedictory. I wouldn't be surprised, should she lose next Tuesday, if the PM rises and declares, 'Ah, sod you all. I'm off to do *Strictly*.'

10 DECEMBER
ALARM BELLS SOUND FOR PRIME MINISTER

A fire alarm rang out in Portcullis House half an hour before Theresa May told her Cabinet that she was abandoning the vote on her Brexit deal. 'An emergency has been confirmed,' declared the public address system in the Commons office block. 'Only the one?' a wry Tory MP remarked.

Perhaps, they joked, this was the Prime Minister's plan B. Rumour circulated that a 62-year-old woman had been seen going into the cellars with an armful of kindling and the look of Bertha Rochester.

It was just a false alarm, unlike the sirens in Downing Street as the Chief Whip finally conceded that the numbers did not look good. Mrs May informed the Cabinet that she had decided on the bold strategy of kicking the vote down the road in the hope that people would forget it.

The reaction when she slipped into the chamber to tell MPs at 3.30 p.m. was underpowered and she was not pushed to her feet by a roar of support. 'I'd like to make a statement on exiting the European Union,' she said, sounding broken. 'We have had three days of debate and I have listened very carefu...' She was drowned out by laughter from the Labour benches.

As she explained that she was going to defer the vote, a chorus of 'weak, weak' taunted her from across the chamber. Her own side were too polite to barrack but their expressions wounded enough.

'Does this House want to deliver Brexit?' Mrs May asked, hoping for a helpful response. 'No!' shouted the SNP cohort, the only MPs with enough enthusiasm to speak. The Brexiteers just looked glum. It was not the response she had hoped for.

Mrs May pleaded with them to see sense. A second referendum would split the country further, a no-deal Brexit would be an economic disaster. There had to be a middle path. Support was threadbare.

When Nigel Dodds of the DUP told her, sadly but firmly, that her vision 'simply isn't credible', the atmosphere in the room was like a vet's surgery after a family has been told that ol' Fluffy isn't going to pull through. There was more sorrow than anger. Yet Mrs May remained oblivious to the apparent direction of her fate. Her policy is going nowhere, but neither is she.

Meanwhile, it seems that Jacob Rees-Mogg's letter-writing circle have yet to find their muse. Dinner at Mogg Towers was disrupted by a call from a member of the European Research Group, concerned about his orders. '*Benedictus benedicat deo gratias*,' The Mogg murmured, laying down a plover's egg to lift the telephone receiver from its cradle.

'Jacob? It's —,' the would-be assassin said. 'Me and the boys are really struggling with that letter to Sir Graham Brady that you dictated for us at our meeting tonight.'

'What ails thee, my child?' The Mogg purred.

'Well, for a start, none of us know how many Ls are in "pusillanimous",' the conspirator replied. 'Or Ss, for that matter. And is "flimflam" one word or hyphenated?' 'Pish and indeed tosh,' The Mogg replied. 'My epistle was a mere template. Yours must come from the heart, composed in your own peculiar vernacular.'

'Yer wot?' 'Oh, just write "May out now" and he'll get the message,' The Mogg snapped. '*Benedicto benedicatur* and all that.' Click, brrr. The backbench rebellion creeps on.

12 DECEMBER
IGNORANCE IS BLISS FOR JUNIOR MINISTER

The Commons debated the tusk problem last night, though not the one they had intended. Instead of the finale of the five-day Brexit brouhaha, we had Thérèse Coffey leading a debate on the Ivory Bill. To remind her of the subject, the environment minister wore a blue scarf covered in elephants. Thick-skinned, slow-moving and facing extinction, Theresa May was meanwhile in Brussels, tackling Tusk of the Donald variety.

More ministers should follow Dr Coffey's lead and dress appropriately for the dispatch box. Matt Hancock could wear a stethoscope; Damian Hinds a mortar board; Gavin Williamson would surely love to have war paint on his cheeks (a knitted scarf may suit him better); and Chris Grayling could honour his transport brief by arriving twenty minutes late.

What should a Chancellor of the Duchy of Lancaster wear? For the present one, nothing but a full hazmat suit would do. David Lidington is a good man for an emergency, completely unflappable, no matter how loud the heckling.

'It's an abject mess,' ranted Jeremy Corbyn, who had secured an emergency debate. Mrs May had 'demeaned her office' by pulling the vote and was now a 'runaway Prime Minister'. Mr Lidington brushed the Labour leader away with a theatrical flourish and reminded MPs that his boss had spent twenty-two hours at the dispatch box in the past two months. 'She has made in that time…' he began. 'A mess!' shouted a heckler, not unfairly.

Pete Wishart, of the SNP, who can get carried away with his own brilliance, went down an ABBA theme. He called Mrs May 'the worst dancing queen in history' and said she should 'come back and face her Waterloo'. Mr Lidington smiled.

'He has been crafting that one for quite some time,' he said, witheringly.

He had more trouble with Labour's Ivan Lewis (Bury South), who observed that it had now reached the point at which ministers didn't actually know if they were telling the truth to the Commons because they were not being told the truth by the Prime Minister. Mr Lidington could only say that the Cabinet were told what they were told when told it.

His was one of two Brexit-related ministerial appearances demanded by the opposition to plug the gap in the timetable. First, we had an urgent question on the legal ramifications of delaying the vote. Labour had asked for the Attorney General but Geoffrey Cox was busy practising his Tennyson for a recital at a carol service last night, so instead they got Robin 'Pipsqueak' Walker, a junior minister.

Mr Walker is not a lawyer – his career before inheriting his father's Worcester seat peaked as Oliver Letwin's press officer – but he has seen a few episodes of *Judge Rinder* so felt qualified to give the legal assurances Labour wanted. His essential message was: look, just trust us, it will be fine. The MPs were not convinced.

'It's a constitutional outrage,' Yvette Cooper said. 'Nonononono,' Mr Walker replied. 'That's just conspiracy theories and scare stories.' He had all the authority of a supply teacher who has been asked to take a class before Christmas and decided just to put a video on.

Labour's Chris Elmore (Ogmore) thought that Mr Walker was being evasive rather than clueless over the date for a rearranged vote. 'He clearly knows something,' he said. Mr Walker found this suggestion immensely flattering. 'I am very honoured that he believes I know something,' he replied. Indeed, it would make him one of the few in government who does.

13 DECEMBER
ASLAN'S ON THE MOVE

A loud drumming erupted from Committee Room 14 just after
5 p.m., the sound of palms, or perhaps heads, hitting wooden
desks as the Prime Minister addressed her tribe. The Tory Party
was showing its loyalty, which is not quite the same thing, of
course, as being loyal. The louder the banging, the more easily
it masks the sound of daggers being sharpened.

Alas, Andrew Bridgen arrived too late to join in the thun-
dering. 'I wouldn't have added much to it,' the North West
Leicestershire Tory remarked. His hands would have been well
muffled. Mr Bridgen has the affection for Theresa May that a
weak-bladdered spaniel has for a lamppost.

Julian Smith, the Chief Whip, left the room with Mrs May
at 5.45, fifteen minutes before voting opened. How did it go?
'Very positive,' Mr Smith said, giving one of those slightly scary
wide smiles that you see in a gangster movie from a hoodlum
just before his rival acquires a third eye.

The PM's supporters talked her up to the press waiting in
the corridor. 'Magnificent,' purred Sir Nicholas Soames. Michael Gove predicted she would 'win and win handsomely'.
Asked to put a number on it, the Environment Secretary said,
'I studied English not maths. I can describe things but not do
figures.'

Jacob Rees-Mogg, that double-breasted Borgia, left the hus-
tings with a smile. The polite assassin did not seem dismayed
by the drums of support. Asked if he would return to vote as
soon as the ballot opened, he said that he might pop into the
cathedral for Mass first. Praying for the soul of the Tory Party?
'Oh, not its soul,' he said. 'Not yet.'

If the moggie was chipper, the lion was sulking. Boris Johnson, whose supporters have been likening him to Aslan in the
Narnia novels, apparently on the grounds that a recent haircut

has unleashed some of that old magic, was said to have been chuntering throughout May's address. His reaction on leaving the room was a throaty growl.

He had been similarly disengaged during Prime Minister's Questions. 'They say Aslan is on the move,' the eager beavers on the Eurosceptic wing had been whispering, but here Aslan was more on the slouch. He sat on the fringe, his arms folded huffily across his chest before finally plonking his head in his paws.

His fellow Brexiteers had similarly glum expressions – Iain Duncan Smith looked as if he was chewing a wasp – as Mrs May grappled with Jeremy Corbyn's exceedingly angry Mr Tumnus. They appeared to be pessimistic about toppling the White Queen, fearing that it will be always winter and never Brexmas.

In PMQs, she was given a loud and loyal reception, with toadies like Michael Ellis ululating like an Alpine shepherd calling to his flock. 'Is that 158?' heckled Labour's Steve Pound (Ealing North), in reference to the number of MPs she needed to win round.

As the day wore on and people confided their voting intention, it appeared she would win by some margin, though drummings and declarations of support do not translate into crosses on a ballot. As one former minister remarked outside Room 14, 'The only thing I'm 100 per cent confident about is that many of my colleagues are liars.'

2019: MAY COMES TO AN END IN JUNE

8 JANUARY

MR CATALOGUE IS A MODEL OF PROCRASTINATION

Here we are, more than a week into the new year and still the same Brexit Secretary as we had at the end of 2018. This must be the famous stability that Theresa May promised. Steve Barclay, who followed... er, oh, you know, the one with the angry face who always ate the same lunch, who had replaced that guy who chuckled all the time and seldom visited Brussels, is not shifting.

Not quickly anyway. Mr Barclay is not a dynamic politician. Nor even a noticeably conscious one. I have seen him in debates and wanted someone to check his pulse. His nickname when he worked in the City, I'm told, was Mr Catalogue because he looked like something in the front window of Debenhams.

Yesterday, the mannequin was required to be a man. Or rather a woman. Jeremy Corbyn had tabled an urgent question to ask Theresa May about the progress she has made with her Brexit deal and, since the Prime Minister was up in Liverpool, Mr Barclay was playing her understudy.

A bit more liveliness was required, therefore, but only a touch. After all, there wasn't anything to report. Moving slowly to the dispatch box, as if he were in stop-motion animation, Mr Barclay explained that it was all going very well and that

MPs will be told about all the developments that have happened in the fullness of time.

This frustrated Mr Corbyn. 'The government are trying to run down the clock in an attempt to blackmail this House into supporting a botched deal,' the Labour leader complained. Mr Barclay sat there with a vacant gaze recently seen selling thermal underwear in Marks & Spencer.

Mr Corbyn conceded that there had been activity in some areas. Chris Grayling, for instance, had awarded a £14 million shipping contract to a company that doesn't own any ships. 'The Transport Secretary has a PhD in incompetence,' Mr Corbyn observed. 'You've only got two O levels,' a Tory heckled, though it wasn't as clever as he seemed to think.

Mr Grayling had fleshed out his no-deal emergency shipping plans – Dunkirk II – in a written statement earlier, explaining that he had, in fact, handed deals worth £100 million to three shipping companies and only one of them doesn't own ships, so stop all this nay-saying. The other two, he said, will be organising new routes from Immingham to Cuxhaven and Vlaardingen, which may be real places but could be somewhere he read about in the *Game of Thrones* miscellany he found in his stocking.

Mr Grayling has also been busy organising a traffic jam in Kent. Or trying to. In order to test a contingency plan designed to handle 5,000 lorries waiting to go through customs at Dover, Mr Grayling had managed to persuade a mere eighty-eight trucks plus a bin van to pootle slowly along the A256. It was not much of a stress test. Perhaps he should have offered more Yorkies.

'Complete waste of time,' huffed Mr Corbyn. 'Shambolic. Too little, too late.' Fair points, but there was no indication of what Labour would do.

Mr Barclay slowly rose, striking a pose soon to be seen promoting the John Lewis range of spring casualwear, and said that it was good to see that Mr Corbyn hadn't troubled his cerebellum with forming any fresh thoughts on Brexit over Christmas. He also welcomed the Labour leader's expectation that he might have any answers. 'Last time we met, you said my role was just ceremonial,' he said. Hah, who's the dummy now?

Meanwhile, the importance of this needless and unenlightening debate to the whole Brexit saga was perhaps reflected in the fact that not a single member of the DUP had shown up.

9 JANUARY
FERRY FARCE THREATENS TO SINK GRAYLING

It was a red-letter day for Chris Grayling, the first anniversary of his greatest period of success as a Cabinet minister. On 8 January 2018, at 11.43 a.m., Tory HQ tweeted that he had been appointed party chairman. Before the clock had ticked round to 11.44 – while party staff were still clearing desks and polishing CVs in joy at the news – it was announced that it had been a mistake.

Historians differ on how long Mr Grayling was in the job. Between ten and thirty-seven seconds. And what a golden era it was. Nothing happened – and this was universally welcomed. Unlike for much of his time as Transport Secretary when nothing happened and Mr Grayling got the blame.

To celebrate the occasion, he came to the Commons for a kicking. Just for a change. He has had a lot of these in the past year. He must be a masochist to keep putting himself through this ordeal. London commuters like him tend to be.

Mr Grayling rose with a fixed grin, looking like a bride who on her wedding day has found her future husband in bed with her aunt's Labrador but knows that she has to go through with the charade as it is too late to cancel the photographer.

Across from him the Labour MPs were doing impressions of Admiral Lord Nelson, raising a telescope and announcing that they could see no ships. Mr Grayling's left cheek started to twitch. It was not true, he said, that he had given lots of money for running a post-Brexit ferry service to a company with no record even for running a bath. Why, it was barely £14 million. A drop in the ocean, if only they had a vessel to drop it from.

He had given three times that to DFDS, he said, and, yes, he has checked that they aren't the people who always seem to have a half-price sofa sale now on. We would not be sending goods off to the Continent on a knocked-down leather recliner, let us be clear, although he has had talks with some people called the Jumblies (green heads, blue hands, very David Cameron c. 2009) who can offer a deal on seagoing sieves.

Labour's Andy McDonald asked why a £14 million contract had been awarded to a company with 'no money, no ships, no track record, no employees, no ports, one telephone line and no working website or sailing schedule'. Mr Grayling could have replied, 'For the same reason you want to put Jeremy Corbyn in No. 10 – blind optimism and the hope that something will emerge to save us.' Instead, he attacked Labour for being anti-business.

'I make no apology for being willing to contract with a new British company,' he said. 'Make no apology' is one of his catchphrases, along with 'I'll take no lessons from'. Never apologise, never explain, as the former First Sea Lord Admiral John Fisher was fond of saying – and, like Mr Grayling, he knew a thing or two about ships.

'There seems to be visceral hatred of small business on the other side of the House,' Mr Grayling preached. He also accused his critics of hating Ramsgate, one end of Seaborne Freight's putative service. 'You'll never win that seat back with this negative attitude.'

His great plan for the Ramsgate–Ostend route was quite

sensible, he explained. Seaborne would not receive a penny if they failed to run a service. This is fair enough, but Mr Grayling was then most unamused when the SNP's Angus MacNeil (Na h-Eileanan an Iar) suggested that he lacked a contingency plan should that happen. 'What a load of absolute tripe,' Mr Grayling replied. I think it was a rebuke rather than a sudden moment of self-awareness.

10 JANUARY
SPEAKER UNITES THE HOUSE WITH PUSH FOR CHANGE

The late Alan Clark had a rule that he followed almost as diligently as his one about never passing up an opportunity to drink or screw. If the annunciator screen in the Commons says 'points of order' for more than two minutes, the former Tory minister wrote, it means a 'good row' has broken out and you should dash to the chamber and enjoy it. The points of order that followed Prime Minister's Questions yesterday went on for sixty-eight minutes. It could have lasted much longer.

Several Tory MPs still wanted to shout at John Bercow about his decision to pour paraffin over Erskine May, the parliamentary manual, and light a match, but Mr Speaker called time. You know how he hates to be the centre of attention.

The fireworks began gently with a piece of buttering-up from Peter Bone. 'I have always regarded you as an exceptional Speaker and a defender of Parliament,' the Wellingborough Tory said. Mr Bercow nodded and purred 'quite so, quite so'. Mr Bone then asked why Dominic Grieve was allowed to table an amendment to a business motion when Mr Bone had been told by officials it was against the rules.

With Julian Smith, the Chief Whip, and Andrea Leadsom, Leader of the House, shooting death stares at the chair, Mr Bercow explained that he had simply formed a different view of the matter. 'I am trying to do the right thing,' he preached. This won him loving cheers from the Labour benches to his left and raspberries from MPs to his right.

Mark Francois, deputy chairman of the pro-Brexit European Research Group, was cross. When he campaigned for Parliament to reclaim its sovereignty, he didn't mean that backbenchers should be allowed to block things he is keen on. 'Ridiculous! Utter sophistry!' he shouted. Mr Bercow gave him the regal brush-off.

Mrs Leadsom asked him to publish the advice his clerks had given, assuming probably correctly that he had ignored it. 'It's private,' Mr Bercow said, amusing Tory frontbenchers who had been forced to publish the Attorney General's private legal advice on Brexit.

David Morris (Morecambe and Lunesdale), a Tory backbencher who once pretended to play the keyboards for Rick Astley on *Top of the Pops*, got to his feet and shouted, 'Publish it!' at Mr Bercow, which was extraordinarily disrespectful. The Speaker didn't even bother to acknowledge him. He has seen off better men than someone who failed an audition to be in Duran Duran.

Adam Holloway (Con, Gravesham) noted that the car parked in front of the Speaker's house has a sticker on it declaring 'Bollocks to Brexit'. This was, he said, proof of bias. 'It's my wife's car,' the Speaker said. 'That sticker is not mine.' Mr Holloway asked if he has ever driven it, which was verging on pathetic.

The more cerebral critics were concerned about precedent. Or rather the lack of it. Mr Bercow was in uncharted waters. Jacob Rees-Mogg, who has such an intimate knowledge of Erskine May that it can only be a matter of time before their engagement is announced in *The Times*, asked the Speaker to turn to page 458 and debate the meaning of the word 'forthwith'.

'Pah!' said Mr Bercow, throwing in 'Tchah!' for good measure. What is all this talk of precedent? Do you not know that I make the rules? *L'état, c'est moi.* Or rather *l'Erskine, c'est lui.*

'If we were guided only by precedent, nothing would ever change,' Mr Bercow explained. 'Exactly!' shouted voices to both his right and left. For once he had united the House even if it was for diametrically opposed reasons.

11 JANUARY
TALKING BOLLOCKS WITH MICHAEL GOVE

I am afraid that today's sketch features a lot of bollocks. Yes, yes, not for the first time, but these bollocks are now part of the official parliamentary record, published in Hansard, a perfectly orderly word for an MP to use, according to Mr John Bercow, that noted exponent of bollocks.

In gentler times a euphemism might have been employed. You may recall *Yes, Minister* when Jim Hacker writes 'Round Objects' on a paper and Sir Humphrey replies, 'Who is Round and to what does he object?' But Michael Gove, the son of an Aberdeen fishmonger, is not afraid of salty language. Anyway, the Environment Secretary was quoting a member of the shadow Cabinet.

On Brexit, Labour's policy is not to have a policy. Like Sting during one of his tantric marathons, they keep changing position to delay reaching a conclusion. Mr Gove said Labour had now offered sixteen different visions of Brexit. 'They are chasing a whole carnival of unicorns across the European plain,' he said.

Yet one of Labour's leading lights, that talented whistler and shadow Trade Secretary Barry Gardiner, had in an unguarded moment revealed the truth of his party's Brexit tests. 'He summed them up pithily,' Mr Gove said, 'in a word which in Spanish translates as *cojones* and in English rhymes with "rollocks".'

Perhaps thinking this was too coy, he gave a mischievous clarification. 'I know, Mr Speaker, that there are some distinguished citizens who have put on their cars a sticker saying "Bollocks to Brexit",' he said. Mr Speaker did not repeat his claim that this was his wife's car. 'But we now know from Labour's own front bench that its position is "bollocks".'

The House erupted. As Mr Gove thanked Mr Gardiner for casting light on 'the testicular nature of their position', Sir Edward Davey (Kingston and Surbiton) could take no more. 'Have you made a new ruling on parliamentary language?' the Lib Dem asked. It was a reasonable assumption. Mr Speaker seems to change the rules so often that the next edition of Erskine May will be written in pencil.

'I have made no new ruling,' Mr Bercow said. 'The word beginning with B and ending in S which the Secretary of State delighted in regaling the House with was orderly. I think it is a matter of taste.'

Never mind the bollocks, here's the Brex pistol: Mr Gove delivered one of the finest speeches heard in Parliament since the referendum, a more eloquent defence of Theresa May's Brexit deal than we have ever had from the Prime Minister. It was full of trademark Govian courtesy, disarming people with politeness. He praised the Speaker and his civil servants, called for respect for the fears of those who do not want Brexit and said that the other EU nations are 'our friends' without sounding sarcastic.

He even digressed to talk up a vegan parsnip soup he had with Labour's Kerry McCarthy last week – 'It was a very nice lunch,' she replied – and saluted the 'many talented SNP members', kindly adding that he would 'not blight their electoral prospects by naming them and explaining how much I admire them'.

Speaking fluently for an hour without a script in front of him, as so few MPs now dare to do, just a few A5 pages of handwritten notes, Mr Gove conceded that the deal has imperfections but said it is the best the country could get. It takes us out of the Court of Justice, the common agricultural and fisheries policies, he said, away from ever-closer union and towards control of our borders and money. The EU hates the backstop more than we do and will be keener to end it.

Have faith, he pleaded, and see this not as the beginning of Brexit's end, merely the end of its beginning.

Many, of course, will still think that the government's withdrawal agreement is a load of round objects, but Mr Gove presented it so reasonably that for that one peaceful hour objections were restrained. It was a soothing piece of rhetoric after the anger of the day before. 'I almost think he believes what he is saying,' Labour's Clive Efford (Eltham) remarked. You had to admire his balls.

12 JANUARY
AN EMPTY HOUSE BUT A CROWDED LIVING ROOM

Perhaps it was Steve Pound's use of the phrase 'Gradgrind utilitarianism of the EU' that did it, or maybe it was the Labour MP quoting Francis Fukuyama or describing a second referendum as a 'chimera', but Sir Mike Penning (Hemel Hempstead) rose with a befuddled look on his chops to make the next speech in the unending Brexit saga.

'It is always difficult to follow someone whose oratory is so… er… difficult to follow,' Sir Mike, a plain-speaking Essex Tory, said. 'Most of my friends would not have understood a single word.'

This was a bit unfair on the colourful Mr Pound, who as a former bus conductor and boxer in the Merchant Navy can claim to be as much a man of the people as Ex-Fireman Penning, but he can get a touch floral in his grandiloquence. There was one sentence, however, the opening one, in which his message was crystal clear.

'When all is said and done, and everything that needs to be said has been said, this House is very good at saying it all over again,' he said. Invoking the Countess of Avon, who said that she felt as if the Suez Canal were flowing through her drawing room, Mr Pound described the border with Ireland taking up too much space in his living room. 'We have spent so much time on this,' he complained. 'Are we any further forward?' Not really.

MPs gassed about the Brexit deal for five hours yesterday, after fifteen hours of rhubarb earlier in the week, and three days in early December before Theresa May pressed the pause button. Some MPs had been disappointed not to give their speeches then, a point made by Ian Murray (Lab, Edinburgh South) yesterday in wishing everyone a merry Christmas, as that was how his intended speech had begun.

Layla Moran (LD, Oxford West and Abingdon) asked why they could not have a vote there and then, rather than wait until next Tuesday. One reason is that hardly anyone had shown up, Friday being normally a constituency day. She was the only Lib Dem there, joined by two Scottish Nationalists and barely a dozen Labour backbenchers. Opposite sat twenty or so Tories. Maybe their Chief Whip missed a trick in not calling a surprise vote.

Opinions may not have been swayed but there were some decent speeches. Sir Nicholas Soames, grandson of Churchill, is burdened by his ancestor's oratory but can turn a fine phrase himself, even if Sir Winston would not be seen dead in the bright cerise socks (Leander Club?) or turquoise reading glasses (Primark?) that his descendant has taken to wearing in the chamber.

'We have known many worse times in this country, and some more dangerous times, but not since the war has this House faced a more important moment,' Sir Nicholas said. 'It is our duty to recover our sense of proportion and restore some dignity, reason and calm to this debate.' While he felt that the country had made 'a historically bad decision' in choosing to leave the EU, he conceded that leave we must and that Parliament must not be 'so wet and timid and lacking in will that it cannot find a sufficient consensus to move forward'. He supported Mrs May's deal, 'warts and all'.

Mark Francois feels the opposite. While he began by rigorously defending Sir Nicholas – 'anyone who calls him a traitor has never met him; such a thing is ludicrous' – he despises the deal. The political declaration, he said, was meaningless words – 'the equivalent of "I promise I will respect you in the morning."'

'This country has never bowed the knee to anyone in almost 1,000 years and I do not believe we should start now,' he said. Comparing the withdrawal agreement to Neville Chamberlain's Munich deal, he then snatched the Churchillian mantle from Mid Sussex and growled, 'We will never surrender.' It only needed Elgar to turn some of his colleagues to goo.

Finally, Theresa May made history. The vote on her Brexit deal, which was meant to have been held before Christmas and was delayed when she smelt the mood, could not be put back any more. The margin of defeat, 230 votes, was the heaviest any government has sustained. Labour immediately tabled a vote of no confidence.

16 JANUARY
COX ROARS AND MAY BORES

Amid the wreckage of the biggest, most humiliating parliamentary defeat a Prime Minister has ever suffered, there came a moment of black humour when a lone Tory voice piped up: 'Could we have a second vote?'

Fat chance. This was no close-run thing, no 52–48 split, but a pasting. When the result, 432–202, was read out, it sounded phonetically like a portrait by Picasso, the eyes and the nose spread far, far apart. In cricketing terms, Theresa May must follow on and hope for better luck in the second innings. Yet this will surely not be a reprise of the miracle at Headingley in '81. The only thing this Prime Minister has in common with Beefy Botham is a love of long walks.

Philip May watched dutifully from the gallery as his wife wrapped up a debate on her deal that had begun on 4 December. Yes, as recently as that. We seem to have been hearing these speeches for months rather than weeks.

At the end of a rambling stream of cantankerousness from Jeremy Corbyn, who could be Prime Minister by Easter, Mrs May gave her papers a shuffle, stared the Labour leader in the eye and rose to a thunder of Tory palms being banged on benches, or perhaps foreheads.

The occasion required the speech of her career. Instead, she gave a piece of humdrum oratory-by-numbers. Not something to stiffen the sinews nor summon up the blood. A few Labour MPs tried to shout her down and were told by John Bercow to 'be more Zen'. They should have saved their breath. She was winning no one round. As rallying efforts go, a one-legged tennis player would do a better job.

Mrs May had entered the chamber towards the end of six hours of debate just as a Labour MP remarked that she had 'failed miserably' in her attempt to convince the House. She appeared to raise her eyebrows at this claim. Did she really think that she might win? Or, like a puppy being taken to the vets, had she no idea that she was about to be castrated? Perhaps she had been influenced by the day's opening speech, a marvellous performance of curlicued rhetoric from Geoffrey Cox, the glorious Attorney General, who roared away like the hammy old thespian he is, the sort who when playing Lear will complain to the stage crew that they have not made the storm scene loud enough for him to shout over.

'Do we opt for ORDER!' he roared, bellowing the last word at a decibel level that Mr Bercow seldom touches, 'or choose change?' People were demanding that Parliament got its act together. 'They would be entitled to say, "What are you playing at?"' he said. 'You are not children in the playground. You are legislators.'

He went on to attack Labour for 'factitious, trumped-up opposition' that he claimed was purely designed to 'create chaos' and said that 'future ages will marvel' should the House reject Mrs May's deal 'because somehow it did not seem enough'.

Mr Cox was given a boost before he rose when Mr Bercow mistakenly announced him as Sir Geoffrey. 'I am extremely obliged to you for promoting me, Mr Speaker,' Mr Cox said. 'Perhaps I can take that as a hint to the Prime Minister.' Indeed, had he swayed the House with his oratory, an earldom would have surely been the least that he deserved. Alas, minds had long been made up.

One of the last speeches came from Tim Farron, the former Leader of the Liberal Democrats. 'I am used to losing elections,' he said. 'I am a very good loser. I have had loads of practice.' He reminded the House, in a lesson that they should heed for the future, that referendums are awful and divisive. 'Unless it is one that no one cares about,' he said, wryly, 'like the one on the alternative vote.'

The House was packed come decision time. Only one MP

of those who were eligible to vote – Labour's Paul Flynn, who has been ill for some time – had failed to turn up. Tulip Siddiq, the heavily pregnant MP for Hampstead and Kilburn who had deferred a caesarean section for this, was seen squeezing past the clerks' table in a wheelchair, although there was actually no need for her to enter the chamber to vote. A point was being made publicly about the long delay to introduce proxy voting.

It soon became clear due to the lack of activity among the Tory whips that the scoreline would not be close. No one was trying to cajole MPs into their lobby. The Chief Whip had a smile on his face. Nothing more could be accomplished at this point. Better to save the thumbscrews for a vote they might win.

As she waited for the verdict, Mrs May sat alone, studying what she would say next. By now, her husband had left the gallery. Maybe Tuesday is the night when the bins are put out in Downing Street. More likely, he had gone to her office to pour her a whisky and be ready with a hug. She looked as if she needed both.

17 JANUARY
BOUNCY GOVE PUTS LIFE INTO THE ZOMBIES

As soon as Theresa May had finished pleading for her life, the government Chief Whip skittled across the chamber and knelt beside the Leader of the DUP. 'OK, Nigel,' Julian Smith seemed to mutter. 'How much are you going to make us sweat for this?'

Reassurance came in just over an hour. Nigel Dodds said at the start of his speech that he had been struck by how many MPs had asked him to support Mrs May and prevent a general election. 'Indeed,' he said, 'some of those entreaties have even come from the government.'

If this were a secret ballot, he claimed, Mrs May would be saved by 'an overwhelming majority'. This has little to do with affection or support for the Prime Minister – there is not much of that even in her Cabinet – but more the shudder that comes when MPs think of Jeremy Corbyn in Downing Street.

How frustrating to be a diligent Labour MP, anxious to improve your constituents' lives, sitting opposite a necrocratic government that shuffles like zombies from defeat to defeat, and know that the greatest impediment to you sitting where they do is your leader? It was a theme that Mrs May played on heavily in the best section of her speech. 'The Leader of the Opposition is asking this House to accept that he could be Prime Minister,' she said before reminding MPs of Mr Corbyn's position on security and foreign policy issues. Glum faces on the Labour benches.

He looked remarkably relaxed. Three hours before the debate, when other leaders might have been rewriting their speech, gnawing at fingernails or making repeated trips to the lavatory, he was seen sitting on his own in an empty Commons restaurant with a coffee and the *Morning Star*. He remains true to himself and this is admirable. Does he really want to be PM, though? The no-confidence motion had seemed to give Mrs May the confidence she lacked the day before. She was much more jolly and eager to defend her record and her MPs picked up on it. Sajid Javid, the Home Secretary, hollered and slapped his thigh like a Bavarian during happy hour at the beerfest.

The first sign that all would be well came from John Baron (Basildon and Billericay), a Brexiteer whose attempt to torpedo her deal had gone down by a margin of 576. He encouraged her 'as someone who was defeated by only 230' to 'keep buggering on'.

Other internal opponents joined him. Mark Francois admitted that they did not see eye to eye on the EU. 'That's because she's taller than you,' Simon Hoare heckled. 'So is everyone,' the diminutive Mr Francois conceded. He looked up to her now.

The toadies were also out in force. Nigel Huddleston (Con, Mid Worcestershire) asked how Mr Corbyn could ever be PM when he is such a misery the whole time. The eternally sunny Rebecca Pow said there was 'so little time' to list all the achievements of the government.

No one was more bouncy than Michael Gove, who summed up the debate with such enthusiasm it will have sent the troops skipping to the lobby. The Tories bellowed 'more' and waved their order papers after his turn. They almost never do that for one of Mrs May's speeches.

Tom Watson, summing up for Labour, was also good. Speaking more in sorrow than anger, he said that such a string of failures as Mrs May had achieved would have finished off weaker people far sooner. But losing by 230 votes on a key policy is 'not a mere flesh wound'. She will be known as 'the nothing-has-changed Prime Minister', he said. 'Is it worth giving her another chance to humiliate the UK?' Apparently it is. The necrocrat lives to die another day.

Meanwhile, across Europe, Greece was having its own vote of no-confidence. Its Prime Minister won by three. Makes Mrs May look as durable as the Parthenon.

22 JANUARY
REPEAT OFFENDER REFUSES TO BEND

We have seen this show before. For the sixth time in the past seven parliamentary weeks Monday afternoon meant a new episode of *Nothing Has Changed*, the political box set in which Theresa May sets out what little progress has been made towards Britain leaving the EU.

The script is pedestrian, the characters one-dimensional, the acting rather hammy and the drama unfolds at the pace of a canal-boat holiday, yet still we watch it. Box set means box set, as Mrs May says.

Perhaps one day there will be a twist. Maybe Tim Farron will walk out of the shower and it will turn out that the past three series have all been a dream. Or Dominic Grieve will win an amendment for Brexit to come into effect on 30 February, which Peter Bonehead, John Deadwood and Co will vote for in their eagerness to leave early.

Until then, we get Mrs May telling us opaquely about the things on which she has been clear in two-hour chunks. She began by saying that last week's vote on her deal, lost by sixty-four votes more than any Prime Minister had lost a vote before, made it clear that her approach had to change. 'And it has,' she said.

Instead of high-handedly telling MPs in the chamber that her deal is the only option and expecting them to vote for it, she has been having them round to Downing Street and telling them there that her deal is the only option and expecting them to vote for it. All apart from Mr Corbyn, of course, who found that her meetings clashed with his South American poetry circle.

Nothing has changed. Her red lines remain of the deepest vermilion. Every single party leader or opposition backbencher who came to see her had asked for a second referendum, she said. And she had taken this consensus on board and immediately rejected it.

They also wanted her to press pause on the Article 50 process until we know what we want to do.

Nothing will be conceded there, either. Extending Article 50 would be just kicking the can down the road, Mrs May told MPs. 'It defers the point at which the decision needs to be taken.' This from a woman who has kicked the can so much that it is now spherical. Her sudden lack of enthusiasm for can-kicking was like a Frenchman saying that he has gone off cheese.

When Mrs May says that she will change her approach, what she really means is that she will act like an Englishman abroad and say exactly the same things but LOUDER and more slooooowly so that everyone understands.

'Her door may be open but her mind is closed,' complained Hilary Benn, chairman of the Brexit Committee, after suffering a night of Mrs May's hospitality. 'She's talking as if she lost by thirty votes, not 230,' added Yvette Cooper, chairwoman of the Home Affairs Committee.

Mrs May pursed her lips, or was it a smile? Perhaps she thinks that all it will take is more stubbornness. She may be right. The PM has given so many concessions in the past week and shown such flexibility that there is every chance she can keep the next defeat down to 225.

24 JANUARY
FILLER AND VANILLA PLAY LUNCHTIME PAT-A-CAKE

I have never seen the Commons so empty at midday on a Wednesday. As the party leaders crept in for their weekly joust, barely raising an eyebrow never mind a cheer from narcoleptic comrades, vast acres of unoccupied green leather could be seen, especially in the back two rows on the Tory side. Surely they couldn't all be in Davos.

Rebel Corner was less populated than usual and Hecklers' Ridge was missing a few regulars, such as the waistcoated bulk of Alec Shelbrooke, whose absence alone left room for three regular-sized backbenchers. A couple of anonymouses were eventually found and shoved into the gap like those placeholders used at the Oscars when actors need to go and shove Colombian marching powder up their nose to beat the boredom.

Even the Bercow bark was silent for a change. Mr Speaker intervened only twice, once almost out of duty to remind MPs not to speak when sitting down and once to tease Tim Farron very gently, but he seemed disengaged. He did not even correct Peter Bone when he said that 'your government is full of Remainer ministers' and 'will you replace them with Brexiters'.

Technically, as Mr Bercow is often very keen to remind MPs, all comments should be directed at him, not the PM. Perhaps he thought the idea that he might want Brexiters in the Cabinet to be highly risible.

Prime Minister's Questions is, let us be honest, not a big draw these days, not with the combatants we have at present. Theirs is a game of lunchtime pat-a-cake, not a prize fight. Boxing promoters might market it as the Grumble and the Bungle or the Filler and Vanilla.

We knew the tactics for this match well in advance. 'Take "no deal" off the table,' demanded Jeremy Corbyn. 'If you want to avoid "no deal" then support a deal,' Theresa May replied. Or at least come to Downing Street to discuss it. Mr Corbyn continues to decline that invitation, knowing that it might force him to reach a decision about his own policy.

'He will sit down with Hamas, Hezbollah and the IRA without preconditions,' Mrs May crowed, 'yet he will not meet me to talk about Brexit.' He retorted that, based on what he had heard from those who had taken up her invitation, it would be a waste of his time. 'The door may be open but the minds inside are completely closed,' he said.

What is worse, a closed mind or an empty mind? Mrs May thinks there isn't much inside the Corbyn cranium and that if they ever do sit together, she can bamboozle him with details. He asked if she supported a customs union. 'What does he mean by that?' she asked. 'Does he mean accepting the common external tariff? The common commercial policy? The union customs code? Accepting EU state aid rules?' Mr

Corbyn's face was blank. 'He hasn't got a clue,' she scoffed. 'It's not complicated,' he replied. Nothing ever is to him. That is the problem.

Yet at some point, surely, the Prime Minister and the man who allegedly wants to be Prime Minister have to meet and see if they can find a common path through this mire. Perhaps she should be generous and invite the whole shadow Cabinet to afternoon tea on the terrace: I'll provide the scones, Jeremy, if you can bring some jam from your allotment.

On second thoughts, that could be a risky idea. We would only end up with another parliamentary schism over whether you put the cream on first or last.

31 JANUARY
AFTERNOON TEA FOR TWO IS RATHER STRAINED

At last the rivals meet. Jeremy Corbyn finally deigned to visit Theresa May's Commons office yesterday to discuss a way through the Brexit mire. It must have been excruciating for both of them. Neither is good at small talk, nor at winning round those who have a differing view. How much of the 45-minute encounter was spent in awkward silence?

'More tea, Jeremy?' Mrs May asked every few minutes in the absence of anything else to say, to which the Labour leader replied that he would not accept the tea she was offering unless she could promise that hot water was off the table.

And then the Prime Minister had to explain, yet again, that both sides had already agreed to boil a kettle and if he wanted to avoid a mug of hot water he had to decide upon a teabag. 'How about Earl Grey?' she offered. 'I will not burn my lips on such an emblem of privilege,' he replied. 'That's a pity,' Mrs May said. 'Philip calls it proper tea.'

Mr Corbyn grunted. 'Proper tea is theft,' he muttered. 'I

want a tea that represents the workers.' But when Mrs May gave him builder's tea, he turned it down because it came in a blue mug. Mr Corbyn's aides later described the encounter as 'cordial'. That probably means he spent it drinking squash.

This was not a meeting of master strategists. Neither had a new plan to sell. These were two dogmatic opponents determined to reject whatever the other said. It was as if Churchill and Eisenhower had decided to take the spring of 1944 off and leave the organisation of the invasion of Normandy to Captain Mainwaring and Warden Hodges.

Few peace summits begin with the participants trashing each other three hours earlier. Prime Minister's Questions was as enlightening as ever, although Mrs May seemed rather buoyant after persuading her party to vote against the deal that she had spent most of the winter trying to sell to them.

Mr Corbyn used the tactic, rare for him, of asking a pithy opening question. They are always much harder to answer than his usual angry ramble. MPs had voted to find 'alternative arrangements' to the hated backstop, he said. 'Will she tell us what they might be?'

'Absolutely,' Mrs May said as she sprang to her feet. And then she realised she did not have the foggiest how to go on. What followed was the sort of ferocious flannelling you get on bath night at an orphanage.

'There are a number of proposals,' she said. Will that do? No? 'We are engaging positively with proposals that have been put forward by...' Here she named four Tories. Enough? No? 'Others have put forward different proposals.'

'What are they?' demanded Emily Thornberry from three seats to Mr Corbyn's right. Her leader looked up as if he hadn't thought to ask that. 'Wait and see,' Mrs May replied and then she gave the flannel another vigorous workout.

'None of that was very clear to me,' Mr Corbyn replied and for once it was not because he is dim. After another succinct question about her red lines, he decided to give question one another go. 'Which options are being explored?' he asked. Mrs May did not even open her folder for this. 'I covered that already,' she sighed. 'Perhaps if he listened he wouldn't need to repeat himself.' And she sat straight down.

That was the peak of their tussle. Mr Corbyn asked a couple more times for details. Mrs May said that there were 'a number of options that we are working positively on' and then repeated to him that the only way to prevent 'no deal' was to back a deal. 'He has no plan,' she scoffed. And nor, really, does she. They have two weeks in which to find one.

6 FEBRUARY

RAINY-DAY THERESA TAPS INTO THE SPIRIT OF THE BEIGE

The Lord's Prayer, depending which translation you go for, gets its message across in between sixty and seventy words. The Ten Commandments take up fewer than 400. The Gettysburg Address lasted a mere 271 words, three more than Mark Antony needed to whip up Rome into rebellion, if you believe Shakespeare.

Sometimes you need a few more words to convey your message. Harold Macmillan took 882 words to sell the winds of change; Winston Churchill expended 729 over nothing but blood, toil, tears and sweat; Franklin Roosevelt needed 1,880 words to say that Americans had nothing to fear but fear itself; and Martin Luther King banged on for 1,624 words about having a dream.

Yesterday, Theresa May topped them all. The Prime Minister, that Pericles of our age, visited a tech company on the banks of the Lagan in Belfast and set out her plans for Brexit in 3,237 of her speechwriting team's beigest words. What a waste of printer ink. The message could have been condensed to just three words: nothing has changed.

As the rain streamed down the window behind her, Mrs May tried to speak of sunshine. Sure, her withdrawal agreement had received a record pasting in the Commons and she was still struggling to find an alternative plan that might win favour, but let's accentuate the positive. Britain and Ireland could stage a joint bid to host the football World Cup in 2030, when the post-Brexit transition period might even be nearing completion.

Her mission, she said, was to give Northern Ireland 'the brightest future for generations'. The province was no longer a place of violence, but one of 'dynamism and success'. Not that dynamism is a word you often hear used around Mrs May. She spoke yesterday in the same bland tones that you get from an optician who is going through the motions of an eye examination.

'Which withdrawal treaty looks better? Is is the first one? Or the second one? The first? Or the second?' And you just nod and pick an answer at random, because frankly you can't see a difference.

Her main message, which must have occupied at least 2,500 of her 3,237 words, was that there would be no return to a hard border between Britain and Ireland once she had eradicated the hated backstop. 'I am here to affirm my commitment,' she said, using that polished phrase three times. Her desire to avoid a hard border is 'unshakeable'. Advances in technology would help to prevent that, she added, though the message was spoilt by the TV feed from Belfast repeatedly breaking down.

Mrs May's big problem is that her government is being kept afloat by a political party, the DUP, whose view on Brexit is closer to the Tory Eurosceptics than to the majority of people they represent. Northern Ireland is 56 per cent in favour of staying in the EU, but if you only look at Ulster politics through a Westminster lens you might assume that they are all Brussels-bashers like East Antrim's Sammy Wilson.

The Prime Minister seemed surprised, therefore, when the lukewarm applause ended almost as soon as it had started and she opened the room up to questions. It turned out that the majority of her audience didn't want to ditch the backstop and felt uneasy at these 'alternative arrangements' she has agreed to find.

'Many business leaders feel you've shafted them,' one said. 'Why would anyone trust you?' Mrs May gulped. Just her luck to come to the one part of the country that actually liked her withdrawal agreement.

8 FEBRUARY
SPEAKER AND LEADER HAVE AN INCREDIBLE WAR OF WORDS

It was another incredible day in the life of Andrea Leadsom. Many politicians have a cliché, a favourite word or phrase they return to when they have nothing else to say. For David Cameron it was 'let me say this'; Theresa May has 'I have been clear'; and Mrs Leadsom, the Leader of the Commons, is fond of saying how incredible everything is.

Hansard records that she passed 250 career uses of 'incredibly' yesterday, three of them in a brief reply to Labour's Ian Mearns (Gateshead), to whom she was 'incredibly sympathetic' and grateful that he had been 'incredibly helpful' over what was an 'incredibly important' matter. For overemployed expressions, the Leadsom 'incredibly' is up there with John Bercow's variations on a theme of 'chunter' (278 instances) and 'from a sedentary position' (442).

Among the things she found incredible yesterday were crime statistics in Somerset, sprinkler systems and the existence of the Bank of England, yet when she came to the matter that most other MPs find beyond incredible, she delivered her words with a straight face.

'The Prime Minister is currently negotiating a revised deal for the UK's departure from the EU,' she reported as hysterical laughter pealed around the chamber. They have heard this song many times before. It would be easier to make revisions to the Rosetta Stone.

The next stage, she explained, would be as follows: if the PM can get a revised deal, there will be a meaningful vote on it next week. If she can't, they get a meaningless one on Valentine's Day, when Mrs May hopes to receive loving support – ballots-doux, you might say – and not a massacre.

This seemed straightforward. Incredibly so. But Mr Speaker was not happy. He suspects that the government will be slippery about this and gave Mrs Leadsom a 500-word lecture, with footnotes, on the need to stick to her promise.

His conclusion seemed more complicated than the withdrawal agreement. 'The dependability of statements made and commitments given, whatever people's views on the merits of the issues, is absolutely critical if we are to retain or, where lost, to restore trust, so there can of course be no resiling from the commitment which I think is explicit and which has been made: no dubiety, no backsliding, no doubt,' he said, before adding, 'I think that is clear.' As mud.

There is no love between Speaker and leader. He clearly thinks that she is an untrustworthy moron and she feels he is a pompous bully. While Mr Bercow pontificated, she refused to look at him, but she soon made her views known in a reply to one of the SNP members.

'I think it is unfortunate, Mr Speaker, that you somewhat muddied the waters' – there was a loud gasp from MPs at this – 'by unresponding to the Business of the House statement.' What a marvellously passive-aggressive word that 'unresponding' is.

'I had made it perfectly clear what was the case,' she went on, 'and I am perfectly able to do that for myself. I will set it out again.' And having done so she tetchily added, 'OK? Is that clear?' There will be no Valentine's cards sent to Speaker's House from her office.

Naturally, Mr Bercow would not let this lie. 'Colleagues,' he began, for he was hoping, like Mark Antony at the funeral, to rouse the mob. 'I have not muddied any waters. What I have done is to quote the factual position.' He then said that no one was going to tell him how to do his job. 'I could not care less who tries to obstruct me. That is my mission and responsibility.'

He also insisted that he always treated Mrs Leadsom with 'great courtesy' (apart from that time he called her a stupid woman, of course) and would ever continue to do so. Of all the things said in the House yesterday, that one most deserved the label of incredible.

12 FEBRUARY
WE WILL SERENADE THEM ON THE BEACHES!
WILLIAMSON SEEKS CRUISE CONTROL

I don't know what effect Gavin Williamson will have upon the enemy but, by God, he amuses me. The Defence Secretary, he of the 'go away and shurrup' threats to Moscow, who was once heckled by his own mobile phone during a statement on terrorism and who plans to defend Gibraltar with paintballs, aspires to greatness. The problem is, he has all the authority of Rodney Trotter at an arms fair.

Now in the second year of his YTS (Young Tory Statesman) placement, Mr Williamson is getting itchy feet. He wants to run the company. It was perhaps no coincidence that his big speech on future objectives was given in the room where Theresa May began her leadership bid. He smells the whiff of cordite and hears the distant drums. It is time to move into position, ready for the big push. And what better way to cheer the Tory faithful than by rolling back the clock to when Britain was Great? In Gavinworld it is always 1895.

'We should be the nation that people turn to when the world needs leadership,' he declared. Invoking Churchill, as they always do, he recalled the darkest hours when Britain stood alone against tyranny. Russia will find that provoking us will 'come at a cost', he warned, while our new aircraft carrier will be sent to put the willies up China. This is the 'new Great Game', he said.

Bless him. It is understandable that he should want to talk tough to a room that contained more gold braid than a Parisian opera house, especially when he looks as though he has borrowed his big brother's interview suit. The Williamson Doctrine is the inverse of Teddy Roosevelt's 'speak softly and carry a big stick'. He thinks we should boast lustily and hope that no one notices that our Navy amounts to a few pedalos armed with peashooters.

Mr Williamson has a big new idea with a grand name: the 'Littoral Strike Ship Concept'. It later turned out that this concept involves converting civilian passenger ferries into warships. Let us hope that Chris Grayling is not in charge of procuring them. What a team: you provide the ferries, Chris, and I'll provide the war!

Some might be sceptical that a fleet of former Channel-crossers with names like *Pride of Margate* will 'enhance our lethality', as Mr Williamson boasted, but just wait until he signs a deal with Viking River Cruises to patrol the Mediterranean. What the Navy lacks in firepower it will more than make up for with the quality of its on-board buffet and speaker list.

Who needs F-35s when you can have Dame Mary Beard? And as for the 'innovative crewing methods' that Mr Williamson said he would be trialling on our ships in the Gulf, well, that can only mean that he intends to press-gang oceangoing cabaret acts into service. Make Jane McDonald the First Sea

331

Lord! God help the Chinese when she is belting out 'The Wind Beneath My Wings'.

19 FEBRUARY
MELANCHOLY WAIL OF THE SMALLER BEASTS

This was more like a therapy session than a schism. The mood was as grey and laden with tears as the sky outside and the seven speeches took the same route: a 'my name is', a personal story and a mournful explanation of why they were leaving. It felt like a meeting of Melancholics' Anonymous.

Luciana Berger was first. She began to introduce herself as 'the Labour MP for...' before realising why they were there. This divorce was real. There was a painful pause as she struggled with dropping the badge she had proudly worn since she was a student before concluding, 'I am the [deep breath] Member of Parliament for Liverpool Wavertree.'

Labour no more but part of a new breakaway given the rather nebulous title of The Independent Group. Tiggers. Not that there was much bounce. This was not a new dawn but an attempt to escape the storm. They had left their family, not through ambition but out of long-festering desperation.

The Momentum wing had been wanting them to go for months. The tweets of abuse had become a cacophony. There must be fifty ways to peeve a brother: just get on your bike, Mike; make a new plan, Ann; give it a miss, Chris. And something unprintable about Chuka.

One by one they stepped up and spoke in sorrow of a party that had become impossible to live with: intolerant, bullying, unwilling to deal with antisemitism and, though this card felt underplayed, facilitating Brexit.

These were not big names. The Gang of Four in 1981 had a

Foreign Secretary, a Chancellor, the most prominent woman on the left and Bill Rodgers. You had to be quite the Westminster nerd to name all seven yesterday. It was a septet of 'and Bill Rodgers' types. This was the desperate wail of the party's smaller beasts, pushed to breaking point: less a Limehouse Declaration than a dormouse lachrymation.

Chris Leslie, who was once shadow Chancellor for the length of an internship, recalled the good old days when Labour won elections and he went straight from being the kid who did Gordon Brown's photocopying to the youngest MP. The former Baby of the House, now a frustrated forty-six, declared that he could not campaign to make Mr Corbyn Prime Minister. 'Many still in the Labour Party will privately admit this,' he said.

Angela Smith (Penistone and Stocksbridge), the only one without a safe seat, said that Labour had forgotten that their voters want a better life. 'I don't want to be patronised by left-wing intellectuals who think that being poor and working class constitute a state of grace,' she said. Take that, Seumas.

Chuka Umunna was the most familiar name, though he spoke in clichés, saying things like 'no more politics as usual', 'forge a new consensus', and 'it doesn't have to be this way'. None of them had much to say about their plans. Desperate people don't always know the next step, they just know they must take the first one.

Unlike Mr Umunna, neither Ann Coffey (Stockport) nor Mike Gapes (Ilford South) could be dismissed as careerists. Both had been elected in 1992 and never troubled the ministerial carpool. If they were Blairites, they went unrewarded.

Ms Coffey spoke of her pride in the 'last Labour government'. Did she mean the most recent one or the final one? By the end of the day, with news breaking that Derek Hatton had been readmitted to the Labour Party thirty-four years after he was expelled, it was hard to tell.

21 FEBRUARY
EVEN CORBYN DISPLAYS RESIGNATION, IF NOT FROM HIS JOB

And so the seven became eleven. The Independent Group of politicians who feel abandoned by their parties had gained as many new MPs in thirteen hours as Tim Farron did with the Lib Dems in two years. At this rate they will be in government by Easter.

Rebel Corner, square of the wicket at the Speaker's end, where Anna Soubry used to barrack, Sarah Wollaston used to plead and Heidi Allen just looked sad, was empty as its former occupants took their new seats diagonally opposite, between Lib Dems, nationalists, the DUP and eight refugees from Labour (Joan Ryan having belatedly followed the less than magnificent seven).

The whole chamber, in fact, felt understocked. Old familiars were absent. Some could be considering a change of party – I can see Michael Fabricant as Leader of the Whigs – but others had kept to their half-term recess plans. The honourable members for Val d'Isère and West Zermatt were on a blue run and it didn't involve crossing the floor to share stationery with Mike Gapes.

Jeremy Corbyn was also heading downhill. Again. The noise when the Labour leader rises for PMQs would seldom stir a hibernating hedgehog, but this time, rising just after a Tory backbencher had asked a patsy question about antisemitism, it was as if someone had pressed the mute button. A few loyal mouths opened, but nothing came out save halitosis.

'Antisemitism has no place in society,' Mr Corbyn began, before Toady, Lickspittle and Creep on the Tory benches shouted about his failure to tackle it in his party. There were glum faces behind the Labour leader and several nodding heads, in agreement with the Tories, not him.

Mr Corbyn could make no capital from the Tory defections since he supports Brexit, their main beef. He attempted a couple of questions on the status of Theresa May's EU deal, which she swerved as effortlessly as if she were the honourable member for Courchevel Central, slaloming down to lunch. Finally, having failed to land a blow, Mr Corbyn sat down with a sigh. 'Go on,' his weary look said. 'Give me the kicking.'

And she did. 'What do we see from his party?' she gloated. 'Hamas and Hezbollah are friends, Israel and the United States enemies; Hatton a hero, Churchill a villain. Attlee and Bevin will be spinning in their graves.' It was easy pickings. The Prime Minister finished, on a day on which three of her party had defected and after giving six pretty feeble and evasive answers on the biggest headache of modern history, to jubilant cries of 'More! More!' from her backbenches. What luck.

22 FEBRUARY
IN PRAISE OF THE WONKY VEG

It is good to indulge in tripe, said Michael Gove with admirable honesty. Some might say that after all the claptrap, hogwash and bilge of the Brexit debates, tripe has not been in short supply in Westminster, but Mr Gove was talking about the rubbery lining of a cow's stomach. An offal idea.

The Environment Secretary is an enthusiast for the unorthodox, so when Philip Hollobone (Kettering), a Tory backbencher, raised a question about supermarkets throwing away 'wonky veg' – carrots that aren't straight, tomatoes that aren't round – Mr Gove grasped his colleague's knobbly parsnip with delight.

'He is absolutely right,' he said. 'When it comes to food, the search for symmetry and perfection is vain. The true joy of food comes in appreciating diversity.' So too in life. Mr Gove then spoke up for 'unconventional cuts of meat'. I look forward to his TripeAdvisor website.

Parliament is full of wonky veg, especially on Thursday mornings. Let's be honest, you have to be a little odd to want to be an MP in the first place, but to be up at the ungodly hour of 9.30 a.m. to ask Mr Gove about deformed beetroot is bizarre. Yet some of my favourite MPs shine at such times, like Peter Aldous (Con, Waveney), a Gussie Fink-Nottle sort from Suffolk, who has an endearing lisp and waves his hands about as if they might come off. He asked what the minister could do to help Lowestoft fishermen. Mr Gove replied that he would end 'pulse fishing'. Quite right. The lentils must keep slipping through the nets.

After that we had the weekly free-for-all with Andrea Leadsom, a session when some MPs like to show off their erudition. Sir John Hayes quoted from Proust in discussing the jihadi bride case, while Sir Desmond Swayne (Con, New Forest West) dusted off his Coleridge to give poetic voice to his concern that the restoration plans for Parliament would result in a 'stately pleasuredome' rather than a Pugin revival.

Valerie Vaz, shadow Leader of the House, chose the Bob Marley songbook instead, since the reggae musician was getting a blue plaque. She said that while some MPs were singing 'Exodus' this week, the Labour front bench preferred 'One Love'. Not 'Iron Lion Zion', obviously.

There was also jollity when the SNP's Pete Wishart discovered that by a printing error next week's business was due to end on 29 February. A plot to extend the Brexit talks, since this isn't a leap year? 'I put that there deliberately,' Mrs Leadsom purred, 'in the hope he might think that I might propose to him.' This was Parliament as it should be: earnest enquiries coupled with playful respect, not a slanging match.

Norman Shrapnel, a former sketchwriter for *The Guardian*, avoided meeting MPs. 'It might spoil the purity of my hatred,' he used to say, which is a decent joke, but rather sad if true. Some deserve scorn, yes; mockery, sure; disappointment, absolutely. Plenty are stupid, lazy, pompous, vain, longwinded or sycophantic – and our job is to prick them – but more MPs, on all sides, are hard-working, principled and honourable. Perhaps we don't say that enough. They are all too human, if a little wonky.

And so, two years after Theresa May triggered Article 50 to begin the process of leaving the European Union, Brexit Day dawned. But it did not bring Brexit. Nigel Farage and an angry mob gathered outside Parliament to protest about betrayal.

30 MARCH
FARAGISTS ASSEMBLE TO MARK BREXIT BETRAYAL DAY

Six years ago, not long after David Cameron raised the idea of a referendum on Britain's membership of the EU (how did that idea turn out, by the way?), I spoke to one of Nigel Farage's former teachers.

He recalled telling this 'cheeky and charming' boy on his final day at school that he was certain he would go far. 'But whether it is in fame or infamy, I cannot say,' he added. Farage, who pronounced his name to rhyme with marriage in those days, gave his teacher a wink and said, 'As long as I go far, sir.'

Even those who loathe the former UKIP leader cannot deny how far he has since come. Not on the Leave Means Leave march from Sunderland that began two weeks ago and arrived in Westminster yesterday, since he did only a couple of dozen miles himself, but as the figurehead of a movement that, in fame or infamy, has changed Britain.

He stood yesterday afternoon on a stage in Parliament Square, looking across at the statues of Churchill and Lloyd George, and heard his name chanted by tens of thousands of Brexit supporters, perhaps many more than the 36,660 in total who had cast votes for him in seven failed attempts to get elected to Parliament. He has made his mark on politics all the same.

'Ni-GEL, Ni-GEL,' they chanted, proving Oscar Wilde's rule that to be really famous you need to be known by one name of five letters. 'Stop it, don't embarrass me,' he replied, not meaning it for a second.

This should have been a moment of triumph for the Faragists. B-Day: the moment Britain left the EU. But the fizz remained unpopped, the bunting stayed unbunted. There was a different 'B' word on their lips now. 'This has been a day of betrayal,' Mr Farage said. 'Boo,' went the crowd. And 'hiss' as well. It was part pantomime, part pent-up rage.

Through the afternoon, as MPs voted to reject the PM's deal, the masses protested. 'Treason May' declared a banner carried in the midst of a skirl of pipes and drums from Musselburgh, East Lothian, accompanied, oddly, by several French tricolours bearing the Gaullist cross of Lorraine. Frexit next? For every slogan that veered towards the sinister, though, such as the woman holding a placard that twisted the Nazi motto to say '*Ein Reich, ein Volk, ein Tusk*', there were more simply showing a British sense of disgruntlement. One man had written on the back of his *gilet orange*, 'It's my birthday today and you've spoilt it, Mrs May.'

'If you see someone weasly in a suit, watch your back,' a man shouted through his megaphone. 'It may be Michael Gove.' A banner called for the return of Cromwell. Oliver, I assume, rather than Hilary Mantel fans. There was a stand protesting for human rights for Kurds. Optimistic.

In the square, Sir Oliver Letwin, Dominic Grieve and, especially, John Bercow drew hearty jeers when denounced from the stage, while bombastically patriotic statements got loud cheers. 'Let's replace French brandy with Australian,' shouted Tim Martin, founder of Wetherspoons' pubs. 'Yeah!' came the reply. 'And champagne with English sparkling,' he said. 'YEAH!' they shouted back even louder.

Then out bounded Mark Francois, deputy chairman of the European Research Group, who has the appearance of Penfold, the timid sidekick of Danger Mouse, but the confidence of a playground rebel with a pocket full of stink bombs. He said he had a message to deliver to 'the Europhiliacs of the *Today* programme'. There was a pause, then he bellowed 'UP YOURS!' Another loud whoop echoed back.

Carried away by his oratory, Mr Francois then quoted from Pericles, which he had read on the memorial to Bomber Command: 'Freedom is the sure possession of those alone who have the courage to defend it.' Casting himself as the Athenian general may go down badly with his fellows in the ERG, who seem to enjoy comparing themselves to the Spartans. (Unless it was misheard and Jacob Rees-Mogg, that lover of Georgian Bath, actually said 'spa towns'.) Not since Alcibiades has anyone switched sides from one Greek city to the other so quickly.

Finally, at last, came the speaker they wanted. Nigel time. Mr Farage came out to a video of his greatest hits, beginning with his rebuke to the European Parliament after the referendum. 'When I said I wanted to lead a campaign to get Britain to leave the EU, you all laughed at me,' he said. 'Well, you're not laughing now.' No, indeed they are not.

19 APRIL
UKIP REACH THE END OF THEIR PURPLE PATCH

In 1895 H. G. Wells imagined a future in which the world is divided between the peaceful and timid Eloi – childlike, work-shy fruitarians – and the angry, cave-dwelling Morlocks who feed on them. Wells set this society 800,000 years hence, but you could get a taste yesterday morning simply by strolling round Parliament Square.

Camped out for a fourth day of singing and clapping hands and glueing themselves to monuments were the Eloi of the Extinction Rebellion, who kept up their campaign to rid the world of carbon emissions by spinning diabolos, sunbathing and listening to Woody Guthrie. Among the placards was one saying 'Buddhists for Bumblebees'.

On the far side of the square, behind Westminster Abbey in an airless room, the Morlocks had also gathered, to launch their European election campaign and feed on the red meat of Brexit resentment. Here were the Continuity UKIP, what was left after Nigel Farage had taken away all his former party's famous optimism and generosity.

Gerard Batten, its leader and one of only four MEPs to remain under the purple banner from the twenty-four elected in 2014, is miffed that Mr Farage's new Brexit Party is four times more popular than UKIP in the polls. Calling them a 'phoney party' led by 'someone on an ego trip', he even had a dig at their colour scheme. 'You can sum it up in one word,' he said. 'Light blue: it's Tory-light.' He is as numerate as he is charming.

To start with, though, Mr Batten's press conference was pretty reasonable. Brexit had not been delivered, he said, and he wanted people to vote UKIP to ensure that it would be. A 'patriotic Prime Minister' would not have gone down the Article 50 route of negotiating to leave – 'It's a trap!' – but would have revoked the European Communities Act 1972 and told the EU to make an offer.

Mr Batten then promised that he would not send MEPs to Brussels to 'get our snouts back in the gravy train'. Realising the metaphor was muddled, he tried to amend it. 'No, you don't put your snout in a gravy train, do you?' he said. 'You put it in a trough. And the trough is on the gravy train.' As clear as Bisto.

He was followed by several amiably batty candidates, all as unspun as a field of cotton. One called the leader of the Tory Brexiteers 'Judas Rees-Mogg'; another said there had been a conspiracy on referendum night by not declaring the result in a Leave area first; a third said that fishing was 'a hot potato that has been battered'. And served with mushy peas?

So far, so harmless. Just like the old days. No one could doubt their sincerity, even if you disagreed with their cause. But Mr Batten then said he wanted to add some 'controversy' and invited up two members of the far-right online world: Sargon of Akkad and Count Dankula, both prospective MEPs.

Mr Sargon, who actually comes from Swindon rather than Akkad, is best known for making rape jokes about the Labour MP Jess Phillips. He explained yesterday that because Ms Phillips was a 'giant bitch' he had every right to act 'like a dick'. He then called the media 'dirty, dirty smear merchants' and refused to answer any questions. The count, really a comedian from Lanarkshire called Mark, taught his dog to give a Nazi salute. He moaned about freedom of speech and said that his comedy was 'literally the opposite of fascism'. And indeed of humour.

As Mr Batten beamed indulgently at his juvenile comrades acting like toddlers smearing excrement up the wall in a cry for attention, I thought of UKIP leaders past – Henry Bolton, who said he could strangle a badger with his bare hands and ended up living in a hotel with a model half his age; His Excellency Sir Paul Nuttall PhD, the Ashes-winning Nobel laureate and CV fabricator; Diane James, who wrote 'under duress' as she signed her leadership form and lasted a fortnight; and Mr Farage, a shy, modest man who always refused to do any broadcasts after more than five pints – and regretted the demise of a party of such dignity and professionalism.

THE WEAK ARE A LONG TIME IN POLITICS

25 MAY
THE TWILIGHT OF THERESA MAY
_____

It was a nice morning for a self-immolation. The flags above Downing Street hung limp on a clear day, the newly planted begonias in the front garden gave a splash of pink to the stern, grey fortress, and Theresa May, the Maidenhead Brünnhilde (not to be confused with that earlier Valkyrie, Margarethilde), rode out into a pool of sunlight to sing one last song before throwing herself upon the Brexit pyre.

She hoped that the sacrifice would finally break her party's European curse; others fear that the flames will bring down the whole Tory Valhalla. *Götterdämmerung*, the twilight of the government, may be entering its final act.

But first the stage needed to be de-catted. For half an hour before Mrs May's statement, Larry the Downing Street mouser sat on the doorstep, his back turned contemptuously against the gathering press pack, occasionally giving a hiss at Palmerston, the Foreign Office cat, whenever he tried to invade Larry's turf.

Mrs May did not want, however, to have ol' sourpuss in the background for her swansong. The door swung open and Larry was invited to come inside. He refused. The door closed, then opened again and a policeman came out and grabbed him, carrying Larry across the threshold like a sullen teenager being made to see his spinster aunt. 'You are going to say goodbye to her whether you like it or not.'

Suddenly there was a tintinnabulation from the pockets of the press pack as an email arrived from the Downing Street press office. 'Please see below the Prime Minister's statement,' it said. There was nothing below. Premature annunciation or a commentary on the past three years of empty promises and forgettable speeches?

Mrs May emerged just after 10 a.m. With her husband and

chief of staff watching away to her right, she performed some of her favourite songs: 'Honour the Referendum', 'A Country that Works for Everyone' and 'Burning Injustices'. She decided not to give us 'Stronganstable', 'Brexit Means Brexit' or 'No Deal is Better than a Bad Deal'. People grew sick of them long ago.

Even in this time of trial, her grammar did not desert her. 'Ever since I first stepped through the door behind me as Prime Minister, I have striven…' she began. How many of the dwarves who seek to steal the ring from her would have said strived?

There was a slightly dissonant note halfway through, when she invoked the wisdom of Sir Nicholas Winton, a former constituent and architect of the Kindertransport of child refugees fleeing the Nazis. Cynics may question whether Mrs May's immigration policy would have allowed them in.

She said that Sir Nicholas had told her that 'compromise is not a dirty word – life depends on compromise'. Good advice, though how often has Mrs May explored give-and-take during the Brexit process? Those red lines may have become a touch pink of late, but they were pretty deep vermilion for a long time.

Now she had reached her peroration and the emotion was beginning to show. Who could blame her? She is human, despite the evidence, and we would all shed a tear at leaving such a stage. A slight wobble when she said that this job had been 'the honour of my life to hold' was followed by a demi-croak on 'enduring gratitude' before it all fell apart as she spoke of serving 'the country I love'.

Irritated, perhaps, at this loss of control, she spun round sharply and stomped back inside. As she left, we suddenly heard from beyond the Downing Street gate a shout through a megaphone that must have haunted her for two years: 'STOP BREXIT!' Someone else's ears can suffer that barrage now.

AFTERWORD

And so she left. The 54th Prime Minister of the United Kingdom departed Downing Street on 24 July 2019, after three years and eleven days and, like the 50th, sought solace in cricket. Sir John Major went to watch a county game at the Oval; Theresa May took in a Test match at Lord's, both of them aware that politics, like their favourite sport, can be cruel and sometimes unfair, but when the umpire raises his finger, it's time to walk. How different it might have been if she had won that election.

The departure of Mrs May was swiftly followed, in that ruthless way in which we replace leaders, by the arrival in Downing Street of Boris Johnson, the overwhelming winner of the leadership contest among both MPs and party members. If you had asked almost anyone in Westminster a year earlier, maybe even six months, you would have been told this would never happen. Knowing that the grassroots would back Boris, the MPs, who generally disliked him, would never put him on the ballot. Momentum and desperation can do funny things to politicians. Those who in private shook their heads and complained about Mr Johnson's laziness and lack of attention to detail then gamely defended him in public, smelling the wind and hoping that loyalty would get them a job.

Perhaps he will defy his critics. Or maybe there will be another twist. As this book went to print, with Mr Johnson ardently promising that Britain would leave the EU on 31 October 'do or die' and his Chancellor finding billions to mitigate the damage of leaving without a deal, my mind went back three years to a lunch I had at the Savile Club with Stanley Johnson, the new Prime Minister's father, just before the referendum.

A couple of bottles in, Stanley was in a creative and playful mood. He said that he had just had a brilliant idea for a novel. 'It would be about a Prime Minister who is a Russian sleeper agent and tries to destabilise the West with a vote on Britain leaving the EU,' he said. Growing into this theme, he went on: 'To achieve it, he puts an old school chum in charge of the Leave campaign. Handsome fellow, called Horace or something. Anyway, Britain votes to leave and the PM has to resign.

'Then here's the twist: Horace eventually takes over and negotiates a great deal for Britain to rejoin the EU. Naturally there will be lots of beautiful women in it.' Gosh, I said, and how does it all end? 'Oh, I don't know,' Stanley replied, pouring himself another glass. 'Polonium, probably.'

While Mrs May has now gone, I often think that the only certainty in politics is that Jeremy Corbyn will remain as Leader of the Labour Party until the end of time. Who could have imagined when the bookies were offering 200 to one against him becoming leader that he would still be there four years later, on to his third Tory Prime Minister, and yet (at time of typing) ten points behind in the polls? Mr Johnson is fortunate to have such a weak opponent.

The Houses of Parliament are crumbling, a metaphor for the state of modern politics. During my time there, play was stopped in the Commons chamber because of a leak in the roof near Mr Speaker's chair, a block of masonry falling from the Victoria Tower almost led to a by-election, and several fires were mercifully spotted and extinguished just in time. The buildings are covered in scaffolding and in winter the floors are covered in buckets. A former clerk of the Commons said that we were one major sewer failure away from an immediate evacuation.

At some point, they will have to move out, for several years, in order to give the place a complete overhaul. Many MPs are opposed to going – ironically, the ones who wanted to leave the EU want to stay in their disintegrating offices, while the ones who wanted to remain are keen on leaving – but the fire at Notre Dame cathedral helped to focus the minds, and the plan is to depart in 2025, with MPs moving into a new chamber down Whitehall while the Lords cross Parliament Square to take a perch behind the Supreme Court. You can't just rush these things, you know. Preparations must be made. It is odd, perhaps, that while we need six years to make the arrangements for leaving a large stately home, many people thought we could easily leave the EU in just two.

So, eventually, in the early 2030s, a refurbished Parliament will welcome back its politicians to their home by the Thames. I wonder if Mr Corbyn, by then in his eighties, will still be Leader of the Opposition. And will they still be trying to find a conclusion to the Brexit neverendum?

ACKNOWLEDGEMENTS

Thank you to everyone who has helped me to stumble through the parliamentary jungle and get out the other side. To James Stephens, Olivia Beattie, Ellen Heaney and their colleagues at Biteback for their enthusiasm in taking on this book; to Times Newspapers for releasing the copyright; to Morten Morland, that wonderful cartoonist, for his generosity in providing the cover illustration; to colleagues in the *Times* parliamentary office and at HQ, especially the subs who bailed me out (and never took it badly when I moaned about edits); to other members of the Guild of Sketchwriters, present and past, particularly two former inhabitants of my chair, Matthew Parris and Ann Treneman, whose support has been really appreciated; and to those MPs and peers who were friendly to me despite everything.

Above all, I would like to thank the dear friends to be found at the four compass points of my life over the past three years: the Old King's Head in Borough, the Savile Club in Mayfair, All Saints Church in Blackheath and my dear family: Ruth, Hattie and Humphrey. I haven't deserved any of you.